Lokayat

HIGHER BUREAUCRACY AND SOCIAL CHANGE

HIGHER BUREAUCRACY AND SOCIAL CHANGE

S.R. Jitha

and

Reinhart, Philip

KALPAZ

ISBN: 978-93-5128-001-9

Price: ₹ 810

First Published, 2014

Published by

Kalpaz Publications
C-30, Satyawati Nagar,
Delhi - 110052
E-mail: kalpaz@hotmail.com
Ph.: 9212142040

Laser Typesetting: Gyan Prints (AB-I)
Printed at: G. Print Process, Delhi

Cataloging in Publication Data—DK
Courtesy: D.K. Agencies (P) Ltd. <docinfo@dkagencies.com>

Jitha, S. R. (Sujatha Reghunathan), 1965-
Higher bureaucracy and social change / S.R. Jitha and Reinhart Philip.
p. cm.
Includes bibliographical references (p.).
ISBN 9789351280019

1. Bureaucracy—India. 2. Public administration—India. 3. Social change—India. I. Philip, Reinhart, joint author. II. Title.

DDC 352.630954 23

Contents

Foreword 7
Acknowledgements 11
Abbreviations 13

1. Introduction 15
2. Bureaucracy in India: Origin and Legacy 31
3. Value Premises of Indian Administration 43
4. Bureaucracy in India: Constitutional and Legal Foundations 57
5. Bureaucracy and Governance in the Era of Globalisation 77
6. Liberalisation and Development in India 91
7. Bureaucracy in the Post-Liberalised India 107
8. Bureaucracy and Corruption 125
9. Liberalisation and Corruption 143
10. Bureaucracy and Human Rights 159
11. Bureaucracy and Health Sector 183
12. Bureaucracy and Environmental Conservation 207
13. Summary and Conclusion 229

Appendix 239
Bibliography 249
Index 261

Foreword

Engines of Change in a New Development Paradigm

The famous French philosopher Pierre Tielhard de Chardin once said, "Some day, after mastering the winds, the waves, the tides and gravity, we shall harness for God the energies of love, and then, for a second time in the history of the world, man will have discovered fire." This new fire, according to none other than Dr A.P.J. Abdul Kalam is what needs to be discovered for achieving the 21st century mission of peace with prosperity. True, because "a global society stands at its defining moment in history — the needs of the times consisting of prosperity with inclusion, development with equity and industrialisation with environmental concern". It is precisely this challenge that is sought to be addressed when one talks of bureaucracy in the overall context of development. This is all the more relevant in today's scenario wherein the TINA factor (There Is No Alternative) and the NIMTO Syndrome (Not In My Term of Office), not to speak of the canker of corruption, often make bureaucrats Ferrari drivers caught up in a traffic jam.

As India's Second Administrative Reforms Commission observed, "The state apparatus is generally perceived to be largely inefficient with most functionaries serving no useful purpose. The bureaucracy is generally seen to be tardy, inefficient and unresponsive. Corruption is all-pervasive, eating into the vitals of our system, undermining economic growth, distorting competition and disproportionately hurting the poor and marginalised citizens...". No wonder why a 2009 survey on 12 Asian Economies done by the Hong Kong-based Political and Economic Risk Consultancy ranked India's "suffocating bureaucracy" as the least efficient.

Development, according to Amartya Sen, is a process of expanding the real freedom that people enjoy. If this rhetoric is to be turned into reality, we should make a frontal assault on the citadels of the persistent and self-defeating neglect of the impoverished sections of society despite the intensity of problems that these people represent. The sad reality is that they are still treated as sacrificial lambs who can be dispensed with in the pursuit of "development". A combination of historical injustice, cultural exclusion and insensitivity has denied them their legitimate space in the development discourse. Unless the fruits of development reach these marginalised citizens, I am afraid that the tryst with destiny to which we redeemed our pledge on the midnight of 14th August 1947 will get demeaned into a tryst with destitution. It is herein — in service delivery at the cutting edge of administration and in integrating the concerns of the voiceless into policies that are framed at the higher echelons of administration — that the bureaucracy should play a catalytic role.

This book addresses the relevance of the bureaucracy as a change agent in the development paradigm. It perches the redefined role of the steel frame in an era of globalisation. Such a change demands a paradigm shift in the mind-set of bureaucrats which is difficult to achieve, but inevitable in a neo-liberal order. Rather than reaping the benefits of an open economy they should be ready to take up the solemn responsibilities entrusted to them by the founding fathers of our Constitution. The importance of this book lies in its portrayal through the experiences of various senior bureaucrats, how bureaucracy can contribute to such a change, a source of inspiration indeed for the successors-in-office.

Diverting from the casual pattern of documentation the present book analyses in depth the nuances of corruption, development, human rights and environmental conservation in a novel fashion. It highlights the multi-faceted aspects of corruption and brings them into a single thread. Its distinctive approach lies in bringing forth the principles of ability-to-pay, willingness-to-pay and mutual-trust in the usual working of corruption in society and the factors that pave the way for "liberalised corruption". The book has brought out in detail the bureaucratic evils prevailing at large in the system as aptly summarised in the words of Lord Curzon himself, "Round and round like the revolutions of earth goes, file goes after file in the bureaucratic daily dance, stately solemn, sure and slow."

The authors firmly believe in the famous rhyme:

Nature is a temple where living pillars,
Sometimes let go off confused utterances,
Man walks amidst forests of symbols,
Watching him with familiar glances.

No wonder, the concepts of green captivism, commodification of air and green bureaucracy are the new additions of this book. In a system where the greens are getting enclosed and destroyed, posing a threat to the basic human rights of billions, bureaucracy needs to be green in nature. To quote Medha Patkar herself, "The victims of development are to be reached out to, mobilised and organised into non-party movements of political relevance based on people's empowerment and people's politics with a new political ideology and consciousness" — *Environmental Democratic Socialism*. That tantamount to abbreviate the contribution required to be made to the concept of environmental jurisprudence.

To summarise, the book in its totality outlines the issues that needs to be addressed for bringing about a change in the society and the responsibility therein of the bureaucrats. In fact, the authors have gone deep into the bureaucratic cobweb in the context of the hydra headed monster that consumer India represents.

Being a career bureaucrat myself, I am reminded of the words of a former chief secretary of Karnataka who believed that, "...the true challenge of a civil servant lies in the manner in which he responds to pressure of the wrong kind, political or otherwise, to do something blatantly illegal or against the public interest. If he has acted according to his conscience, the consequence should not matter, be it losing his position or facing a reprimand".

I am also inclined to quote Rajaji who suggested that "if the parched fields of Indian Administration have to get fresh, green life and grow, we need the monsoon of purity in national character".

If democracy means "speaking truth to power, to make truth powerful and power truthful", the steel frame in a democratic setup should take these words to heart and uphold the principles of good governance.

They should adhere to the major public service values listed in "The World We Could Win"— access to justice, adherence to due process and to the rule of law, respect for human rights and democratic values, care for the need of poorest and vulnerable groups, tolerance for diversity, protection of the environment, sustainability of outcomes and public service professionalism. Equally important for them is to keep off the seven sins of public life pointed out by the Father of the Nation — politics without principles, wealth without work, pleasure without conscience, knowledge without character, commerce without morality, science without humanity and worship without sacrifice. Then nothing can stop them from being agents of change in shaping the rightful destiny of the nation so that the locusts of despair do not destroy the harvest of India's freedom.

For, the Holy Bible says:

"Yea, though I walk through the valley of the shadow of death, I will fear no evil; Thou art with me."

In some faint dawn
In some dim eve
Like a gesture of light
Like a dream of delight...

I am sure that this book will be a readers' delight.

Dr. Raju Narayana Swamy, IAS
(Secretary to Government of Kerala)

Acknowledgements

The present work provided a great learning experience to us in many ways. In executing this work we have received guidance and assistance from several individuals and institutions and we would like to thank all who have contributed directly or indirectly to this work.

We sincerely express our deep sense of gratitude and respect to our teacher, late Prof. (Dr) M. Bhaskaran Nair, Former Head, Department of Political Science, University of Kerala for initiating us into this subject. We greatly cherish his noble ideas though he has left for his heavenly abode.

Our thanks to Dr Shaji Varkey, Head of the Department of Political Science, University of Kerala for his thoughts and suggestions.

We record our thanks to Dr Raju Narayana Swamy IAS, Secretary to Government of Kerala for writing the foreword.

Our special thanks to Kalpaz Publications for the keen interest in this area and also for their appreciation which enabled us to compile a work on *Higher Bureaucracy and Social Change.*

We thank all our teachers and those individuals and institutions that helped us in different capacities for the completion of this work. Sincere thanks to Dr K. Jayaprasad and Dr M.R. Biju, Associate Professors in Political Science, S.N. College, Kollam for their valuable help. Our thanks to Ms Suja S., Guest Faculty, Department of Commerce, S.N. College, Chengannur for the technical support. Thanks are due to Ms Anitha Kumari, UGC-JRF, Political Science, Hyderabad Central University and Ms Anjaly Vimala Stanley, Assistant, LIC of India, Chengannur, for going through the proof of the work.

Jitha S.R. expresses her gratitude and love to her husband Dr A. Thulaseedharan for his encouragement and inspiration to make this attempt a reality. She also thanks her son Anantajit for his patient cooperation.

Reinhart Philip places on record his deep reverence and love for his parents Shri M.C. Philip, Mrs Aleyamma Philip and Sister Rittu Philip, for their encouragement to proceed with the present work.

Above all, we bow before the Almighty God in making this endeavour a success.

S.R. Jitha and **Reinhart Philip**

Abbreviations

ARC	:	Administrative Reforms Commission
AIS	:	All India Service
BJP	:	Bharatiya Janata Party
CAG	:	Comptroller and Auditor General
CBI	:	Central Bureau of Investigation
CMS	:	Centre for Media Studies
CPI (M)	:	Communist Party of India, Marxist
CWG	:	Common Wealth Games
DCRB	:	Death-Cum-Retirement Benefits
DoPT	:	Department of Personnel and Training
ECOSOC	:	Economic and Social Council
ED	:	Enforcement Directorate
FDI	:	Foreign Direct Investment
GDP	:	Gross Domestic Product
GoI	:	Government of India
GoK	:	Government of Kerala
HDI	:	Human Development Index
HUNGaMA	:	Hunger and Malnutrition
IAS	:	Indian Administrative Service
ICS	:	Indian Civil Service
IIPS	:	Indian Institute of Population Studies
IMF	:	International Monetary Fund
INC	:	Indian National Congress
IPCC	:	Inter-Governmental Panel on Climate Change
IPS	:	Indian Police Service
ISIS	:	Institute of Science in Society
LBSNAA	:	Lal Bahadur Shastri National Academy of Administration

MIB	:	Ministry of Information and Broadcasting
MNC	:	Multi National Corporation
NFHS	:	National Family Health Survey
NIOH	:	National Institute of Occupational Health
PIB	:	Press Information Bureau
POSCO	:	Pohang Steel Company
PTI	:	Press Trust of India
RTI	:	Right to Information
TII	:	Transparency International India
UDHR	:	Universal Declaration of Human Rights
UN	:	United Nations
UNDP	:	United Nations Development Programme
UNEP	:	United Nations Environment Programme
UPSC	:	Union Public Service Commission
US	:	United States
WB	:	World Bank
WCED	:	World Commission on Environment and Development
WWF	:	World Wildlife Federation

1

Introduction

Bureaucracy is an important institution in every society, be it developed, developing or underdeveloped. Everywhere bureaucracy is large in size and great in importance. The higher bureaucracy, which is an integral part of an organised society, plays a crucial role in the socio-economic transformation and development of all societies. Although politicians are in command, it is the higher civil servants who provide input into various development policies and schemes. Their deep understanding and experience would benefit the political leadership in the correct formulation of development strategies. Bureaucracy gets importance due to them being steering the wheel of administration. When the government is involved in developmental activities, bureaucracy becomes the main instrument of the implementation of government programmes. In a developing society like India, bureaucracy is considered as the backbone of developmental programmes and social change. The higher bureaucracy is defined as a relatively permanent top group of civil servants who are placed between the political decision-makers and the rank and file bureaucracy and who share in different degrees the task of directing various administrative agencies (Lee 1970: 108).

Bureaucracy

The term bureaucracy has become a commonly used one and in the day-to-day life one may use that term more often as a curse than praise. Be it in the railway station, bus stand, way side or in front of any government office, from the most illiterate to the literate have many stories to tell about their 'dealings' with bureaucrats. Of all, majority will be related to the bitterness they have to face from the government servants, including matters related to bribes. Thus, bureaucracy has become a term that the common man looks up with fear, contempt and scorn. Instances of bureaucracy, being praised is very much limited and this is because of the attitude of bureaucrats who wants to see themselves as a group apart from the society.

Originating from the word 'bureau' and using from the early 18th century France, bureaucracy refers writing desk in workplace where the officials work. In simple sense it denotes a body of regular government employees mostly in the specific sense, of Civil Service especially the higher government service (Ramakanth and Mathur 1994: 46). The person first used this word by speaking of it as bureaucratic was Vincent de Gourney, an eighteenth century French Minister of Commerce. The new word gained acceptance and soon spread to other countries. It came into considerable vogue in the 19th century Germany, where a highly developed civil service existed. The real flowing of the word in many languages and the systematic description and analysis as a part of modern government is a recent development. Modern democracies arose as the governments grew large during the modern period, especially industrial revolution, with the multiplication of the functions of the government; there has been the expansion in the number of officials as also in the rules and procedures.

The term Bureaucracy was used in many ways, rational organisation, rule of the officials, organisational efficiency, self- serving rather than serving the society, top civil service etc. Thus, the meaning depends upon the intension of the user. Simply put, bureaucracy is a hierarchical organisation of officials appointed to carry out certain public objectives or the great number of government employees who carry on the process of administration. In the broad sense, bureaucracy includes the entire array of government employees from local to the national level, in the narrow sense it indicates the top brass of civil servants, to say the IAS officers in India. Bureaucracy is being used in a negative sense too, a government by officials for their own aggrandisement. Laski sees, "Bureaucracy as a system of government, the control of which is so completely in the hands of officials that their power jeopardises the liberties of ordinary citizens." The classical writings on bureaucracy can be traced to several sources, Max Weber, Karl Marx, Peter Blaue, R.Michel and others.

The most important contribution to bureaucracy comes from the German Sociologist, Max Weber. Max Weber's name became synonymous with bureaucracy, for he enjoys a unique place in the galaxy of social scientists who have attempted to explain the concept of bureaucracy. Perhaps, he was the first scholar to make a systematic analysis of bureaucracy and the credit of formulating bureaucratic theory systematically, first, goes to him. For Weber, bureaucracy was inseparable from the term rationality, as he prefers a legal-rational bureaucracy, which is legitimised by being in accordance with formally correct rules and regulations. Weber defined bureaucracy as a legal, rational organisation based on certain important characteristics like division of labour, fixed remuneration of officials, a system of rules and files, officials are subjected to discipline and control during the performance of his duties, hierarchy and merit form of selection (Weber 1947: 333). Weber claimed that purely from a technical point of view, bureaucracy is capable of attaining the highest degree of rationality and effectiveness. The division of labour minimises duplication of tasks and hierarchy in organisational structure facilitates centralised control, planning and co-ordination. Merit based selection ensures persons of talent in administration. The impersonal feature of bureaucracy promotes objectivity in decision making and there by curbs irrational actions, favouratism and discrimination.

When an organisation comes closer to display these features, the more rational and effective it would be. An organisation that does not possess several of these features is not a fully developed bureaucracy. Bureaucracy according to Max Weber is the most efficient organisational form for the large scale complex administration that has been developed in modern world (Weber 1947: 333). He insists that bureaucracy as an independent entity is an indispensiable component of every society and its influence is inescapable. However, Weber was not blind towards the negative consequences of bureaucracy. Recognising the potential of the bureaucracy to do serious damage to valued social and political institutions, Weber was pessimistic about the ability of democracy to maintain control over the bureaucratic apparatus of the state.

Karl Marx's explanation of bureaucracy was assessed on its impact on the power structure of the society. Bureaucracy was not central to Marxian thought, though he made more than passive reference to bureaucracy in his *Critique of Hegel's Philosophy of Right*. Marx's interpretation of bureaucracy is within the general framework of his theory of class conflict, the crisis of capitalism and advent of communism. Marx sees bureaucracy as an instrument of the dominant class to exercise its domination over other classes in the society. Viewed in this regard, the interest of bureaucracy is closely linked to those of the dominant class, the bourgeoisie. According to Marx, bureaucracy constitutes a very specific and particular social group. It is not a social class altogether, its existence is linked to the division of society into classes. Bureaucracy does not occupy an organic position in the social structure, it leads a parasitic existence, a parasitic body designed to maintain status quo and the privileges of its masters, the dominant section of the society (Naidu 1996: 90). In Marxian thought, bureaucracy's main function is to maintain the status quo and the privileges of the master. It acts as a mechanism for the perpetuation of exploitation of the weaker sections by the dominant class.

Within the broader frame work of class struggle specific instances of alienation could be found. In this process of alienation, that the social forces escape from the control of man and bureaucracy becomes an autonomous and oppressive force. Majority of the people felt that it is incompetent, mysterious and a distinctive entity.

Robert Michels (1954) was another key contributor to the classical formulations of bureaucracy. He concentrated on the internal politics of large-scale organisations, including socialist parties and labour unions in Europe before World War I, for his analysis of bureaucracy. His studies revealed that there is a tendency in every organisation, to centralise the power of decision making, in an active minority of leaders. Based on his observation of the internal structure of the German Socialist Party, Michels formulated his *Iron Law of Oligarchy*, which states that in large organisations power is necessarily concentrated in the hands of a few, a law that applies equally to all organisations including the government. All organisations try to develop a bureaucratic structure, including the state. Michels regards bureaucracy as a highly rational and efficient instrument for implementing the goals of the few of the oligarchy.

Peter Blaue (1965: 50) describes an element of positivism when he emphasises efficiency as the core and goal of bureaucracy. He describes bureaucrats as ritualistic and explains their ritualism in terms of their fear of the superior and feeling of insecurity. Bendix is of the view that bureaucracy is a component of an extensive social system. According to him, it is inevitable that bureaucracy is constantly affected by individuals and their views in turn vitally influencing the totality of organisational and process spheres (Bendix 1959: 2006). Michel Crozier (1964: 320), in his book *The Bureaucratic Phenomenon* suggests bureaucracy as a part of social system, which consists of a distinctive culture, and a system of shared values.

V.A. Pai Panandikar and S.S. Kshir Sagar in their study of bureaucracy in India say that structural and behavioural characteristics of bureaucracy are only moderately related. The functional context of bureaucracy, and, the type of office and its level of mass contacts to meet programmatic needs, and the level of skill composition have a significant bearing on the behavioural characteristics (Pai and Sagar 1978: 6). Higher bureaucracy constitutes a small group in the governmental service largely drawn from members of the generalist administrative cadre. They are selected through competitive examinations after formal education. The civil servants engaged in development activities constitute the development bureaucracy (Victor 1964: 91). The development role of higher bureaucracy can be divided into: (i) policy formulation (ii) advice on financial and administrative matters (iii) implementation of public policies (iv) training, and (v) political dimensions (Sapru 1994: 276).

At the level of policy formulation the political leadership in the developing countries, which took over the administration from colonial domination, is preoccupied with several problems. In many cases, political leadership lacks required experience and professional skill for development planning, thus the role of higher bureaucracy in the formulation of development policy becomes more important. In certain instances, their advisory role transforms itself into the most effective factor in the determination of policies.

The higher bureaucracy has the responsibility of advising on the financial and administrative implication of decisions. This was necessitated by lack of understanding of political leadership about the intricacy and complexity of financial matters. Thus, administrators have to play a crucial role in the allocation of funds for different development schemes according to priorities. Besides the role in the policy making the higher bureaucrats are involved in implementing them and giving directions to the lower level bureaucracy as well as monitoring the implementation process. It should also be noted that after having formulated the policy, the senior bureaucrats have a very important responsibility of interpreting the policies to the lower level bureaucracy and train them in the methods to be adopted to achieve the goal. However, the political leadership in India has nurtured a different notion about the bureaucracy. Mostly regard bureaucracy as an instrument for facilitating and carrying out political dictates and it can be used for achieving their own self interests.

The top-level bureaucrats function as a conveyor belt between politician and administrative machinery and thereby make political control feasible (Jitha 2007: 51). With the task of public service being more numerous, complex and varied, there is need for competent and achievement oriented senior administrators to cope with the changing needs of the society. However, the knowledge, experience and superior skill are often not in agreement with the political leadership. They almost become integrated into political set up sharing the spoils in power. Thus, they became partners in the political and administrative system.

Development

Development in the third world became a very powerful analytical category in American social science thinking in the 1950s. It was looked at as a strategy against insurgency and growth of communism in the third world countries. The Comparative Public Administration Group in US perceives modern administration as a mechanism for the attainment of developmental goals. To them, bureaucratisation was a functional pre-requisite for maintaining stability and legitimacy in the political order. Thus, bureaucracy was looked upon as a machinery for the implementation of development policies.

The Western, especially, the American political thinkers did the conceptualisation and elaboration of development administration after the Second World War. This term has been used with reference to the developing nations of Asia, Middle East and Latin America (Dwivedi 1994: 3). The newly liberated countries of this region were concerned with the complex process of nation building and rapid socio-economic change. The emerging problem is how to combine skills which exist in these countries and bring them to bear more effectively in action programmes which will accelerate economic growth, expand social well being and improve public services (Milton and John 1969: 508).

Development is the top priority of national governments in third World countries. Literally, it means growth or improvement into a higher stage or status. It is widely conceived as a participatory process of directed social change in a society intended to bring about both social and material advancement. This broader sense conveys the ideas of progress, improvement, well-being and an aspiration for a better life. In a narrow sense, the term development refers to narrow goals such as increasing the rate of economic growth. Development in its economic dimension is associated with the maximisation of outputs, economic growth and in one word, economic development. Development as a process that stands for the transformation of society is significant as far as a third world country is concerned. From such a perspective, development can be defined as the efforts to improve the economic well being and quality of life of a community by encompassing the principles of participation, distribution and harmony, which rejects monopolies, special privileges and other exclusionary social barriers (Reinhart 2009: 48). Development thus has an intimate relation with social justice, which speaks of a society that offers individuals and groups fair treatment and an impartial share in the benefits of societal development.

The concept of development has numerous definitions. Edward Weidner (1970: 8) considers development as "a state of mind, a tendency or a direction rather than a fixed goal; it is a rate of change in a particular direction". According to John Montgomery (1966: 59) "development is an aspect of change that is desirable, broadly predicted or planned or influenced by governmental actions". Fred. W. Riggs (1970: 27) defines development in terms of "rising levels of autonomy or discretion in the sense of ability to choose among alternatives not of course in the sense of caution or moderation." Esman sees development as a rational process of organising and carrying out prudently conceived and staffed programmes or projects as one would organise and carry out military or engineering operations. To Colm and Geiger, development is change, change coupled with growth. Baron says that development means far-reaching transformations of society's economic, social and political structure of dominant organisation of production, distribution and consumption (Arora 2010: 13.4). These different definitions means development help us highlight a number of its features or implications. Some of these are:

- Development is a dynamic concept. It is an ever-changing one, always evolving, always moving forward and always advancing.
- Development is a multi-dimensional concept. This means that development is not only economic but also social and one that touches every aspect of human and social life.
- Development implies growth that is planned.

The term *Sustainable Development* in place of development has become increasingly popular in discussions among all the social scientists, organizations, statesmen, politicians etc. (Allam and Stein 2004: 5). The industrial-technological-economic development registered by human kind during the past 100 years has not proved to be a real development as far as it has created imbalances in the environment as well as among the nations. Degradation of environment resulting from unprincipled and excessive exploitation of resources of our planet earth has threatened to negate and has already adversely affected the development registered by various societies.

Sustainable development stands for sustainability and it represents an approach to development which is concerned with such fundamental concerns like poverty, environment, equality, democracy, development and peace. The Brundtland Commission on Environment and Development defined sustainable development as *the development that meets the needs of the present generation without compromising the ability of the future generations to meet their needs* (WCED 1987: 43). The four indicators of sustainable development includes: (i) Development in no way should lead to environmental degradation; (ii) Development should be in tune with the health of land, water, air, forests and other natural features of planet earth; (iii) The earth and its resources are the common possession of our civilisation and benefits must be shared equally; and (iv) Development in the present should in no way hinder or damage the developmental needs and abilities of the future generation.

Sustainable development involves the concept of "prudent management of available global resources and environmental capacities and the rehabilitation of the environment previously subjected to degradation and misuse" (Johan 2003: 15). It is the duty of the bureaucracy to ensure that development in no way should lead to environmental degradation and the development should be in tune with the health of land, water, air, forest and other natural resources. They also have to ensure that development should benefit all classes of people living in all parts of the world. So the role of bureaucracy in ensuring sustainable development is manifold and multi-dimensional.

Bureaucracy and Citizens

The relation developed by administrators with the people is of considerable importance, because the citizens depend upon the state to create necessary infrastructure and to find the necessary resources for development. Thus, the duty of the administrator is to understand the problems of the people and to create a balanced socio-economic and political environment, so that the citizens could lead a meaningful life. At the same time, the people must realise the limitations of rules and procedures, with which the administrators has to function and will be reasonable in making their demands. Such an attitude of mutual trust and confidence is necessary for the success of our socio-economic development.

Before independence, civil servants seldom met the public in any sense face to face and were confined to the collection of land revenue and maintenance of law and order (GoK 1958: 132). After independence, the leaders felt that the bureaucracy alone provide men of experience that would meet socio-economic demands of socially puzzled and politically unstable society of free India. In the post-independent period government has come closer to the daily life of citizens. The need and opportunity for contact between them have increased due to welfare and development schemes the five years plans. The number of rural development activities increased. A nation-wide programme of Community Development took shape (Dubashi 1998: 106). The National Extension Service was established to extend specific technical know-how and service to millions of farmers. A new strategy of agriculture was introduced. Again, during the middle of the second plan (1959-60), the idea of Panchayati Raj originated (Dubashi 1998: 106). Benefits of co-operative and commercial banking is being provided to the citizens belong to the weaker sections. The Public Distribution System, Health, Education and Family Welfare programmes were extended to the well being of the people of both the rural and urban areas. The starting of public sector undertaking brought the administration in direct contact with the people.

The extension of governmental responsibility over wide field of activities does not reached into its goals. There exists a wide gap between the aims and achievements, and a feeling that administration has not come up to the expectation of the welfare state. Its performance in its dealing with citizens leaves much to be desired. The common man does not always look upon the administration with any expectation of service to him. Instead, he feels to be carrying the burden of the administration in his shoulders (Bhaskaran Nair 1988: 30). Why people get alienated from the administration? Why are they denied the basic minimum services that they deserve from the administration? How the entire bureaucracy in a way has become irresponsible and unaccountable? The reasons for such a feeling are that policies are not being implemented effectively. The discretionary powers and unnecessary delay and inconvenience, which it creates, restrict individual freedom caused general dissatisfaction among the people. The chances of getting justice from the lower level functionaries are negligible. Very often the functionaries are not responded to the applicants. Sensitivity to public grievance at the lower level has gone down.

Another aspect is lack of transparency in administration. Civil servants usually function in an atmosphere of secrecy and they like to be a closed society. Normally, they dislike sharing information to the public and wants restricted access of the public to the records and files they keep. This can be seen even after the passing of the Right to Information Act 2005, by which it is mandatory to provide the sought information, as per the rules. But there is lots of complaint that information in a document concerned with a citizen or a petitioner is not often given properly, claiming confidential nature of the document. K.J. Alphonse IAS (1996: 56) states, "I do not understand why we have to be secretive in dealing with such papers. If a decision is taken based on objective analysis, there is no reason to hide decision from the public."

The bureaucracy ignored the criteria to be objective, neutral and value laden. Trends have emerged like; rules and regulations are modified or even ignored to suit their convenience. Complaints of favouratism to friends and relatives or men of position and money are regular ailments of the people. There is a feeling among the ordinary people that the administrators consider their entry into the service as a means of attaining power. They felt that they are not treated with due respect and regards. Citizens have to face so many hurdles to reach the higher officials. No consideration is shown for the value of time of the citizen. If at all, they manage to meet the officers they get a cold response. This type of approach of the officials is infuriarating and frustrating for the people and has alienated the citizens from the officials (Rao 1980).

There is also a general feeling among the administrators that the citizens very often fail to look after the difficulties of administration. They put unreasonable demands upon the administrators, without considering rules and procedures. The administrators also complain that the people who have sufficient political pull have a tendency of bringing political pressure upon civil servants for their personal gain (Rao 1980). If the officials are not in a position to fulfill such demands, they become the victims. This section of the people would prefer to take all their problems directly to the politicians instead of approaching the administrators.

Emergence of coalition politics and coalition governments created vacuum in the political system. Erosion of political system and its authority started since long, but now the intensity and magnitude of all the atrocious activities like scams and illegal deals have become a day-to-day affair. Parliamentary democracy is a number game, the sovereign people in a democratic set up is having nothing to do except wait and watch. This degenerating situation is because of the linkage of administrators with social, political and legal system. In the ecology of administration, people too have accepted their destiny to be exploited by them. Bureaucrats in this crisis-ridden situation either becomes headless or with overheads having many commands at a time. This created conflict between the vested interests forcing them to find out new ways and means of this relationship. Some of the smart officials decided to take a middle path, that they can change their interests and loyalty according to their needs and convenience.

Corruption

Corruption is the misuse of public power for private gain or misuse of public office for private gain (Guham and Samuel 2001: 246). Corruption can assume many forms to cover a wide variety of transactions and helps in the spread of administrative corruption to all levels. If the top is not clean obviously the bottom is bound to be unclean. Without face or shame, illegal qualifications are now openly demanded for official business small or big. No law, rule or regulation comes in the way. Corruption operates at various levels in public sphere which influences political and administrative behaviour. It can do so independently among politicians and bureaucrats. But more commonly there is nexus between corrupt politicians and bureaucrats. The common men are denied of basic justice in the hands of corrupt officials.

Neither rules nor regulations come on the way and illegal and impermissible transactions are carried out quickly. Black money exceeds the accounted money (Guham and Samuel 2001: 246). The latest estimates of the black economy in India by the Global Financial Integrity put the quantum of black money at Rs. 22.5 lakh crore or half of India's GDP (Dhiraj and Sandheep 2011: 19). Black money really keeps Indian exchequer poor and weak and has been the root cause of growing economic inequalities, monopolisation of wealth and resources and continued ill-health of the national economy. This aggravates inequality in an already unequal society. Due to corruption and maladministration, the common man does not look upon the administration with any good expectation of service to him; instead they consider it as a burden or liability (Bhaskaran Nair 1988: 30).

Liberalisation and Globalisation

Liberalisation and Globalisation are both part of the programme of economic reform undertaken by dozens of countries in the last decade to give a new shape and direction to their economies. This programme represents a most radical departure from the theory and practice of state intervention that had a powerful grip in the backward economies of Asia, Africa and Latin America in the post war years. Liberalisation is the progressive elimination of the control of the state over economic activities. It is driven by the neo-liberal idea that government involvement should be as low as possible, leaving the field to the operation of self-interest driven market forces of demand and supply. The programme of liberalisation has two dimensions, internal and external. Globalisation or external liberalisation as a deliberately adopted economic policy is intimately connected with the phenomena of globalisation as a process that has been sweeping the world over the last couple of decades.

Armand Mattelart refers to globalisation as, "one of those tricky words, one of those instrumental notions that, under the effect of market logics and without citizens being aware of it, have been naturalised to the point of becoming indispensable for establishing communication between people of different cultures." He argues that globalisation has a hegemonic role in organising and decoding the meaning of the world (Tony and Webb 2006: 1). To Samir Das Gupta (2006: 144) "Globalisation is a powerful tool of capitalism, which comes dripping with blood and dirt from every pore, from head to foot, of ordinary people in the Third World." James Petras and Henry Veltmeyer (2001: 8) argue that "globalisation is little more than imperialism in a new form." To them, globalisation has a class project behind it.

Alfred Saad sees, "globalisation as merely the international face of neo-liberalism: a worldwide strategy of accumulation and social discipline that doubles up as an imperialist project, spearheaded by the alliance between the US ruling class and locally dominant capitalist coalitions" (Saad and Deborah 2005: 2). He further states, this ambitious power project centered on neo-liberalism at home and imperial globalism abroad is implemented by diverse social and economic political alliances in each country, but the interests of local finance and the US ruling class, itself dominated by finance, are normally hegemonic. Globalisation and imperialism cannot be analysed separately.

Globalisation, as propounded as a process of economic integration has its roots entrenched in the capitalist mode of production. Capitalism is, no doubt the by-product of Industrial Revolution and is the highest form of commodity production. Marx and Engels has quoted in the *Manifesto,* "The need for a constantly expanding market for it products chases the bourgeoisie over the whole surface of the globe. It must nestle everywhere, settle everywhere, and establish connections everywhere." When the home market of the bourgeoisie becomes not sufficient to consume all the products, they will be forced to set up new markets. That is what happened in the world, especially after the industrial revolution and the capitalists annihilated all the national and geographical barriers through its concerted efforts. New commodities were exported which ultimately destroyed the indigenous markets and productive system. After the Second World War the physical conquest of one nation by another got replaced by economic conquest or as Kwame Nkrumah (1999: 43) says, "in place of colonialism as the main instrument of imperialism we have today neo-colonialism." The essence of neo-colonialism is that the state which is subject to it is, in theory, independent and has all the outward trapping of international sovereignty. In reality its economic system and thus its political policy is directed from outside. Foreign capital is used for the exploitation rather than for the development of the less developed parts of the world. Investment under neo-colonialism increases rather than decreases the gap between the rich and the poor countries of the world (Dave and Ellen 2009: 202).

Samir Amin (2001) refers to this stage (globalisation) as the third wave of imperial devastation. The first phase of this devastating enterprise was organised around the conquest of the Americas, in the framework of the mercantilist system of Atlantic Europe at the time. The second phase of imperialist devastation was based on the industrial revolution and manifested itself in the colonial subjection of Asia and Africa. Opening the markets and seizing the natural resources of the globe formed the real motive behind this devastation. The third wave of devastation of the world by imperialist expansion was encouraged by the collapse of the Soviet system and of the regimes of populist nationalism in the Third World. The control of the expansion of markets, the looting of the earth's natural resources, the exploitation of the labour reserves in the periphery, etc. forms the main objectives of the dominant capital even during its third wave of devastation.

The big push towards globalisation was both political and economic. Politically the big push was a result of the dramatic change in political power away from leftist, populist and nationalist regimes towards globalist governments. The big push from the political side was the counter-point of a confluence of economic developments that engineered the dynamics of globalisation. Four factors have preceded and contributed to the big push: (i) the over-accumulation crisis; (ii) profit squeeze resulting from labour/capital relations; (iii) intensification of International Capitalist Competition; and (iv) massive growth of financial market. As a practical solution to the over-accumulation crisis, i.e., shrinking of profit when capital grew within the bounds of nation state, the neo-liberalists advocated a break down in the internal constraints on external movements to overseas markets. Globalisation thus became a solution to the over-accumulation crisis.

Many of the nations of Asia, Africa and Latin America entered the circle of globalisation during the crisis of 1980s and 1990s. To come out of the crisis, the IMF and the World Bank provided conditional loans and these nations were forced to undertake the Structural Adjustment Policies (SAP), which can be called as a trap to globalisation. Accepting SAP made these nations implement neo-liberal policies of: dismantling of state regulations, liberalisation of export-import laws, de-licensing, flexible laws including labour laws, corporate tax reduction, increased subsidies to corporate, hegemonious control of employers in hiring, firing, outsourcing, sub-contracting and so on.

Globalisation is nothing but the expansion of capitalism or the higher stage of capitalist expansion. It can be said that, capitalism, imperialism and globalisation are different stages of the same process of unfolding of capital. Colonialism emerged when the domestic markets became insufficient to consume all that is produced. New markets were created around the world by the industrial powers. The creation of new markets was through the creation of colonies, which benefited the colonial powers not just through market for their commodities but also by providing abundant raw materials and cheap labour. Capitalism expanded further and reached a monopoly stage in which capital (finance) itself became a commodity, the stage defined by Lenin as Imperialism, the monopoly stage of capitalism. Imperialism hasn't been washed away with the Second World War. Instead colonialism and imperialism emerged in their new guise neo-colonialism and neo-imperialism. As a solution to the over-accumulation crisis and profit-squeeze resulting from labour-capital relations, the capitalists advocated a free market economy, which got sway under neo-liberalism. The neo-liberal advocacy created a favourable climate for the emergence of what is known as Globalisation.

Not only the reason but also the features or consequences of colonialism, imperialism and globalisation are the same: exploitation of labour; concentration of wealth in the hands of a few and deprivation of majority out of the means of production. In all these stages we can see an unequal relation between the dominant and the dominated, i.e., between the haves and the have-nots (Reinhart 2012: 38). Exploitation of wage labour by the one holding capital forms the basis of a capitalist system and the haves exploited the have-nots from the very beginning stages and it is still continuing. Exploitation perpetuates unequal relations both at the domestic and at the international level. The call for a New International Economic Order (NIEO) is the clear manifestation for the unequal relations that exists between the developed North and the developing and under-developed South. In all these stages, those who controlled the means of production, especially capital controlled the system. The advantaged position of one creates disadvantages for the other, that too the case under globalisation.

Social Change

By social change is meant in simple, an alteration in the social order of a society. In other words social change is the transformation of political, social and economic systems and institutions to create a more equitable and just society. The terms economic development, social change, nation building, modernisation etc. are interchangeably used. Esman defines socio-economic progress (change) as the "sustained and widely diffused improvement in material and social welfare and nation building as the deliberate fashioning for integrated political community within fixed geographical boundaries in which the nation-state is the prominent political institution" (Esman 1966: 59). The New Public Administration exhorts realisation of social equity as a purpose of public administration and social equity means that public administrators should become champions of the underprivileged sections of the society (Nigro and Nigro 1984: 15). The public administrators must become active agents of economic and social change. Bureaucracy as an agent of social and economic change has added significance in this era of globalisation, where market economy threatens equality and social justice (Jitha and Reinhart 2012: 54). The policies of globalisation have resulted in serious social crisis, making the rich richer and the poor poorer by concentrating wealth in the hands of a few and keeping the majority out of the benefits of development.

References

Alfred, Saad-Filho and Deborah, Johnston (eds) (2005): *Neo-liberalism: A Critical Reader*, Pluto Press, London.

Allam, Ahmed and Stein, Josephine (2004): "Science, Technology and Sustainable Development: A World Review," *Inderscience*, 1(1).

Alphons, K.J. (1996): *Making a Difference*, Viking Publishers, New Delhi.

Arora, N.D. (2010): *Political Science*, McGraw Hill Education, New Delhi.

Bendix, R. (1959): "Bureaucracy" in *International Encyclopaedia of Social Sciences*, MacMillan, New York.

Bhaskaran, Nair M. (1989): "Evolving New Values in Civil Service and Combating Corruption," *Kerala Journal of Social Sciences*, Vol. III and IV, No. 1 and 2, July/December.

Dasgupta, Samir and Kiely, Ray (2006): *Globalisation and After,* Sage, New Delhi.

Dave, Hill and Ellen, Rosskam (2009): *The Developing World and State Education: Neo-liberal Depreciation and Egalitarian Alternatives*, Routledge, New York.

Dhiraj, Nayyar and Sandheep, Unnithan (2011): "The Great Indian Robbery," *India Today*, XXXVI(5), January 31, 18-24.

Dubashi, P.R. (1998): "Restructuring and Reforms of Indian Political, Administrative and Economic System", in T.N. Chaturvedi, *Fifty Years of Indian Administration: Retrospects and Prospects*, Indian Institute of Public Administration, New Delhi.

Dwivedi, O.P. (1998): "Development Administration: An Overview", in Chaturvedi, T.N (ed.), *Fifty Years of Indian Administration: Retrospect and Prospects*, Indian Institute of Public Administration, New Delhi.

Edward, W. Weidner (1970): "The Elements of Development Administration", in Weidner (ed) *Development Administration in Asia*, Duke University Press, Durham.

Esman, Milton J. (1966): "The Politics of Development Administration", in Montgomery and Siffin, *Approaches to Development Politics, Administration and Change*, McGraw Hill, New York.

Fred, W. Riggs (1970): "The Idea of Development Administration", in Weidner (ed) *Development Administration in Asia*, Duke University Press, Durham.

GoK (1958): Government of Kerala, Report of Administrative Reforms Committee, Vol. I and II, Government Press, Thiruvananthapuram.

Guhan, S. and Samuel Paul (2001): "Corruption in India", in S. Subramanian (ed) *India's Developmental Experience*, Oxford University Press, New Delhi.

Jitha, S.R. (2007): *Higher Bureaucracy and Development*, Kalpaz Publications, New Delhi.

Jitha, S.R and Reinhart, Philip (2012): "Higher Bureaucracy, Liberalisation and Social Change", *South Asian Journal of Socio Political Studies*, XII(2), Jan-June, 53-6.

Johan, Rockstrom (2003): "Rethinking Water Management: Innovative Approaches to Contemporary Issues", *Earthscan*, London.

John, Montgomery (1966): "A Royal Invitation: Variation on Three Classic Themes", in Montgomery and William Siffin (eds) *Approaches to Development: Politics, Administration and Change*, McGraw-Hill, New York.

Lee, Hahn-Been (1970): "The Role of Higher Civil Service Under Rapid Social and Political Change", in Edward Weidner (ed.), *Development Administration in Asia*, Duke University Press.

Max, Weber (1947): *The Theory of Social and Economic Organisation*, Oxford University Press, New York.

Michel, Crozier (1964): *The Bureaucratic Phenomenon*, The University of Chicago Press, Chicago.

Milton, J. Esmon and John D. Montgomery (1969): "System Approaches to Technical Cooperation: The Role of Development Administration", *Public Administration Review*, 29(5), September-October.

Naidu, S.P. (1996): *Public Administration, Concepts and Theories*, New Age International, New Delhi.

Nigro, F.A. and Nigro, L.G (1984): *Modern Public Administration*, Horper Collins.

Nkrumah, Kwame (1999): "Excerpt from Kwame Nkrumah's Neo-Colonialism: The Last Stage of Imperialism", *The Crisis*, July-August.

Peter, Blaue (1965): *Bureaucracy in Modern Society*, Random House, New York.

Petras, James and Veltmeyer, Henry (2001): *Globalisation Unmasked*, Madhyam Books, New Delhi.

Priya, Ranjan Dash (2008): "Slowdown, my Foot; Economy is in the Black", Dec. 18, http://www.mydigitalfc.com/economy/slowdown-my-foot-economy-black-483.

Ramakanth, Rao M.G. and Mathur, Prashant K. (1994): *Advanced Public Administration: Policy, Planning and Decision-Making*, Kanishka Publishers, New Delhi.

Rao, T.M. (1980): "The Civil Servants are Not on the Job", *The Statesman*, Calcutta, November.

Reinhart, Philip (2012): "Globalisation: The Higher Stage of Capitalist Expansion", *University College Journal of Politics and Society*, Research Journal, Department of Political Science, University of Kerala, 7(1 and 2), March, 27-40.

—— (2009): "Economic Development and Social Justice", *Competition Success Review*, XLV(11), May, 48-50.

Robert, Michel (1954): *Political Parties: A Sociological Study of the Oligarchical Tendencies of Modern Democracy*, Dover Publishers, New York.

Samir, Amin (2001): "Imperialism and Globalisation", *Monthly Review* 53(2), July.

Sapru, R.K. (1994): *Development Administration*, Deep and Deep Publications, New Delhi.

Tony, Schirato and Jen, Webb (2006): *Understanding Globalisation*, SAGE Publications, New Delhi.

Victor, A. Thompson (1964): "Administrative Objection for Development Administration", *Administrative Science Quarterly*, Vol. 9, June.

WCED (1987): *Our Common Future*, Report of the World Commission on Environment and Development, Official Records of the General Assembly, 42nd Session, Supplement No. 25 (A/42/25).

2

Bureaucracy in India: Origin and Legacy

In India the concept of bureaucracy as it presently understood was first introduced by the British. British administration in India was established through the agency of trading corporation namely the English East India Company formed in 1600 under the Charter of Queen Elizabeth. The Act gave the company the right of trading to different parts of Asia, Africa and Latin America. Thus, company established its factories at several places in the country. Gradually factories in Bombay, Madras and Calcutta become the chief Presidencies. This company of small traders slowly developed into an empire of the country. This mainly happened because at that time the country did not have any powerful rulers capable of maintaining law and order. The then Mughal Empire was came to an end and power vacuum developed in all parts of the country especially in Bengal where the company was involved in trading in the second half of the 18th century. In 1765, the East India Company secured the right of revenue collection and judicial administration of Bengal, Bihar and Orissa (Aravind 1992: 4). It did not made any large scale changes in the administration of provinces.

The officers of the East India Company were not concerned with good administration. The company fall into bankruptcy and there was the charge of corruption. Thus, the British Parliament appointed a committee to enquire into the affairs of the company and on the basis of the report of the committee; the Regulating Act of 1773 was passed. This marked the first constitutional advance over the earlier system of Government. A Supreme Government was constituted with a Governor General and four councillors. This Act constituted the first landmark in the transformation of the company's commercial council into a political apparatus of the British Government. It laid the foundation of a central administration and marked the beginning of the company's transformation from a trading corporation to an administrative concern (Narayanan 1973: 14).

Evolution of Civil Service in India

The creation of Indian Civil Service was the most important legacy of the British rule in India. The ICS on the one hand represented the visible presence of British rule in India and on the other hand formed the authority through which they expanded their network in India. In the beginning, the servants of the company who were engaged in its commercial affairs were called as "civil servants" to distinguish them from the military and naval personnel of the company. In 1675, the Company created a regular gradation of posts: Apprentice, Writer, Factor, Junior Merchant and Senior Merchant. Later on, when the Company acquired control over territories, the civil servants also assumed administrative tasks. By 1765, the term "civil servant" came to be used in the company's official records.

It was the efforts of Lord Warren Hastings and Lord Cornwallis that led to the rise of modern civil service in India. Hastings laid the foundations of civil service and Cornwallis reformed, modernised and rationalised it. Hasting introduced the post of District Collector, which still occupies a unique position in Indian administrative system. In 1772, Warren Hastings appointed the employees of East India Company as Collector in charge of Revenue in each district which was the basic territorial unit for administration. Thus, the office of "Collector of Revenue" came into existence symbolising the transformation of the company into a regular administrative organisation. But, the East India Company did not have a clear idea of the function of the collector, when they first established the office in Bengal and Bihar. When Cornwallis assumed office, in 1787, he united the administration of revenue, civil justice and magistracy in the office of District Collector. The District Collector became powerful machinery and the symbol and mainstay of imperial rule in India. Gradually, the functions of the collector evolved as time passed and at different needs came to the forefront (Aravind 1992: 3).

In appreciation of his efforts to standardise the civil service in India, especially the post of District Collector, Lord Cornwallis came to be known as the "Father of Civil Service" in India. He was doubtful about the integrity and ability of Indians and thought that the task of establishing and consolidating the British rule in India could not be left to the natives. Thus, he introduced the *Covenanted Civil Services* (higher civil services) which were different from the *Uncovenanted Civil Services* (lower civil service). He believed that an administration-based on the British model could be strongly established in India only by the Englishmen and not by the natives. He wanted to preserve the lucrative posts in civil services for the influential class of British society. So the covenanted civil service became the exclusive privilege of the whites who entered into a covenant to serve the Company (Mishra 1970: 201) faithfully and received a salary of 500 pounds (Malley 1965: 228). The service consists of different categories like judicial, political, revenue and mercantile. The uncovenanted civil service did jobs of mercantile nature such as registering, posting accounts and keeping diaries. The members of this service did not sign any covenant with the company and served the company on temporary basis. This twofold division was retained by the Aitcheson Commission and in 1892 christened as the Indian Civil Service and the Provincial Civil Service.

In 1800, Lord Wellesley established a college at Fort William in Calcutta to provide training to the civil servants of the Company. Three years training in oriental and European studies was imparted in the college, with great stress on learning the local languages of India in order to facilitate the communication between the British and Indians. The Court of Directors did not favour this move of Wellesley; so they established the East India College at Hartford Castle in 1806, later moved to Haileybury in 1809, for the same purpose. The college at Fort William continued as a language training school untill 1854.

The Charter Act of 1833 attempted to introduce a system of open competition as the basis of selection of civil servants of the Company, and stated that the Indians should not be debarred from holding any place, office and employment under the company. But this was negated due to the opposition of the Court of Directors. At the same time the increasing workload in the offices of the English judges and magistrates made possible the entry of large number of Indians, but to subordinate positions (Moreland and Chatterjee 1953: 400). The Charter Act of 1853 abolished the system of patronage and introduced the system of open competition. The patronage powers of the Court of Directors were deprived and the covenanted civil service was open to competition. The Macaulay Committee (the committee on the Indian civil service) was appointed in 1854 to suggest measures to give effect to the provisions of the Act. The committee made the following recommendations in its report submitted in 1854:

(i) The candidates for higher government jobs should be appointed on the basis of an open competitive examination.

(ii) The age of candidates for admission to the tests should be 18 to 23 years.

(iii) The competitive examinations should be held in England.

(iv) After finishing the training in England, there should be a probationary period for the candidates, in which they have to undergo district training.

(v) The East India College at Haileybury should be abolished.

(vi) The competitive examination should be of a high standard and should ensure the selection of candidates with thorough knowledge.

All the recommendations of the Macaulay Report were accepted and implemented by the Board of Control. Based on the report, the first competitive examination was held in London in 1855 under the Board of Control. Later on in 1858, this responsibility was transferred to the British Civil Service Commission (set up in 1855). Similarly, the East India College was abolished in 1858 and training to the civil servants was imparted in British Universities. The competitive examination aimed at testing the proficiency of the candidates in subjects like English Language, European Literature, Mathematics, Sanskrit, Arabic, Moral Science, Philosophy, Logic, Natural Science etc. (Ramesh and Rajani 2011: 43). The Macaulay Committee Report came to be known as the Bible on competitive recruitment and training. Since then the British Government, under the seal of the Crown, appointed various committees, commissions, boards, and study teams etc. for specified areas of administration. The most important among them includes the Aitchision Commission (1886-87), Islington Commission (1912-1915) and the Lee Commission (1923-1924). The Indian Civil Service Act of 1861 provided for the reservation of certain principal posts for members of the covenanted service. The next statutory Civil Service Act of 1870 remedied the defects of 1861 Act and provided for the Indianisation of services. However, it could be implemented only in 1879 by Lord Lytton, the then Viceroy.

From 1858 to 1919, the Indian Civil Service attracted the best talented of the British society. Queen Victoria's proclamation of 1858 declared that her subjects whatever race, creed were entitled to be appointed in all public services. This resulted in the recruitment of a band of administrators from Oxford and Cambridge Universities designated as Indian Civil Service (Jain 1976: 37). The ICS officers who so selected were gently but very quickly push up very high in society, to a ruling position by the colonial bureaucracy and accepted as such by the Indian Society.

The foundation for other services required at the central and provincial levels to ICS and Indian Police Service in the administration of the country was also laid by the British after 1858, through the establishment of various services at the central and provincial level. These services were in general and technical sphere. Organisations like Railway, Road, Telegraph and Departments like public works, irrigation, and forest were established in all the provinces. These services were profitable to the British trade and they would not do anything which affects the British trade and commerce (Letha 1990: 824). In the course of time, the British also took interest in undertaking certain welfare measures like means of education, health facility, legal system, making of roads, bridges, digging of canals etc. These services gradually developed into one of the most efficient and powerful civil service. It is important to note that these services with certain modifications continue to be utilised, to man the position in administration at the centre and state even today (Aravind 1992: 26).

Throughout these years British maintained the *English* character of the civil service. In order to address the increasing demand for Indians to higher and more extensive employment in public service, a public service commission under the chairmanship of Charles Aitchison was appointed in 1886. The Aitchison Commission submitted its report in 1887, and made the following recommendations:

1. There was to be a local civil service to be called the Provincial Civil Service.
2. The two-tier classification of civil services into covenanted and uncovenanted should be abolished.
3. Three services were carved out, viz., the Imperial Civil Service, the Provincial Civil Service and the Subordinate Civil Services.
4. The maximum age for entry into civil services should be fixed at 23 years.
5. The statutory civil service system of recruitment should be abolished.
6. The competitive examinations should not be held simultaneously in England and India.
7. Certain percentage of the posts in the imperial civil service should be filled by promotion of the members of the provincial civil service.

The recommendations of the Commission was largely accepted and implemented. The covenanted civil service was renamed the Indian Civil Service (ICS) and the uncovenanted civil service was named as Provincial Civil Service (PCS). The members of the Provincial Civil Service were recruited from the provinces to which it belonged. The Subordinate Civil Service was created by including the lowest ranks of the uncovenanted service. Though educational qualification was indispensible for entry to the PCS, element of reservation was included to secure due representation of different classes of the community in the public service. In matters related to promotion to higher posts of the ICS from PCS, the government framed rules in 1892 that stipulated that promotion must be by special selection and not on grounds of seniority alone (Mishra 1977: 140). It was also laid down that not more than one-sixth of the posts in the cadre of the ICS might be made available for promotion.

In 1912, the British Government appointed a Royal Commission on public services under the Chairmanship of Lord Islington. The Islington Commission submitted its Report in 1915, but it could be published only in 1917. By the time, the recommendations contained in it became outdated due to the first World War and the August Declaration of 1917. The commission recommended that recruitment to the superior posts should be made partly in England and partly in India. But, it did not favour the idea of holding the competitive examinations simultaneously in England and in India. The services under the Government of India should be categorised into class I and class II and 25 per cent of the superior posts should be filled by Indians partly by direct recruitment and partly by promotion. A probationary period of two years for direct recruits and three years for the ICS was also recommended.

The Montague–Chelmsford Report of 1918, known as the Montford Report or Report on Indian Constitutional Reforms, was the next milestone in the evolution of civil service in India. The report suggested that the members of the ICS should be given fair salary, pension benefits and allowances. Other important recommendations includes: 33 per cent of the superior posts should be recruited in India and this percentage should be increased by 1.5 per cent annually; and the competitive examinations should be held simultaneously in England and India. The recommendations were accepted and implemented by enacting the Government of India Act of 1919.

As a result of the reforms of 1918 and 1919, the first competitive examination for the ICS in India was held at Allahabad in 1922 under the supervision of the British Civil Service Commission. By this time there were a total of five methods of entry into the Superior Civil Services: (i) by open competitive examinations in England; (ii) by separate competitive examinations in India; (iii) by appointments from the Bar (in case of judicial positions, generally for the post of district and sessions judge); (iv) by promotion from the Provincial Civil Services; and (v) nomination in India to facilitate communal and provincial representation. The procedure of nomination was a strict departure from the Weberian model of recruitment by merit.

The number of All-India Services was nine by that time. That includes:

1. Indian Civil Service,
2. Indian Police Service,
3. Indian Forest Service,
4. Indian Forest Engineering Service,
5. Indian Service of Engineers,
6. Indian Civil Veterinary Service,
7. Indian Medical Service,
8. Indian Educational Service,
9. Indian Agricultural Service.

The Indian Agricultural Service was the last to be added to the list of All-India Services, in 1906-1907. The members of these services were recruited and controlled by the Secretary of State for India. Hence, these services were also known as the Secretary of State's Services. Notably, the term 'All-India Service' was first coined in 1918 by the Committee on Division of Functions, chaired by M.E. Gauntlett (Laxmikanth 2011: 1.6). A Staff Selection Board was set up by the Government of India in 1922 for the recruitment to the lower services. It functioned until 1926, when its functions were taken over by the newly established Public Service Commission.

In 1923, the Royal Commission on Superior Civil Services in India was appointed by the British Government, under the chairmanship of Lord Lee. The recommendations of the commission were striking and included:

1. Establishment of a public service commission provided by the Government of India Act of 1919.
2. Among the All-India Services only the Indian Civil Service, Indian Police Service, Indian Medical Service, Indian Service of Engineers (irrigation branch) and Indian Forest Service (except in the Bombay province) should be retained.
3. No further recruitment should be made to other All-India Services, viz., the Indian Agricultural Service, Indian Veterinary Service, Indian Educational Service, Indian Service of Engineers (roads and building branch) and Indian Forest service (only in Bombay province). The members of these services should in future be appointed and controlled by the provincial governments.
4. Direct recruitments should be in equal proportions for Indians and Englishmen.
5. For effecting Indianisation of services, twenty per cent of the superior posts should be filled by promotion from the Provincial Civil Service.
6. The British officers should be allowed to retire on proportionate pensions if they are not willing to work under Indian Ministers.

The recommendations of the Lee Commission were accepted and implemented by the British Government. A Central Public Service Commission consisting of a chairman and four other members was set up in 1926. It started functioning from 1st October of the same year and was entrusted with the task of recruiting civil servants. Sir Ross Barker, a senior member of the British Home Civil Service, was the first chairman (Laxmikanth 2011: 1.6). When the Government of India Act of 1935 was made operative in 1937, the commission was replaced by the Federal Public Service Commission which was finally replaced by the UPSC on 26th January, 1950, when the Constitution of India came into force. The Government of India Act of 1935 provided for the protection of the rights and privileges of the members of civil services. It also provided for the establishment of not only a Federal Public Service Commission but also a Provincial Public Service Commission and Joint Public Service Commission for two or more provinces.

The grant of provincial autonomy by the 1935 Act had its impact on the role of higher civil servants. The Governor Executive Council was replaced by Council of Ministers. They lost their share in the determination of policy of the government, except advisory functions. In the post-1935 period ICS officials learnt to tolerate the elected representative and ministers (Narayanan 1973: 16). The Higher Civil Servants in India from 1919 to 1939 enjoyed the major functions of: maintenance of order and security, efficiency in administrative matters; concern in regard to public works and irrigation without injuring the basic economic system and diverse type of rural development activities (Dwarakadas 1958: 21).

When the Second World War ended, the Government appointed a commission under, Sir Richard Tottenham to suggest measures for reorganisation of the structure, functions and form of administration. The report of commission was significant that it recommended a change from police administration to welfare administration. The commission recommended expansion of functions of PSC and the machinery for the selection of Secretarial Officers should come under the public service commission.

When Great Britain decided to quit India in 1946, unlike Nehru and G.B. Pant, Sardar Patel, emphasised the neutrality of the qualified administrators to maintain continuity in administration, stability and order, and to build a new India. The Indian Civil Service was allowed to continue in Independent India, with all its tradition, background and attitude (Jain 1976: 38). In 1947, the number of All-India Services was reduced to two: the Indian Civil Service and the Indian Police Service. Various Central and State services came in and the Central services were classified into four categories — Class I, Class II, Subordinate, and Inferior services. The Indian Administrative Service created after independence on the model of ICS has the legacies of ICS such as status consciousness, inclusiveness, aloofness and elitist background.

The Important Acts that Influenced Indian Administration and Civil Service

The landmarks in the development of the Constitution during the British rule which laid down the legal framework for the organisation and functioning of administration in British India were the Regulating Act of 1773; Charter Act of 1833; Indian Councils Acts of 1861, 1892; the Government of India Acts of 1858, 1909, 1919, 1935 and the Indian Independence Act of 1947.

The Regulating Act 1773: The Regulating Act of 1773 was the first step taken by the British Government to control and regulate the affairs of the East India Company in India. The Act formed the basis of all subsequent legislations for determining the form of government and is chiefly applied to the presidency of Bengal. It laid the foundations towards the centralisation of the governmental system of the company. The Governor of Bengal was designated as the Governor-General of Bengal. The first such Governor General was Lord Warren Hastings. The Governor-General and Council were empowered of superintending and controlling the presidencies of Bombay and Madras. It also established Supreme Court at Calcutta as the highest court and directed the company to pay annual salaries to the Governor-General and Council, the Chief Justice of Supreme Court and other judges.

Pitts India Act of 1784: The Act placed the Indian affairs under direct control of the British Government. The Act established a Board of six commissioners called "Commissioners for the Affairs of India", popularly known as the Board of Control. The Board represents the British Cabinet and has control over the Court of Directors, the governing body of the East India Company. The Act made provisions for the prevention and punishment of corruption, disobedience, etc., on the part of the company's servants in India.

Charter Act of 1833: By the Charter Act of 1833, the East India Company became a purely administrative body under the crown. The Board of Control was given responsibility to superintend, direct and control the affairs of the company relating to Government or revenues of the Indian Territory. The Governor-General of Bengal became the Governor-General of India. All civil and military powers were vested in him. In addition, the Government of Bombay and Madras were deprived of their legislative powers. This was the final step towards centralisation in British India. The Act created for the first time, the Government of India having authority over the entire territorial area possessed by the British in India. The Act also provided for the Codification of Law in India and a Law member was added to the Council of the Governor General. Other significant step of the Act was the disfavouring of excluding Indians from higher posts which was introduced by Cornwallis and reinforced by the Charter Act of 1793.

Charter Act of 1853: This Act separated, for the first time, the legislative and executive functions of the Governor-General's Council. A Law Commission was appointed for the codification of Indian laws. The Directors lost their power of patronage and there introduced a system of open competition as the basis of recruitment for civil servants of the Company. All vacancies in India were to be filled in by competitive examination.

The Government of India Act of 1858: This Act transferred the real powers of government, territories and revenues of India from the East India Company to the British Crown. In other words, the rule of company was replaced by the rule of the Crown in India. The Board of Control and Court of Directors were abolished and all their powers were transferred to the Secretary of State for India. The Secretary of State was a member of the British Cabinet and was assisted by Council of India, having 15 members. He was vested with complete authority and control over Indian administration through Governor

General as his agent, and he was responsible ultimately to the British Parliament.

Indian Council Act of 1861: The Council Act of 1861 was the first charter of Indian Legislative Assembly. It introduced for the first time the representative institutions in India. It thus provided that Governor-General's Executive Council should have some Indians as non-official members while transacting legislative business. Another significant move was the introduction of portfolio system in the Governor General's Executive Council. Each member of the Council was to be assigned charge of one or more departments, with the power to issue orders with regard to matters which concerned their department.

Indian Council Act of 1892: The Act introduced the principle of election but in an indirect manner. The Governor-General still had the power of nomination even though the members were indirectly elected. Also, it enlarged the functions of Legislative Councils and gave them the power of discussing the Budget and addressing questions to the Executive.

Indian Council Act of 1909: This act, also known as Minto–Morley Reforms was the opening of an important chapter in constitutional reforms in India. The size of central Legislature and provincial legislature, along with their functions were enlarged. The name of Central Legislative Council was changed to Imperial Legislative Council and the official majority in it was retained. The provincial Legislative Councils, on the other hand, were allowed to have non-official majority. The Act empowered the members to discuss the budget and move resolutions; ask supplementary questions and discuss matters of public interest. The most unfortunate feature of this act was the introduction of communal representation for Muslims by accepting the concept of 'Separate Electorate'.

Government of India Act of 1919: The Government of India Act of 1919 or the Montagu-Chelmsford Reform introduced dyarchy. The administrative subjects were divided into central list and provincial list. The Central control over the provinces was reduced by demarcating and separating the Central subjects from that of provincial subjects. The Central and provincial legislatures were authorised to make laws on their respective list of subjects. The Act further divided the provincial subjects into two parts — Transferred and Reserved. The transferred subjects were to be administered by the Governor with the aid of ministers responsible to the Legislative Council. The reserved subjects, on the other hand, were to be administered by the Governor and his Executive Council without being responsible to the Legislative Council.

The Act set up a bicameral legislature at the centre, consisting: Council of State (upper house) and a Legislative Assembly (lower house). The legislature was to have both elected and nominated members. The elective seats were distributed among the provinces on the basis of communities and classes. For the first time direct elections were introduced in the country. But the franchise was restricted. The Act also required that the three of the six members of the Governor General's Council (other than the Commander-in-Chief) were to be Indian. The Government of India Act of 1919, contained a provision for establishment of public service commission to discharge about recruitment and control of public services.

Government of India Act of 1935: The Government of India Act of 1935 provided for establishing an All-India Federation consisting of provinces and princely states as units. Consequently, the Act divided the powers between the Centre and units in terms of three lists, namely, Federal List (for Centre, with 59 items), Provincial List (for provinces, with 54 items) and the Concurrent List (for both, with 36 items). The residuary powers were given to the Governor-General. However, the federation never came into being, as the princely states did not join it.

The Act abolished Dyarchy in the provinces and introduced 'provincial autonomy' in its place. Thus, the provinces were freed to a large extent from the Central control. They are allowed to act as autonomous units of administration in their defined spheres. Moreover, the Act introduced responsible governments in provinces, that is, the Governor was required to act with the advice of ministers responsible to the provincial legislatures. This part of the Act came into effect in 1937 and was discontinued in 1939. Dyarchy was adopted at the Centre. Consequently, the federal subjects were divided into Reserved Subjects and Transferred Subjects. However, this provision of the Act did not come into operation at all.

The Act introduced bicameralism in six out of eleven provinces. Thus, the Legislatures of Bombay, Bengal, Madras, Bihar, Assam and the United Provinces were made bicameral consisting of a Legislative Council (upper house), a Legislative Assembly (lower house). However, many restrictions were placed on them. The Act provided for the establishment of Public Service Commission for the Provinces and Joint Public Service Commission for two or more provinces. A new authority, the Federal Railways Authority, was created for the control of railways. The Act also provided for the office of Advocate General and Financial adviser, to the Governor General.

Until 1947, the Government of India functioned under the provisions of the 1919 Act as the provisions of 1935 Act relating to federation and Dyarchy did not come into operation. Thus, the Executive Council provided by the 1919 Act continued to advise the Governor-General till 1947.

Indian Independence Act of 1947: The Act provided for the establishme... of two nations, India and Pakistan. India was declared as an independent sovereign state and the responsibility of the British Parliament for administration of India was brought to an end. Responsible government was established both at the Centre and at the Provinces. The Governor-General of India and the Provincial Governors were designated as constitutional heads (nominal heads). In other words, it made them to act on the advice of the respective council of ministers. The Constituent Assembly was to function as the Central Legislature of the Dominion to which it belonged. So, the dual function of constituent as well as legislative was assigned to the Assembly.

References

Aravind, S. (1992): *Indian Administration*, Himalaya Publishing House, Bombay.

Bhambhri, C.P. (1973): *Public Administration in India*, Vikas Publishing House, New Delhi.

Dwarakadas, R. (1958): *Role of Higher Civil Service in India*, Popular Book Depot, Bombay.

Jain, R.B. (1976): *Contemporary Issues in Indian Administration*, New Vishal Publications, New Delhi.

Laxmikanth, M. (2011): *Governance in India*, Tata McGraw-Hill, New Delhi.

Letha, Sinha (1990): "Role and Rationale of All India Services," *Indian Journal of Public Administration*, XXVI(4), Oct-Dec.

Malley, L.S.S.O. (1965): *The Indian Civil Service*, Frank Class and Company, London.

Mishra, B.B. (1977): *The Bureaucracy in India*, Oxford University Press, New Delhi.

——- (1970): *The Administrative History of India*, Oxford University Press, New Delhi.

Moreland, W.H. and Chatterjee, A.C. (1953): *A Short History of India*, Longmans, London.

Narayanan, Nair (1973): *The Civil Service under the Law and the Constitution*, The Academy of Legal Publications, Thiruvananthapuram.

Ramesh, K. Arora and Rajni, Goyal (2011): *Indian Public Administration*, New Age International, New Delhi.

3

Value Premises of Indian Administration

After Independence, the broad framework for Indian Administration was laid down by the Constitution of India which provided for a democratic and welfare state. The constitution is the highest law of the country and reflects the fundamental principles on which the system of government and administration of the country is based. The nature, structure, powers and role of Indian administration are determined and influenced by the principles and provisions of the Constitution of India. The influence of the Constitution on administration is direct by prescribing the configuration of the administrative system and indirect by determining the role, responsibility and responsiveness of the administrative system. It also influences the character and the behaviour of the administrators. Every constitution has its philosophy, values and some basic principles upon which the government structure is build up. The preamble of the Indian Constitution embodies these principles and set out the goals of the nation.

Constitutional Framework of Indian Administration

The Indian Constitution is the largest written constitution in the world, the lengthiest and most detailed one. The Original Constitution consisted of 395 Articles, 8 Schedules and 22 Parts. The number of articles remains the same, even today, but the number of Schedules was increased to 12 and the number of parts increased to 24. In framing the Constitution, the founding fathers drew inspiration from several foreign constitutions, like that of the United States, Ireland, Canada, Australia, England, Germany, etc., But such a process was not a bag of borrowing, instead, a tailoring to suit the needs of the Indian environment and to meet the aspirations of the people of India. The ideas and values of the National Movement got due recognition while framing the Constitution. The Constitution is the supreme law of the land and all agencies of the government, viz., the legislature, executive and judiciary is expected to act within the limits prescribed by the Constitution.

Preamble

The Preamble is the most precious part of the constitution which describes its philosophy. It describes the nature of the Indian state and the objectives which are to be achieved for all the citizens. Acting as the guiding star for the government, the Preamble enshrines the principles of Justice, Liberty, Equality and Fraternity. The Preamble of the Indian Constitution reads as follows:

WE, THE PEOPLE OF INDIA, having solemnly resolved to constitute India into a *Sovereign Socialist Secular Democratic Republic* and to secure to all its citizens:

JUSTICE, social, economic and political;

LIBERTY of thought, expression, belief, faith and worship;

EQUALITY of status and of opportunity; and to promote among them all

FRATERNITY assuring the dignity of the individual and the unity and integrity of the Nation;

IN OUR CONSTITUENT ASSEMBLY this twenty-sixth day of November, 1949, do **HEREBY ADOPT, ENACT AND GIVE TO OURSELVES THIS CONSTITUTION**.

The preamble through the words "We, the people of India" testifies the fact that the people are the ultimate source of all authority. Thus, preamble emphasises the principle of popular sovereignty. India is declared as a "Sovereign Democratic Republic". Later, by the 42nd Constitutional Amendment of 1976, the terms Socialist and Secular were added to the Preamble. India is a sovereign state from 14th August, 1947 and is not subject to the control of any foreign domains. A spirit of socialism was epitomised by the constitution. But now-a-days, a radical departure from this spirit can be seen, starting with the neo-liberal reforms of 1991. From a unique mixed economic pattern, India moved towards the pattern of Globalisation that works on the principle of the survival of the fittest. By secular is meant the absence of a state religion and freedom of conscience and religion for all, according to individual preferences. The state does not interfere with the religious freedom of the individual, until and unless warranted by public order, morality and health. India is a democracy where people elect their representatives and democracy prevails in the grass-root level too, in the form of Panchayati Raj Institutions. A parliamentary form of government was established in the nation, where the executive is a part of the legislature and is responsible to the legislature. India is a Republic, as the President of India; the head of the nation is elected and not adorns the office through heredity.

The preamble exhorts the objectives of justice, liberty, equality and fraternity. The dimensions of justice includes, social, economic and political. Ample provisions have been made in the Directive principles to ensure a social order in which justice triumphs. The second objective pertains to liberty with regard to belief, thought, expression, faith and worship. Article 19(1) guarantees the fundamental freedoms of speech and expression and Articles 25 to 28 guarantees freedom with regard to practice, profess and propagation of one's religion. Equality finds expression in the fundamental right to equality enshrined in Articles 14 to 18 of the constitution. Equality before law and equal protection of law is guaranteed to all under the constitution. Fraternity represents a moral and philosophical ideal of the Indian Constitution and has relevance in a multi-racial and multi-religious society like India. In short the Constitution provides a frame work of ideals and values for the administration to follow.

Fundamental Rights

Normally rights are those conditions of social life, without which no man can be at his best. Rights are needed for the fullest development of one's personality. Rights arise from the social nature of man and outside the circle of society there is no question of rights. While living in the society the rights of the man are not unlimited, it is limited by the rights of other persons. Rights can be better enjoyed only when we respect the similar rights of others. State exists there to regulate the claims of individuals and it is the duty of the state to see that everyone enjoys his or her rights, to have a decent life. Democratic governments usually enshrine these rights in their constitution itself. This incorporation will set some limitations on the powers of the legislature and executive, as a means for securing the enjoyment of such rights. The judiciary will serve as an impartial umpire to protect these rights, if encroached upon by the legislature or the executive.

Indian Constitution that is loudly solicitous about the rights of individuals has set apart a separate part for Fundamental Rights. Part III of the Indian Constitution, starting from Articles 12 to 35 deals with fundamental rights. The peculiarity of fundamental rights enshrined in Indian Constitution is that non-citizens of the state can enjoy some of the rights also. Rights like equality before law and equal protection of law (Article 14), protection in respect of conviction of offences (Article 20), right to life and personal liberty (Article 21), right against exploitation (Articles 23 and 24), freedom of conscience and religion (Articles 25 to 28), and quite naturally the rights to constitutional remedies (Article 32) are applicable both to citizens and aliens alike. At the same time, there are some limitations on the fundamental rights ensured by the Constitution. Subject to Articles 358 and 359, there can be suspension of rights mentioned in Article 19 (six fundamental freedoms) and on the right to approach courts for the enforcement of fundamental rights (except those mentioned in Articles 20 and 21), during a proclamation of emergency. Fundamental rights are also amendable by the Parliament.

Article 12 clarifies the word *state*, “the State” includes the Government and Parliament of India and the Government and the Legislature of each of the States and all local or other authorities within the territory of India or under the control of the Government of India. Article 13 deals with laws inconsistent with or in derogation of the fundamental rights. Article 13(1) reads that, all laws in force in the territory of India immediately before the commencement of this Constitution, in so far as they are inconsistent with the provisions of this Part (III), shall, to the extent of such inconsistency, be void. Clause 2 prohibits the State from making any law which takes away or abridges the rights conferred by the Part III and any law made in contravention of this clause shall, to the extent of the contravention, be void. Clause 3 defines law and law in force: (a) “law” includes any ordinance, order, bye-law, rule, regulation, notification, custom or usage having in the territory of India the forces of law; (b) “laws in force” includes laws passed or made by a Legislature or other competent authority in the territory of India before the commencement of this Constitution and not previously repealed, notwithstanding that any such law or any part thereof may not be then in operation either at all or in particular areas.

The fundamental rights guaranteed by the Constitution are as follows:

1. Right to Equality (Articles 14, 15, 16, 17 and 18);
2. Right to Freedom (Articles 19, 20, 21 and 22);
3. Right against Exploitation (Articles 23 and 24);
4. Right to Freedom of Religion (Articles 25, 26, 27 and 28);
5. Cultural and Educational Rights (Articles 29 and 30);
6. Right to Constitutional Remedies (Article 32).

Right to Equality

Article 14 states, “the State shall not deny to any person equality before the law or the equal protection of the laws within the territory of India.” All are equal before the eyes of law and enjoys equal protection of law.

Article 15 deals with prohibition of discrimination on grounds of religion, race, caste, sex or place of birth. Article 15(1) provides — the State shall not discriminate against any citizen on grounds only of religion, race, caste, sex, place of birth or any of them and; (2) No citizen shall, on grounds only of religion, race, caste, sex, place of birth or any of them, be subject to any disability, liability, restriction or condition with regard to — (a) access to shops, public restaurants, hotels and places of public entertainment; or (b) the use of wells, tanks, bathing ghats, roads and places of public resort maintained wholly or partly out of State funds or dedicated to the use of the general public. All these did not affect the powers of the state to make special provisions for women, children (Clause 3), any special provision for the advancement of any socially and educationally backward classes of citizens or for the Scheduled Castes or the Scheduled Tribes (Clause 4).

Article 16 provides for equality of opportunity in matters of public employment — (1) There shall be equality of opportunity for all citizens in matters relating to employment or appointment to any office under the State; and (2) No citizen shall, on grounds only of religion, race, caste, sex, descent, place of birth, residence or any of them, be ineligible for, or discriminated against in respect of, any employment or office under the State. However the constitution does not debar (3) the Parliament from making any law prescribing, in regard to a class or classes of employment or appointment to an office under the Government of, or any local or other authority within, a State or Union territory, any requirement as to residence within that State or Union territory prior to such employment or appointment.

Nothing in Article 16 prevents the State from making any provision for the reservation of appointments or posts in favour of any backward class of citizens which, in the opinion of the State, is not adequately represented in the services under the State.

Article 17 abolishes untouchability — "Untouchability" is abolished and its practice in any form is forbidden. The enforcement of any disability arising out of "Untouchability" shall be an offence punishable in accordance with law.

Article 18 ensures equality of status. The provisions are: (i) No title, not being a military or academic distinction, shall be conferred by the State; (ii) No citizen of India shall accept any title from any foreign State; (iii) No person who is not a citizen of India shall, while he holds any office of profit or trust under the State, accept without the consent of the President any title from any foreign State; and (iv) No person holding any office of profit or trust under the State shall, without the consent of the President, accept any present, emolument or office of any kind from or under any foreign State.

Right to Freedom

Article 19 gives six fundamental freedoms to the citizens. All citizens shall have the right:

(a) to freedom of speech and expression;

(b) to assemble peaceably and without arms;

(c) to form associations or unions;

(d) to move freely throughout the territory of India;

(e) to reside and settle in any part of the territory of India; and

(f) to practice any profession, or to carry on any occupation, trade or business.

These six fundamental freedoms constitute the backbone of the right to freedom defined in the Constitution. Originally, there were seven fundamental freedoms. But by the 44th Constitutional Amendment of 1979, the right to hold, acquire and disposal of property Article 1(f) was deleted from the Constitution. The rights guaranteed in Article 19 are not without restrictions. The state can imposes reasonable restrictions in the interests of the sovereignty and integrity of India, the security of the State, friendly relations with foreign States, public order, decency or morality, or in relation to contempt of court, defamation or incitement to an offence.

Article 20 provides protection in respect of conviction for offences: (i) No person shall be convicted of any offence except for violation of a law in force at the time of the commission of the Act charged as an offence, nor be subjected to a penalty greater than that which might have been inflicted under the law in force at the time of the commission of the offence; (ii) No person shall be prosecuted and punished for the same offence more than once; (iii) No person accused of any offence shall be compelled to be a witness against himself.

Article 21 gives protection of life and personal liberty: No person shall be deprived of his life or personal liberty except according to procedure established by law. It provides the right not to be subject to imprisonment, arrest or physical coercion in any manner without legal justification. The rights mentioned in Articles 20 and 21 are inviolable even during the proclamation of emergency.

By the 86th Constitutional Amendment of 2002, a new article has been incorporated as 21A, Right to Education — The State shall provide free and compulsory education to all children of the age of six to fourteen years in such manner as the State may, by law, determine.

Article 22 guarantees protection against arrest and detention in certain cases. Two rights are guaranteed under Article 22(1) No person who is arrested shall be detained in custody without being informed, as soon as may be, of the grounds for such arrest nor shall he be denied the right to consult and to be defended by, a legal practitioner of his choice; (2) Every person who is arrested and detained in custody shall be produced before the nearest magistrate within a period of twenty-four hours of such arrest excluding the time necessary for the journey from the place of arrest to the court of the magistrate and no such person shall be detained in custody beyond the said period without the authority of a magistrate.

However, these rights, in Clauses 1 and 2 shall not apply — (a) to any person who for the time being is an enemy alien; or (b) to any person who is arrested or detained under any law providing for preventive detention. Prolonged detention is prevented by Clause 4: No law providing for preventive detention shall authorise the detention of a person for a longer period than three months unless — (a) an Advisory Board consisting of persons who are, or have been, or are qualified to be appointed as, Judges of a High Court has reported before the expiration of the said period of two months that there is in its opinion sufficient cause for such detention; (b) such person is detained in accordance with the provisions of any law made by Parliament (under sub-clauses A and B of Clause 7 of Article 22).

Right Against Exploitation

Under Article 23 (1) Traffic in human beings and beggar and other similar forms of forced labour are prohibited and any contravention of this provision shall be an offence punishable in accordance with law. Selling and buying of human beings, especially women for the purpose of immoral purposes, exploitation of people by forcing them to work as bonded labourers, or work without remuneration are made an offence under this article. The state can impose compulsory service for public service under Clause 2: Nothing in this article shall prevent the State from imposing compulsory service for public purposes, and in imposing such service the State shall not make any discrimination on grounds only of religion, race, caste or class or any of them. Article 24 prohibits employment of children in factories—No child below the age of fourteen years shall be employed to work in any factory or mine or engaged in any other hazardous employment.

Right to Freedom of Religion

Article 25 guarantees freedom of conscience and free profession, practice and propagation of religion— (i) Subject to public order, morality and health and to other provisions of this Part, all persons are equally entitled to freedom of conscience and the right freely to profess, practise and propagate religion. The state can regulate or restrict any economic, financial, political or other secular activity which may be associated with religious practice.

Under Article 26, Subject to public order morality and health, every religious denomination or any section thereof shall have the right:

(a) to establish and maintain institutions for religious and charitable purposes;
(b) to manage its own affairs in matters of religion;
(c) to own and acquire moveable and immoveable property; and
(d) to administer such property in accordance with law.

Article 27 provides freedom as to payment of taxes for promotion of any particular religion—No person shall be compelled to pay any taxes, the proceeds of which are specifically appropriated in payment of expenses for the promotion or maintenance of any particular religion or religious denomination.

Article 28 gives freedom as to attendance at religious instruction or religious worship in certain educational institutions— (i) No religious instruction shall be provided in any educational institutions wholly maintained out of State funds; (ii) Nothing in Clause 1 shall apply to an educational institution which is administered by the State but has been established under any endowment or trust which requires that religious instruction shall be imparted in such institution; (iii) No person attending any educational institution recognised by the State or receiving aid out of State funds shall be required to take part in any religious instruction that may be imparted in such institution or to attend any religious worship that may be conducted in such institution or in any premises attached thereto unless such person or, if such person is a minor, his guardian has given his consent thereto.

Cultural and Educational Rights

Articles 29 and 30 protect the interests of minorities, both linguistic and religious. These rights are absolute as the state cannot impose any restrictions on it. The objective is to protect the language, script and culture of the minorities and to prevent the majority from imposing their language and culture on the minorities.

Article 29 (1) lays down that, any section of the citizens residing in the territory of India or any part thereof having a distinct language, script or culture of its own shall have the right to conserve the same. Clause 2 mentions that no citizen shall be denied admission into any educational institution maintained by the State or receiving aid out of State funds on grounds only of religion, race, caste, language or any of them.

Article 30 guarantees the minorities the right to establish and administer educational institutions: (i) All minorities, whether based on religion or language, shall have the right to establish and administer educational institutions of their choice. Clause 1A moves one step forward that: In making any law providing for the compulsory acquisition of any property of an educational institution established and administered by a minority, referred to in Clause 1, the State shall ensure that the amount fixed by or determined under such law for the acquisition of such property is such as would not restrict or abrogate the right guaranteed under that clause. Further Clause 2 states that, the State shall not, in granting aid to educational institutions, discriminate against any educational institution on the ground that it is under the management of a minority, whether based on religion or language.

Right to Constitutional Remedies

Article 32 provides remedies for enforcement of rights conferred by the Constitution. In case of violation or infringement of these rights, Article 32(1) confers the right to move the Supreme Court by appropriate proceedings for the enforcement of the rights. By Article 32(2) the Supreme Court shall have power to issue directions or orders or writs, including writs in the nature of *habeas corpus, mandamus, prohibition, quo warranto and certiorari*, whichever may be appropriate, for the enforcement of any of the rights conferred by the Part III.

The fundamental rights incorporated in the Indian Constitution acts as a check on the arbitrariness of the administrative system. Clear parameters have been drawn and the administrative system is expected to function within that. Moreover, it is the duty of the administrative system to ensure and enforce the fundamental rights of the individuals. The state cannot also encroach upon the rights without sufficient reasons, the reasons being mentioned within the Constitution itself. Critics, argue that these rights exist only in theory and what the Constitution gives with one hand, takes away with the other. This view is based on the contention that there are so many restrictions and exemptions attached to the rights. But we have to keep in mind that uncontrolled freedom and rights can be enjoyed either in vacuum or out of the society. Reasonable restrictions are to be imposed on one's rights, so as to ensure the similar rights of others, or in the larger public interest. Growing interest can be seen from the part of the individuals and the governance system to protect the rights of the individual. This itself is the clear manifestation for the importance of fundamental rights.

Directive Principles of State Policy

A separate part in the Constitution has been devoted to the Directive Principles of State Policy (DPSP). Part IV of the Indian Constitution, from Articles 36 to 51 deals with these principles. These principles by its very nature is not enforceable in a court of law, but remains as directives to governments both at the centre and in the states, in matters of governance. Article 37 reads, the provisions contained in this Part shall not be enforceable by any court, but the principles therein laid down are nevertheless fundamental in the governance of the country and it shall be the duty of the State to apply these principles in making laws. Even though there is no judicial remedy available in case of violation of the directive principles, they are sacrosanct as they place an ideal before the legislators of the country. The major provisions in the DPSP are:

Article 38: State to secure a social order for the promotion of welfare of the people— (i) The State shall strive to promote the welfare of the people by securing and protecting as effectively as it may a social order in which justice, social, economic and political, shall inform all the instructions of the national life.; and (ii) The State shall, in particular, strive to minimise the inequalities in income, and endeavour to eliminate inequalities in status, facilities and opportunities, not only amongst individuals but also amongst groups of people residing in different areas or engaged in different vocations.

Article 39: Certain principles of policy to be followed by the State—The State shall, in particular, direct its policy towards securing:

(a) that the citizens, men and women equally, have the right to an adequate means of livelihood;
(b) that the ownership and control of the material resources of the community are so distributed as best to subserve the common good;
(c) that the operation of the economic system does not result in the concentration of wealth and means of production to the common detriment;
(d) that there is equal pay for equal work for both men and women;
(e) that the health and strength of workers, men and women, and the tender age of children are not abused and that citizens are not forced by economic necessity to enter avocations unsuited to their age or strength; and
(f) that children are given opportunities and facilities to develop in a healthy manner and in conditions of freedom and dignity and that childhood and youth are protected against exploitation and against moral and material abandonment.

Article 39A: The State shall secure that the operation of the legal system promotes justice, on a basis of equal opportunity, and shall, in particular, provide free legal aid, by suitable legislation or schemes or in any other way, to ensure that opportunities for securing justice are not denied to any citizen by reason of economic or other disabilities.

Article 40: The State shall take steps to organise village panchayats and endow them, with such powers and authority as may be necessary to enable them to function as units of self government.

Article 41: The State shall, within the limits of its economic capacity and development, make effective provision for securing the right to work, to education and to public assistance in cases of unemployment, old age, sickness and disablement, and in other cases of undeserved want.

Article 42: The State shall make provisions for securing just and human conditions of work and for maternity relief.

Article 43: The State shall endeavour to secure, by suitable legislation or economic organisation or in any other way, to all workers, agricultural, industrial or otherwise, work, a living wage, conditions of work ensuring a decent standard of life and full enjoyment of leisure and social and cultural opportunities and, in particular, the State shall endeavour to promote cottage industries on an individual or co-operative basis in rural areas.

Article 43A: The State shall take steps, by suitable legislation or in any other way, to secure the participation of workers in the management of undertakings, establishments or other organisations engaged in any industry.

Article 43B: The State shall endeavour to promote voluntary formation, autonomous functioning, democratic control and professional management of co-operative societies.

Article 44: The State shall endeavour to secure for the citizens a uniform civil code throughout the territory of India.

Article 45: Provision for early childhood care and education to children below the age of six years—The State shall endeavour to provide, early childhood care and education for all children until they complete the age of six years.

Article 46: Promotion of educational and economic interests of Scheduled Castes, Scheduled Tribes and other weaker sections—The State shall promote with special care the educational and economic interests of the weaker sections of the people, and , in particular, of the Scheduled Castes and the Scheduled Tribes, and shall protect them from social injustice and all forms of exploitation.

Article 47: Duty of the State to raise the level of nutrition and the standard of living and to improve public health—The State shall regard the raising of the level of nutrition and the standard of living of its people and the improvement of public health as among its primary duties and, in particular, the State shall endeavour to bring about prohibition of the consumption except for medicinal purposes of intoxicating drinks and of drugs which are injurious to health.

Article 48: Organisation of agriculture and animal husbandry—The State shall endeavour to organise agriculture and animal husbandry on modern and scientific lines and shall, in particular, take steps for preserving and improving the breeds, and prohibiting the slaughter, of cows and calves and other milch and draught cattle.

Article 48A: Protection and improvement of environment and safeguarding of forests and wild life—The State shall endeavour to protect and improve the environment and to safeguard the forests and wild life of the country.

Article 49: Protection of monuments and places and objects of national importance—It shall be the obligation of the State to protect every monument or place or object of artistic or historic interest, declared by or under law made by Parliament to be of national importance, from spoliation, disfigurement, destruction, removal, disposal or export, as the case may be.

Article 50: Separation of judiciary from executive—The State shall take steps to separate the judiciary from the executive in the public services of the State.

Article 51: Promotion of international peace and security—The State shall endeavour to:

(a) promote international peace and security;
(b) maintain just and honourable relations between nations;
(c) foster respect for international law and treaty obligations in the dealings of organised peoples with one another, and
(d) encourage settlement of international disputes by arbitration.

Attempts have been there to implement the principles enshrined in the DPSP. Special care is being given to the advancement of the weaker sections of the people. Besides, reservation, a number of programmes and projects are being implemented for the advancement of the SCs, STs and the OBCs. Steps are there to ensure the participation of the workers in the management of industries. The Panchayati Raj system has been introduced through the 73rd Constitutional Amendment to implement local self-government system. A number of social security schemes are there to take care of the old aged, widowed, destitute, disabled and injured. At the same time principles like uniform civil code has been left, owing to its sensitivity. But it is clear that both the governments, at the centre and in states are giving respectability to the majority of directive principles. Even the Constitution has been amended (25th Constitutional Amendment of 1971) to ensure validity to actions which tries to implement those principles enshrined in Article 39 (b) and (c), even if its implementation abridges the fundamental rights mentioned in Articles 14 and 19.

Fundamental Duties

The Constitution of India imposes duties not only on the state, but also on the citizens. The original constitution did not have a part on fundamental duties. It has been incorporated by the 42nd Constitutional Amendment of 1976, by adding a new clause, Clause A to Article 51. Originally there were 10 fundamental duties (Article 51A (aj), but by the 86th Constitutional Amendment of 2002, an eleventh duty has been added up (k).

Article 51 A states that it shall be the duty of every citizen of India:

(a) to abide by the Constitution and respect its ideals and institutions, the National Flag and the National Anthem;
(b) to cherish and follow the noble ideals which inspired our national struggle for freedom;

(c) to uphold and protect the sovereignty, unity and integrity of India;

(d) to defend the country and render national service when called upon to do so;

(e) to promote harmony and the spirit of common brotherhood amongst all the people of India transcending religious, linguistic and regional or sectional diversities; to renounce practices derogatory to the dignity of women;

(f) to value and preserve the rich heritage of our composite culture;

(g) to protect and improve the natural environment including forests, lakes, rivers and wildlife, and to have compassion for living creatures;

(h) to develop the scientific temper, humanism and the spirit of inquiry and reform;

(i) to safeguard public property and to abjure violence;

(j) to strive towards excellence in all spheres of individual and collective activity so that the nation constantly rises to higher levels of endeavour and achievement.

(k) who is a parent or guardian to provide opportunities for education to his child or, as the case may be, ward between the age of six and fourteen years.

There are no legal sanctions against the violations of fundamental duties. It is up to the citizen to decide whether to perform his/her duties. Because of this the impact of fundamental duties on the national life is minimal. A visible apathy can be noticed among the majority of citizens towards these national and social obligations and responsibilities. Fundamental rights remain as a part without much substance and force. But its existence stands accepted as a part of constitutional morality, which is based on the moral power and conscience of the citizens as human beings. Advocacy to make this fundamental duties binding and enforceable have come from various corners, recently.

References

Avasthi, Amreshwar and Avasthi, Anand Prakash (2008): *Indian Administration*, Lakshmi Narain Agarwal, Agra.

Bakshi, P.N. (2008): *The Constitution of India*, Law Publishers, Allahabad.

Basu, D.D. (2000): *An Introduction to the Constitution of India*, Nagpur, Wadhwa.

—— (1981): *The Shorter Constitution of India*, Prentice-Hall, New Delhi.

Pylee, M.V. (1995): *An Introduction to the Constitution of India*, Vikas, New Delhi.

GoI (2007): *The Constitution of India*, Ministry of Law and Justice, Government of India, New Delhi.

Ramesh, K. Arora and Rajni, Goyal (2011): *Indian Public Administration*, New Age International, New Delhi.

4

Bureaucracy in India: Constitutional and Legal Foundations

In India, the actual moulding of the bureaucracy started after independence. India adopted socialist philosophy and centralised planning and the hopes and aspirations of the people of independent India created new tasks and responsibilities, which were assigned to the newly created IAS, successor of ICS, but with no radical break with the British administrative tradition (Jitha 2007: 40). The national leaders felt that the bureaucracy alone provide men of experience that would meet socio-economic demands of socially puzzled and politically unstable society of free India. Sardar Patel, the first Deputy Prime Minister of India has emphasised the necessity of qualified administrators to maintain continuity in administration, stability and order, to build a new India (Premlatha 1974: 11). In the post independent India, the IAS has emerged as the elite corps to man the important decision-making positions in the administrative system. The pattern of IAS supremacy is also visible in the state government and local bodies. Today IAS is the core of the country's administrative structure, sharing its tasks with a number of All India, Central and State services, providing strong administrative links throughout the country.

The post-independence period witnessed a sharp change in the nature and goals of administration in India. After independence, the total environment and ethos of the country underwent a qualitative change and the nature of governmental tasks shifted from mere care and maintenance of law and order to social welfare and individual progress. Elections, political parties, competitive politics, parliament and ministers came on the scene. A federal political system with division of powers between the union and the states were introduced and the division of powers has been done in the constitution itself. India adopted a parliamentary form of government both, at the centre and in the states. There established the supremacy of political executives over civil servants and subordination of civil servants to political executives, with the civil servants working on the basis of anonymity and political neutrality.

India launched a massive programme of community development with a view to liberating the millions of people from poverty illiteracy, ignorance, unemployment, disease, overpopulation etc. Planning was adopted to ensure social equality and economic justice to every citizens of the country. There occurred a growth in the number of welfare and development departments at both the levels of polity. This change had brought about new responsibilities pertaining to economic development and social welfare on the shoulders of the higher bureaucrats. Civil servants are made agents of change in the process of socio-economic development. But bureaucracy remained largely indifferent with their legacies of exclusiveness and class-consciousness, which they had inherited from the ICS.

India inherited at the time of freedom, the legacies of a generalist higher civil service, not used to any tasks of gigantic nation-building, trained in the traditions of law and order machinery based on fear and awe and without any institutionalized system of accountability to the people. An irresponsible, unresponsive, autocratic, and bureaucratic structure was inherited by the country which operated in the context of a poor and backward agricultural economy. Such a system could no longer carter to the needs of the independent India. So a change in the role of the Indian bureaucracy became one of the major issues of those times. Commenting on the role, T.N. Chaturvedi, himself a distinguished member of the IAS, says:

> The Civil Service in India is expected to play manifold roles. There is need to match the role perception and role expectation so that the role performance by the civil service is the optimum and may satisfy the diverse needs and urges of the community.......(It) is an instrument for implementation of people's will and aspirations as expressed in the constitution. It is the focal point of stability and order in the shifting sands of politics. At the same time, as an elitist class, it is an instrument of modernization and social change. It is an instrument of planning and economic development. It may be expected to safeguard the rights of the under-privileged sections in society. It has to be all the time aware of the political milieu and the democratic context in which it has to operate.

He concludes thus:

> The civil service has to undergo radical structural, procedural and attitudinal changes if it has to serve as an effective instrument of change and progress in a developing society. The civil service has to cultivate much wider social awareness and responsiveness as well as social base apart from the traditional virtues of integrity, functional efficiency and a sense of fair play and impartiality.

Higher Bureaucracy — All-India Services and Central Services

All-India Services are those services which are common to both central and state governments. Presently, India has three all-India Services – the Indian Administrative Service (IAS), the Indian Police Service (IPS) and the Indian Forest Service (IFS). Recruitment to IAS and IPS are done through the common annual competitive examination conducted by the Union Public Service Commission (UPSC). Separate examination is there for the post of the Indian Forest Service. The personnel of the All-India Services serve the central government, union territories and the states. But their cadre controlling authorities are the ministries or departments of the central government. The Ministry of Personnel, Public Grievances and Pensions is the cadre controlling authority of the Indian Administrative Service, in case of the Indian Police Service it is the Union Home Ministry, and the Ministry of Environment and Forests is the cadre controlling authority of the Indian Forest Service. Indian Administrative Service and Indian Police Service enjoy enormous status and prestige and are known as premier services.

The Central Services belong to the central government and mans various departments of the central government. These personnel's are controlled by the respective ministries or departments. The members of the central services serve in central government and the offices of the central government in states and union territories. Unlike the officers of the IAS, IPS and IFS, the central service officials do not work under the state governments while working in the states. Central Services in India have four classifications: Central Services, Group A; Central Services, Group B; Central Services, Group C and Central Services, Group D. Group A comprises of 34 important services, including the Indian Foreign Service, Indian Audit and Accounts Service, Indian Postal Service, Central Secretariat Service and so on. Group B consists of 25 corresponding services to Group A. Recruitment to Group A and B services are done by the UPSC. The Group C Central Services consists of clerical personnel and their recruitment is made by the Staff Selection Commission. Group D consists of manual personnel like peons, gardeners, sweepers etc. Thus, Group A and Group B comprises gazetted officers while Group C and Group D are non-gazetted class.

Indian Foreign Service (IFS) is the top most Central Service in terms of prestige, status, pay and emoluments. Though a Central Service it competes with the All-India Services in position, status and pay scales. It comes next to the IAS in ranking and its pay scale is higher than the IPS. It is managed by the Ministry of External Affairs and its recruits serve the Indian missions and embassies abroad.

Constitutional Provisions Regarding Recruitment

Part XIV of the Indian Constitution, starting from Article 308 to 323, exclusively mentions about the services under the Union and the States. Elaborate provisions with regard to recruitment and service conditions of All-India and Central Services are laid down in this part:

1. Article 309 deals with *Recruitment and conditions of service of persons serving the Union or a State*— "Subject to the provisions of this Constitution, Acts of the appropriate Legislature may regulate the recruitment, and conditions of service of persons appointed, to public services and posts in connection with the affairs of the Union or of any State". Thus, the Parliament was empowered to regulate the recruitment and service conditions of persons appointed to Central Services and posts.
2. Article 310 provides that the members of All-India Services and Central Services and posts hold office during the pleasure of the President. "...every person who is a member of a defence service or of a civil service of the Union or of an all-India service or holds any post connected with defence or any civil post under the Union holds office during the pleasure of the President..."
3. Article 311 deals with *Dismissal, removal or reduction in rank of persons employed in civil capacities under the Union or a State*— (i) No person who is a member of a civil service of the Union or an all-India service or a civil service of a State or holds a civil post under the Union or a State shall be dismissed or removed by an authority subordinate to that by which he was appointed. (ii) No such person as aforesaid shall be dismissed or removed or reduced in rank except after an inquiry in which he has been informed of the charges against him and given a reasonable opportunity of being heard in respect of those charges.
4. Article 312 authorises the Parliament to create new All-India Services (including an All-India Judicial Service) and regulate the recruitment and service conditions of persons appointed to these services. "...if the Council of States has declared by resolution supported by not less than two-thirds of the members present and voting that it is necessary or expedient in the national interest so to do, Parliament

may by law provide for the creation of one or more all India services (including an all-India Judicial Service) common to the Union and the States, and, subject to the other provisions of this Chapter, regulate the recruitment, and the conditions of service of persons appointed, to any such service."

It also says that the services known at the commencement of the constitution as the Indian Administrative Service and the Indian Police Service shall be deemed to be services created by Parliament under this Article. Moreover, the All-India judicial service shall not include any post inferior to that of a district judge. Though the 42nd Amendment (1976) made the provision for the creation of All-India Judicial Service, no such law has been made so far.

5. Article 320 speaks about the powers of the Public Service Commissions— (1) It shall be the duty of the Union and the State Public Service Commissions to conduct examinations for appointments to the services of the Union and the services of the State respectively.
6. Article 323A authorises the Parliament to provide for the setting up of an Administrative Tribunal for the adjudication or trail of disputes and complaints with respect to recruitment and service conditions of persons appointed to central services and posts.
7. Article 335 lays down that the claims of the Scheduled Castes and the Scheduled Tribes to services and posts—The claims of the members of the Scheduled Castes and the Scheduled Tribes shall be taken into consideration, consistently with the maintenance of efficiency of administration, in the making of appointments to services and posts in connection with the affairs of the Union or of a State...

System of Recruitment

The present system of recruitment to All-India Services and higher Central Services in India is based on the recommendations made by the: (i) The Macaulay Committee, (ii) The Kothari Committee, and (iii) The Satish Chandra Committee. In recent times, two or more committees were appointed (i) Alagh Committee (July 2000–Oct. 2001), and (ii) Hota Committee (February 2004 – July 2004).

The report of the Macaulay Committee on the Indian Civil Service laid down the basic policy governing recruitment to civil service for the first time in 1854. The most important aspects of this policy were the system of open competition and the scholastic nature of the examination. The present scheme of examination to test the merit and suitability of candidates for direct recruitment to the All-India Services and higher Central Services is laid down by the Kothari Committee and the Satish Chandra Committee. However, the basic policy laid down, and the philosophy of recruitment advocated by the Macaulay Committee continues to influence the system.

Apart from this direct recruitment, a method of recruitment by promotion is also followed. The All-India Service Act of 1951 specifies that senior duty posts not exceeding 33.3 per cent in the Indian Administrative Services (IAS), Indian Police Service (IPS) and Indian Forest Service (IFS), are required to be filled in by promotion of officers employed in the State Services. Such promotions are made on the recommendations of the Selection Committee constituted for this purpose in each state. Each such committee is presided over by the Chairman or a Member of the UPSC.

Therefore, the IAS, the top most All-India Service-consists of officers recruited by the following three methods:

1. By direct recruitment through a combined, open competitive Civil Services Examination.
2. By direct recruitment, that is, promotion of officers of State Civil Services.
3. By special selections from those holding gazetted posts under state governments but who are not members of the State Administrative Services.

Rationale of All-India Services

The need and significance of all-India services have been well recognised. The arguments put forward in favour of the All-India Services are:

1. They are the continuation of the old administrative arrangement developed during the British period. The members of these services during the British rule constituted the highest rung of the administrative hierarchy. The IAS, the only multi-purpose All-India Service, is the direct descendent of the erstwhile ICS which was called as the 'Heaven- born Service'.
2. They promote national integration as the members of these services are posted in states other than their own. So, they can function beyond the regional, linguistic and communal interests. Moreover, these services have a national vision and perspective.
3. Since the members of these services are recruited on the basis of all-India competitive examinations, their calibre is substantially high. All-India Services attract the best talent in the country due to the wide field of recruitment, high remuneration, status and prestige. During the British period, they were called *the Steel-frame of administrative structure*.

4. They help to ensure uniformity of the administrative system throughout the nation. The members of these services are rotated between the Centre and the States.
5. They facilitate liaison, co-operation, coordination and joint action on the issues and problems of common interest, between the centre and the states.
6. When the President's Rule is in operation in any state, he can depend on the loyalty and cooperation of these offices for efficient administration. This is because; they are appointed and removed only by the President of India.
7. All-India Services promote independence and impartiality of civil service at the highest level. As members of these services enjoy the constitutional safeguards, they are free from regional and local pressures and influences. Hence, they can afford to give free and frank advice to the state ministers.
8. They facilitate the interchange of rich experience among different states. The officers of all-India services serve not only the state governments and central government but the union territories and local governments as well (both urban and rural). Thus, their rich experience can be used for the benefit of the whole country.
9. It is beneficial to the states as the talent mobilised through national recruitment to these services is distributed among the states. Hence, the states which are deficient in their manpower supply to fill the high and strategic positions will be benefited.

The arguments put forward against the All-India Services are:

1. The All-India Services were just the hang-over of the past. These services were created during the period of British rule in India. At that time, the structure of government was unitary and nature of state was authoritarian. After independence, the structure of government and the nature of state underwent a radical transformation. In this changed scenario, the All-India Services have no place.
2. These services are against the federal system of government provided by the constitution. They restrict the autonomy and patronage of the states. Since 1950, they have been a point of dispute and problem area between the Centre and State. The states have not supported the creation of more All-India Services in spite of a constitutional provision in this regard.

   The Rajamannar Committee, constituted by the Tamil Government in 1969, in its report of 1971 recommended for the abolition of IAS and IPS.

3. All-India Services violate the principle of ministerial responsibility at the state level. The ministers in the states have to work with the aid and advice of those civil servants (Secretariat) who are appointed and trained by the Central Government, which also enjoys the ultimate control over them.
4. The states of Indian Union are not equally represented in these services. The states of the Punjab, UP, Bihar, Tamil Nadu, Andhra Pradesh are represented more than others. Thus, they lack the national character due to regional loyalties.
5. These services involve larger expenditure on state governments due to high salary scales. This is done to attract the best talent from all over the country and to maintain their efficiency. Hence, a financial burden is to the states.
6. The service conditions of All-India Services including pay and promotional avenues are very favourable compared to the State Services. Also, the members of State Services are made to work under the officers of All-India Services. All this demoralises the State Services.
7. The members of the All-India Services who come from outside the state may not be familiar with the local languages, cultural and general environment. Hence, they cannot understand the problems of the people properly.
8. The continuation and creation of new All-India Services hampers the effective spread of State Services. They reduce employment opportunities for the local people, that is, 'Sons of the Soil'.
9. The All-India Services, especially IAS, do not facilitate specialisation, which is so essential in the modern age. It is said that the IAS officers are *Jack of all trades but master of none*.

Administrative Reform

Administrative reform refers to the process of improving the administrative machinery of a government with a view to making it fulfil the preset goals. Such a process involves enhancement in the capacity of the administrative system to achieve the assigned goals. Reforming the system includes in its ambit; improvements in structure, processes, behaviour and components of the administrative machinery. Lee Hahn's defines administrative reforms as, "an effort to apply a new idea or combination of ideas to an administrative system with a conscious move to improving the system for positive goals of national development". To John Montgomery, administrative reform is a "political process designed to adjust the relationship between a bureaucracy and other elements in a society or within the bureaucracy itself in order to change the behaviour of the public service". What administrative reforms meant to Blackoff is "improving the performance by identifying the attributes and rates of bureaucratic adaptability".

Administrative reform is a continuing necessity in a society when the society confronts a quantum jump in its basic framework of governance including its goals. Thus, viewed India started its career of an independent state with a profound contradiction. The policy that was adopted after independence was new but at the same time the machinery to implement its new tasks was inherited from the British Raj. This constitute nothing short of a qualitative change in the goal as well as role of the state in India. Consequent upon the changes in goals and objectives, it is axiomatic that the instrument of public administration required be re-engineering and re-casting. As pointed out by Mrs. Indira Gandhi, former Prime Minister of India, "Our pattern of administration were drawn or defined at a time where government's main business was to keep law and order. They are inadequate for the challenges which we face today. What we need therefore is revolution in the administrative system without which no enduring change can be brought about in any field" (Vishnoo and Vidhya 2011: 445).

Since independence, there has been on a rough estimate, more than six hundred committees and commissions at the central and the state level, appointed under the rubric of administrative reforms. The bigger share of this comes from the state governments, and there have been some comprehensive reports such as that of the Kerala Administrative Reforms Commission (1958), Andhra Pradesh Reforms Enquiry Committee (1960), Rajasthan Administrative Reforms Committee (1963) and the Administrative Reforms Committee of West Bengal (1963). The rest have been on strengthening few specific components of the administrative system, like local government agencies, revenue administration etc. The reform efforts of the central government have been broader and more far-reaching, like the First Administrative Reforms Commission (1966) and the Second Administrative Reforms Commission (2005). Among the various commissions/committees appointed in India for the purpose of reviewing the administrative machinery and to make suggestions to improve the same, the most important ones includes the A.D. Gorwala Committee (1951), the Paul H. Appleby Committee (1953), the First Administrative Reforms Commission (1966), and the Second Administrative Reforms Commission (2005).

Recommendations of A.D. Gorwala Committee

In 1951, the Planning Commission of India set up a Committee under the chairmanship of A.D. Gorwala, a retired Civil Servant to find out whether the administrative machinery was adequate and also sufficiently equipped to meet the requirements of planned development. Gorwala recorded that the public was experiencing delay in execution, and that there was lack of integrity and undue interference as well as corruption and lack of involvement of officials. He recommended a re-organisation of the government for greater speed, efficiency, effectiveness and responsiveness. He submitted his report in the first quarter of 1951 and made the following main recommendations:

1. Parliamentary government with a cabinet system on the British model cannot be effective, unless the standard of morality of those who work it is high and the public believes it to be so. Gorwala insists on the maintenance of moral standards among ministers, legislators and administrators and ascribes the fall in standards of public administration to corruption, patronage and influence. It vitiates policy weakens administration and undermines public confidence.
2. He suggested proper relationship between Administrative Ministers and the Finance Ministry. Financial control is desirable but financial interference should be avoided.
3. The Minister should confine himself to matters of policy and leave the initiative to the Secretary.
4. There should be created an O and M branch in the government and a Board of two members should be set up to provide necessary drive and direction to administration.
5. Parliamentary control over the working of ministries and more especially over expenditure is most desirable.
6. More junior officers and less clerks should be appointed.
7. Discipline in government offices has been the first victim of independence. To bolster the discipline, he recommended promotion on the basis of good work.
8. Whitley Councils on the pattern of UK should be established.
9. Training, besides aiming at precision and surety in the conduct of business and improvement of staff morale, must also encourage the civil servant to see his work in its widest context and to persevere with his own educational development. It must prepare him for higher work and greater responsibilities and attune his outlook and methods to the needs of changing times.
10. The Principal of the IAS Training School would be absolved of other departmental responsibilities.
11. Director of Training and Organisation and methods with requisite staff and office should be immediately appointed.
12. Recruitment to all grades of government service should be conducted in a manner which eliminates scope for patronage and suspicion of patronage. All posts, whether temporary or permanent, should be filled up by the Public Service Commission.

Recommendations of the Report of Paul H. Appleby

Paul H. Appleby was an American Professor of Public Administration, appointed to enquire into the administrative machinery. He surveyed and reported on Public Administration Reforms in India in 1953 at the invitation of the then Prime Minister Pt Jawaharlal Nehru. He submitted two reports: *Public Administration in India: Report of a Survey, 1953; and Reorganisation of India's Administrative System with Special Reference to Administration of Government's Industrial and Commercial Enterprises, 1956*. Only two of the recommendations were implemented, the setting up of Institute of Public Administration (IIPA 1954) and the establishment of Organisation and Management Division (O&M 1954). The first report was submitted in January 1953 and the main recommendations are as follows:

1. An Organisation and Management of Public Administration office directly under a minister of the Government should be set up. It should focus attention and study on proposals concerning the improvement of governmental structure and procedures.
2. An Institute of Public Administration for India should be established. It should serve as a nucleus of a professional journal, expansion of studies and development of literature towards advancement of administrative knowledge.
3. An academic graduate programme in public administration should be evolved for young persons in association with this institute.
4. Procedures at different levels of government should be simplified and expedited in all developmental and social action fields.
5. The administrative hierarchy should take a more truly pyramidal form with more executives at most levels. The number of levels should be increased.
6. More flexibility and discretion should be allowed to administrative agencies in co-operation with the P.S.C in regard to recruitment of personnel.
7. Extensive and sustained Personnel Development Programmes to maximise the potentialities of public personnel should be undertaken.

Appleby produced his second report in 1956. The main recommendations are as follows:

1. New levels of co-ordination below the level of cabinet and below the level of Minister should be provided structurally.
2. Provision should be made for recruitment and training of generalist administrator and technical administrator.
3. Structural and Procedural arrangements should be made for the growing size of administration.

4. An official called Programme Expediter or Plan Expediter should be appointed in the Central Secretariat who will be responsible for overcoming all hurdles, viz., red tape, inadequate staff, and for overseeing the fulfilment of the Plan.
5. There should be appointed a Finance Officer with the parent ministers to develop financial and budgetary competence.
6. There should also be appointed an Expenditure Secretary in the Finance Ministry to accelerate decision-making. None of the three officers should be deemed permanent additions to the administrative structure but should be set up as temporary expedient to hasten reviewing and decision making functions and to provide speed to governmental processes by eliminating reviewing agencies at all stages.
7. The Reports of the Comptroller and Auditor-General contain too much grave matters. These ought to be shorter and selective.
8. The principle of delegations should be applied to the field of administration. The Parliament should not go into petty details in the name of parliamentary control and pursue accountability. It should raise itself to the appropriate high level of direction. Its outlook should be a positive one where it would stop looking for things to criticise and begin looking for things to praise.
9. Board of Directors for companies and corporations should work on the principle of delegation. The Board should have two functions, one of evaluation and the other co-ordination.
10. Central purchase and central construction retard operation of large undertakings.
11. The Comptroller and Auditor-General should be relieved of the responsibility of audit. The auditors should not assume the role of judges of policy administrative judgements or public interest.
12. The layout, the hierarchical structure and the location of plant or the public undertaking should be determined with a view to future growth and enlargement.
13. The public employees should be paid adequate salaries. "Since future prosperity of the country is dependent on the success of the Indian Government, people must be willing to pay what adequate and successful government will cost."

The First Administrative Reforms Commission (ARC), 1966-1970

The Government of India set up a Commission of Inquiry by a resolution dated 5th January 1966, to *examine the public administration of the country and make recommendations for reform and reorganisation wherever necessary*, under the Chairmanship of Sri Morarji Desai (later by Sri K. Hanumanthiya). The Commission comprised of a Chairman, four members and a member secretary.

The Commission during its four and a half years submitted twenty reports, with 581 recommendations. Of these 20 reports the momentous ones are on — (i) The Machinery of Government and its Procedures; (ii) Personnel Administration; (iii) State Administration; (iv) Problems of Redress of Citizens Grievances; and (v) Centre-State Relations. The report on Personnel Administration ranks perhaps as the weightiest and its recommendations includes:

1. There should be specialisation among civil servants, even among the 'heaven born' IAS. The eight areas of specialisation includes — Economic Administration, Industrial Administration, Agriculture and Rural Administration, Social and Educational Administration, Personnel Administration, Financial Administration, Defence Administration and Internal Security, and Planning.
2. Selection to the top posts was to be based on merit.
3. Posts entailing similar qualifications and responsibilities were to be grouped in the same grade.
4. The upper age for competitive examination should be raised to 26 from 24.
5. Only two chances should be given to candidates competing for all-India services.

The implementation of the Commission's recommendations was weak, colourless and tardy. Out of all recommendations only a few were implemented and others out rightly rejected. The upper age for competitive examination was raised to 26. The accepted recommendations under other heads are — creation of a separate Department of Personnel (1970) and the creation of Lok Pal and Lok Ayukthas. A bill entitled "The Lok Pal and Lok Ayuktha Bill 1968" was introduced in the Lok Sabha and got passed on 20th August 1969 and in Rajya Sabha on 1970. But the institution of Lok Pal still lies on the shelf.

The Second Administrative Reforms Commission, 2005

The Second Administrative Reforms Commission (ARC) was constituted by the Government of India (Department of Administrative Reforms and Public Grievances, Ministry of Personnel) in August 2005 under the chairmanship of Sri Veerappa Moily, a senior Congress leader and former Karnataka Chief Minister. It was constituted as a Commission of Inquiry to prepare a detailed blueprint for revamping the public administration system. It completed its work in May 2009. The commission suggested measures to achieve a proactive, responsive, accountable, sustainable and efficient administration for the country at all levels of the government. The commission, *inter alia,* considered the following:

1. Organisational Structure of the Government of India;
2. Ethics in Governance;
3. Refurbishing of Personnel Administration;
4. Strengthening of Financial Management Systems;
5. Steps to Ensure Effective Administration at the state level;
6. Steps to Ensure Effective District Administration;
7. Local Self-government/Panchayati Raj Institutions;
8. Social Capital, Trust and Participative Public Service Delivery;
9. Citizen-centric Administration;
10. Promoting E-governance;
11. Issues of Federal Polity;
12. Crisis Management;
13. Public Order.

Detailed examination of administration of Defence, Railways, External affairs, Security and Intelligence, and also subjects such as Centre-State relations, judicial reforms etc., which are already being examined by other bodies were excluded from the purview of the commission. The commission was; however, free to take the problems of these sectors into account in recommending re-organisation of the machinery of the Government or of any of its service agencies.

Reports of the Commission

The Commission submitted 15 reports to the Government. They are mentioned below in the order of submission:

1. Right to Information: Master Key to Good Governance (2006);
2. Unlocking Human Capital: Entitlements and Governance – A Case Study (2006);
3. Crisis Management: From Despair to Hope (2006);
4. Ethics in Governance (2007);
5. Public Order: Justice for Each: Peace for All (2007);
6. Local Governance: An Inspiring Journey into the Future (2007);
7. Capacity Building for Conflict Resolution: Friction to Fusion (2008);
8. Combating Terrorism: Protecting by Righteousness (2008);
9. Social Capital: A Shared Destiny (2008);
10. Refurbishing of Personnel Administration: Scaling New Heights (2008).

11. Promoting e-governance: The SMART Way Forward (2009);
12. Citizen Centric Administration: The Heart of Governance (2009);
13. Organisational Structure of Government of India (2009);
14. Strengthening Financial Management Systems (2009);
15. State and District Administration (2009).

Recommendations of the Commission

On Right to Information:

1. The Official Secrets Act 1923, be repealed as it is incongruous with the regime of transparency in a democratic society. It stated that the safeguards for state security should be incorporated in the National Security Act.
2. Total reorganisation of public records for effective implementation of the Right to Information (RTI) Act.
3. An office should be set up in each state as a repository of expertise, to monitor all records. One per cent of the funds for all flagship government programmes should be earmarked for five years for updating records and building infrastructure.
4. At least half the members of the Information Commission (IC) should be drawn from a non-civil service background. Thus, the members will represent variety and experience in society.
5. The IC should be entrusted with monitoring implementation of the RTI Act in all public authorities. For this purpose, clear guidelines should be evolved to determine which non-government organisations came under the Act.
6. Most requests for information are for redressal of grievances. The states may be advised to establish independent public authorities to deal with complaints of delay, harassment and corruption.
7. A roadmap should be chalked out for effective implementation of the Right to Information Act in the legislature and the judiciary at all levels.
8. Files and noting *per se* are not confidential and should not be inaccessible to the public unless exempted under the Right to Information Act.
9. Para 118(1) of the Manual of Office procedure should be deleted as it is totally violative of the RTI Act. The rulebook currently deems file noting to be confidential for the eyes of those within the secretariat.
10. The provisions regarding unauthorised communication of official information and confidential character of notes/files will have to be amended.

11. Every government servant should make available to the public or any organisation full and accurate information which can be disclosed under the RTI Act.

On Ethics in Governance:

1. The Commission has called for providing in the Constitution a national ombudsman, Rashtriya Lokayukta, which will cover all the Union Ministers and Chief Ministers, MPs and others will not cover the PM's office.
2. In the electoral and political spheres, it suggested partial state funding of elections, tightening of anti-defection law, a collegiums for appointment of Chief Election Commissioner and other Commissioners, code of ethics for ministers and law to define "office of profit".
3. It recommended abolition of schemes under which MPs and MLAs are allocated funds for their local area development.
4. It proposed the establishment of National Judicial Council that will decide on appointment of judges by a collegiums consisting of representatives from executive, legislature and judiciary.
5. It suggested a collegium headed by the PM and comprising the Lok Sabha Speaker and the Opposition leader, among others, for appointment of the CEC and ECs.

On Local Governance:

1. The commission has recommended promotion of local democracy, which is much more than decentralisation and which seeks to build up local bodies as self-governing institutions.
2. It recommended that the government place before Parliament a framework law for local bodies on the lines of the South African Act for laying down the broad principles of devolution of power, responsibilities and functions to the local bodies.
3. At the district level, a third tier of democratic government is proposed to replace the present system, which is a colonial legacy. In its place a district council, representing both urban and rural areas, should be constituted and the district collector should work as the chief secretary of the council while reporting to the State government for regulatory functions. This will ensure convergence of planning and developmental activities for rural and urban areas.
4. Parliament is to make provision for constitution of a legislative council in each State. It would comprise members elected by the local bodies in order to strengthen the voice of local bodies.

5. To reform the electoral process, the task of delimitation and reservation of constituencies should be entrusted to the state election commission.
6. To strengthen local bodies finances, it recommended that a state finance commission be constituted in such a manner that it can take into account the recommendations of Central Finance Commission.
7. It recommended that local bodies take total responsibility for the functions entrusted to them under the Constitution and bodies such as electricity boards and water authorities made responsible to them. For ensuring accountability and transparency in the functioning of local bodies, it was suggested that a local body ombudsman be constituted to look into complaints of corruption and maladministration.
8. To suggest steps to deal with rapid urbanisation, it recommended the setting up of a national commission of urbanisation. It also favoured direct election of Mayors by popular mandate.
9. It recommended abolition of octroi and suggested that the government evolve mechanisms to compensate local governments for revenue loss.
10. To tackle the problem of urban transport, particularly in larger cities, it suggested that a unified metropolitan transport authority be set up in all one-million plus population cities for coordinated planning.

On Refurbishing of Personnel Administration:

1. The Government of India should establish National Institute of Public Administration to run Bachelor's Degree courses in public administration/governance/management. The selected universities should also be assisted to offer such graduate level programmes in public administration/governance/public management. These graduates from the National Institute of Public Administration and selected universities would be eligible to appear in the Civil Services Examination. Further, other graduates would also be eligible to appear in the Civil Services Examination provided they complete a Bridge Course in the core subjects. The Bridge course should be run by the same national institutes/universities.
2. The permissible age for appearing in the Civil Services Examination should be 21 to 25 years for general candidates, 21 to 28 years for candidates from OBC and 21 to 29 years for candidates from SCs/STs as also for those who are physically challenged.
3. The number of permissible attempts in the Civil Services Examination should be 3, 5, 6 and 6 respectively for general candidates, candidates from OBC, candidates from SCs/STs and physically challenged candidates' respectively.

4. The Preliminary Examination should consist of an objective type test having one or two papers on general studies including the Constitution of India, the Indian legal system, Indian economy, polity, history and culture. There should be no optional subjects.
5. The Main Examination should consist of two papers only in the compulsory subjects. These compulsory subjects may include Constitution of India, Indian legal system, Indian economy, polity, history and culture, etc. The question papers should be of the conventional descriptive type. Besides, there should be a separate essay paper as a part of the Main examination.
6. The induction of officers of the State Civil Services into the IAS should be done by the UPSC based on a common examination.
7. Every government servant should undergo a mandatory training at the induction stage and also periodically during his/her career. Successful completion of these training programmes should be a minimum necessary condition for confirmation in service and subsequent promotions. Mandatory induction training programmes should be prescribed for Group D staff also before they are assigned postings.
8. A national institute of good governance may be set up by upgrading one of the existing national/state institutes. This institute would identify, document, and disseminate best practices and also conduct training programmes.
9. For making appraisal more consultative and transparent, the performance appraisal systems for all services should be modified on the lines of the recently introduced performance appraisal rules (PAR) for the all India services.
10. The Government should expand the scope of the present performance appraisal system of its employees to a comprehensive Performance Management System (PMS).
11. Annual performance agreements should be signed between the departmental minister and the Secretary of the ministry/heads of departments, providing physical and verifiable details of the work to be done during a financial year. The actual performance should be assessed by a third party.
12. For a transparent system of appointments in the government, covering all ranks, the Commission has suggested the setting up of a Central Civil Services Authority. The Authority should be a five member body with the Chairperson appointed by the President on the recommendations of the Prime Minister and the Leader of the Opposition to make it totally a political.

13. The commission is of the view that in order to avoid any conflict of interest, government officials should not be allowed to go on deputation to private commercial organisations.
14. In order to increase accountability, the Commission suggested a periodic review of the performance for which it recommended a system of two intensive reviews — one on completion of 14 years of service and the other on completion of 20 years. The first review will primarily serve the purpose of intimating individual about his/her performance and the second is mainly to assess the fitness of the officer for his/her future continuation in service. The employees found unfit after 20 years should be dispensed with.

Compared to the reports of other administrative reforms commissions, the report of the second ARC got warm welcome from all quarters. Many of its recommendations got light; the important among them is the Right to Information. The Right to Information Act was passed on 2005 and is a revolutionary step towards transparency in administration. Second, one is relating to the implementation of the Rural Employment Guarantee Act, popularly known as MNREGA (Mahatma Gandhi National Rural Employment Guarantee Act). The recommendations of the commission with regard to muster rolls, jobs cards, evaluation of the programme, etc., got reflected in the Act. Crisis management is the other area that got attention. A change in the pattern of civil service recruitment also got started with the introduction of the Civil Service Aptitude Test (CSAT). Unfortunately, the measures to bring ethics and integrity in administration are not getting any grip.

The efforts to administrative reforms in India have been, no doubt successful to a good extent, but not more than half of what is needed. Good changes have been occurred in the staffing pattern, work arrangement and execution of them in various departments. New departments have been created and innovations such as O&M, vigilance commissions and committees, citizen's grievance redressal organisations, Whitley system have been made. But all these could produce only limited success due to one reason or other. It is a fact that the path of administrative reforms in India bristles with difficulties and problems. The most importance reasons for that includes the prevalence of the VIPism, corruption, intricate nature of administrative reforms, inadequate political and community support, insufficiency of resources allotted and the mindset to resist reforms. In this changed administrative milieu, the old bureaucratic rule book needs drastic re-writing, then only it is possible to ensure good governance to all, a challenge since 1947, i.e., independence.

References

Avasthi, Amreshwar and Avasthi, Anand Prakash (2008): *Indian Administration*, Lakshmi Narain Agarwal, Agra.

Basu, D.D. (2000): *An Introduction to the Constitution of India*, Nagpur, Wadhwa.

—— (1981): *The Shorter Constitution of India*, Prentice-Hall, New Delhi.

GoI (2007): *The Constitution of India*, Ministry of Law and Justice, Government of India, New Delhi.

Jitha, S.R. (2007): *Higher Bureaucracy and Development*, Kalpaz Publications, New Delhi.

Laxmikanth, M. (2011): *Governance in India*, Tata McGraw-Hills, New Delhi.

Premlatha, Bansal (1974): *Administrative Development in India*, Sterling Publishers, New Delhi.

Ramesh, K. Arora and Rajni, Goyal (2011): *Indian Public Administration*, New Age International, New Delhi.

Vishnoo, Bhagvan and Vidhya, Bhushan (2011): *Indian Administration*, S. Chand & Co., New Delhi.

5

Bureaucracy and Governance in the Era of Globalisation

The term globalisation today enjoys immense popularity. It is used as a key word not only in the dominant theoretical and political discourse but also in everyday language. In the present day world "globalisation" is at the centre of diverse intellectual and political agendas, raising crucial questions about what is widely considered to be the fundamental dynamic of our time. James Petras and Henry Veltmeyer (2001: 8) note, "As both a description of widespread, epoch-defining developments and a prescription for action, it (globalisation) has achieved a virtual hegemony that disarms the imagination and prevents thought of and action towards a systematic alternative – towards an another, more just social and economic order."

Globalisation is not a new phenomenon. Business has been carried on by states, transcending boundaries, in manufactured goods, services, communication and so on. However, in recent times a new thrust has been provided to the international business and this happened in the developed world during the eighties and in the developing world during the nineties. Many tumultuous events of the 1980's and 1990's have led to the enthronement of globalisation as the dominant force and the ideological anchor of the late 20th century. These in a nutshell include: collapse of Soviet Union, sweeping political-economic changes in Eastern Europe, end of cold war, ascendance of neo-liberalism, proliferation and expansion of TNCs and MNCs, the growing clout of IMF and the World Bank, emergence of macro economics, establishment of WTO, communication and internet revolution, collapse of third world, ascendance of mono-cultures, decline of counter cultures, erosion of plurality etc. (Satyanarayana 2003: 25; Avasthi and Avasthi 2008: 515). Among the contenting views regarding globalisation there is a near consensus on the point that globalisation process of today, with its major impetus with the demise of Soviet system has certain features that distinguish it from the earlier forms. The important distinction is that while the older version of globalisation was bi-polar or multi-polar, the newer one is uni-polar under the US hegemony.

The rise of uni-polarity in international relations changed the nature of the prevailing capitalist system. With the disintegration of Soviet Union we can see, as Samir Amin (2009: 30) says, a collective imperialism of the triad of the United States, Europe and the Japan. To him the collective character of imperialism is expressed through the management of the world system by the triad's common instruments – the WTO, the IMF, the World Bank, the OECD, the European Union, the G7/G8 and the NATO. The hegemonic project of United States is implemented even through the programme of military control. The best example for this is the invasion of Iraq. After its conquering neo-liberal policies were implemented on it. The US$680 billion contract having been awarded to American-owned Bechtel in 2003 for service delivery management and upgrades in Iraq is an example (McDonald and Ruiters 2005: 8). What makes this imperial coalition dangerous is, Samir Amin (2009: 29) gives the answer, it deepens the polarisation between the centre and the periphery.

Globalisation as the higher stage of capitalist expansion is a model of economics rooted in the belief that liberal market economics constitute the one and only one choice for the whole world. Capital account liberalisation, interest rate set by the market and flexible exchange regimes created the framework for the globalisation of financial transactions. Liberalisation of national legislation has been performed in order to encourage the presence of multinational business. Industries previously closed to Foreign Direct Investment (FDI) have been opened, state properties have been privatised, procedures have been simplified and incentives and concessions (for corporates) have been introduced. The world witnessed the dismantling of state regulations, liberalisation of export-import laws, de-licensing, flexible laws including labour laws, corporate tax reductions, increased subsidies to corporates, hegemonies control of employers in hiring, firing, outsourcing, subcontracting and so on. In short, globalisation created an atmosphere free of restrictions, allowing the corporates to have an unbridled play. Special Economic Zones, Privatisation and FDI became the watchwords of development.

Neo-liberalism's economic roots began with the re-establishment of Bertten Woods Agreement, which fixed currencies to the US Dollar and US Dollar to gold. Neo-liberalism has different conotational interpretations such as neo-classical liberalism and libertarianism. The main thrust of neo-liberalism is to re-establish the *laissez-faire* individualism. To that end it denounces the functions of welfare state and in a reactive fashion; it opposes state interference in relation to economic activities of the individuals or the groups (Scholte 2005: 38). The main proponents of neo-liberalism are Friedrich Hayek, Milton Friedman and Robert Nozick. In the latter half of the 20th century these thinkers perceived the idea that welfare state was hindrance to individual freedom, as it is based on the principle of forced transfer of resources from the more competent to the less competent (Chopra 2009: 260). They propagated the idea of *laissez-faire* not only in the economic sphere but also in socio-political sphere. Neo-liberalism treats man as the maker of his own destiny. To enhance individual freedom and dignity it opposes all social and legal restrictions imposed on individual's freedom of action by the state.

Neo-liberalism is a theory of political economic practices that proposes that human well-being can best be advanced by liberating individual entrepreneurial freedoms and skills within an institutional framework characterised by strong private property rights, free markets, and free trade. The role of the state is to create and preserve an institutional framework appropriate to such practices. The state has to guarantee, for example, the quality and integrity of money. It must also set up those military, defence, police, and legal structures and functions required to secure private property rights and to guarantee, by force if need be, the proper functioning of markets. Furthermore, if markets do not exist (in areas such as land, water, education, health care, social security, or environmental pollution) then they must be created, by state action if necessary. But beyond these tasks the state should not venture. State interventions in markets (once created) must be kept to a bare minimum, because, according to the theory, the state cannot possibly possess enough information to second-guess market signals (prices) and because powerful interest groups will inevitably. distort and bias state interventions (particularly in democracies) for their own benefit (Harvey 2005: 2).

The slow and quantitative development of neo-liberalism after World War II became more rapid in the 1970s and not always by peaceful means. One of the often touted neo-liberal success stories is General Pinochet's Chile, which began with a CIA backed coup, violently ousting the democratically elected government of Salvador Allende (Chopra 2009: 502). The Allende government had pursued radical social-democratic policies and has been labelled as a "Marxist," by the neo-liberalists. The rise of the "Chicago Boys" was the first instance of a reinvigorated belief in market forces and anti-statist economic thought, in 1980s and 1990s. The Chicago Boys derive their philosophy from the University of Chicago's economic programme, which stress control of money supply as the primary economic policy tool (Hira

1998: 76). Hayek and Friedman are the two main economists who inspired the programmes of the Chicago School.

The rise of the wave of neo-liberalism culminated with the Regan government in the United States and Thatcher in Britain in 1980s (Harvey 2005: 9). The Regan and Thatcher governments not only shifted their own countries' policies towards *laissez-faire* but used their control over the Bretton Woods institutions to impose their policies on the rest of the world. The IMF and World Bank imposed their neo-liberal agenda on heavily indebted developing countries in return for much-needed loans. The 1991 demise of Soviet Union and the acceleration of market-oriented reforms in communist China led to the unprecedented dominance of the neo-liberal model in the 1990s (Steger and Roy 2010: 10). Some regard neo-liberalism as synonymous with *Washington Consensus*. The major axiom of the neo-liberal school is that, quoting Thatcher, "there is no alternative" to globalised capitalism (Mittelman 2000: 242). Often abbreviated as "TINA," inherent in the meaning of this slogan is that globalisation is here to stay, globalisation is inevitable and globalisation is right.

Neo-liberalists advocate the "trickle-down theory." In general the trickle-down theory holds that the poor are best served by policies that directly improve the welfare of the most prosperous (Persky *et al.* 2004: 70). In theory, trickle down works as follows: *If one individual or a small group suddenly becomes much richer than the rest of the community, this will not distort any trend towards the equity in that community, in the long run. Neo-liberalists says, we should applaud those rich because they still need the community; they need workers to run their estates and building, architects, mechanics and engineers to build and service the complex infrastructure required by all that to sustain that wealth. Therefore, everyone will eventually benefit as the rich few spend their money* (Theodore 2009: 11). This theory needs an outright rejection because, in real life such winners often do not spend that money in the community in which they gained it, but salt it away in investments abroad.

To the trickle-down theory, under free market capitalism, economic growth and technological change benefit even the poorest countries and people, even if the process is dominated by multinational corporations, rich domestic elites, and organisations such as the IMF dominated by rich countries' financiers (Chopra 2009: 505). The free mobility of capital between sectors, regions, and countries is regarded as crucial. All barriers to that free movement; such as tariffs, punitive taxation arrangements, planning and environmental controls, or other locational impediments, have to be removed. Harvey (2005: 66) points, state sovereignty over commodity and capital movements is willingly surrendered to the global market. International competition is seen as healthy since it improves efficiency and productivity, lowers prices, and thereby controls inflationary tendencies. States should therefore collectively seek and negotiate the reduction of barriers to movement of capital across borders and the opening of markets (for both commodities and capital) to global exchange. In short by this advocacy, neo-liberalists created an atmosphere favourable for a free market economy.

The theory of neo-liberalism has two main tenets: The first is that close economic contact between the industrial core and the periphery is the best way to accelerate the transfer of technology, which is inevitable for making poor economics rich. The second is that government in general lack the capacity to run large industrial and commercial enterprises, hence for core missions and a few others, government should shrink and privatise. These two principles represent parts of the trickle-down theory which states under free market capitalism, economic growth and technological change benefit even the poorest countries and people, even if that process is dominated by multinational corporations, rich domestic elites and so on.

Neo-liberalists succeeded in implementing this theory through Structural Adjustment Policies (SAPs) which required countries to devalue their currencies against the dollar, lift import and export restrictions, balance the budget, reduce public spending, remove price controls and cutting back subsidies. The world ascendancy of globalist classes has provoked a series of social crisis affecting wageworkers, peasants, employees and the self-employed throughout the world. The growth and penetration of globalist policies have engendered a significant increase in inequity between the minority and the majority. Taxes have become increasingly regressive, government tax revenues increasingly come from waged and salaried groups while the percentage from multinational corporate capital is declining. State subsidies for multinational corporate capital grow while the share for wageworkers, pensioners, low wage families, the ill and the injured, children etc. declined.

Governments became mere spectators in the market. The role of state was reduced to a facilitator rather than a regulator and controller. The withdrawal of state from the economy allowed the free play of corporates. MNCs and TNCs became the major actors in International Politics and Economics. Prices of essential commodities, life saving medicines and other necessaries shot up. Everything has become for sale, even those areas of life, such as social services and natural resources including the commons (land, water and seed) that were once considered the common heritage of humanity. The inglorious play of corporates undermined the basic rights and needs of common man all over the world and that is what happened in Cochabamba (Bolivia), Grenoble (France), Plachimada and Puthuserry (Kerala, India), Durban (South Africa), Ghana, Uruguay, Colombia, Canada and even in the US. Privatisation became a license to exploit the nature, without constraint, degrading the environment (Reinhart 2009: 50). The worst affecters of this were the farmers, fishermen, tribals, and those who are directly dependent upon land, water and forest for their livelihoods. The hegemonies play of corporates led to the decline of cottage, small scale and other indigenous industries.

The greatest social crisis is in the countries that have advanced furthest in globalisation. The number of workers without medical coverage, non-unionised workers and temporary or part-time workers with less or no social benefits is greatest in the US followed by the UK. Argentina and Brazil have unemployment rates of 18 and 15 per cent respectively, rates that have been multiplied with the globalisation of their economies. In East European Countries living standards have fallen between 30-80 per cent and in Mexico a fall of 30 per cent of wage earning became evident. In third world nations SAPs acted as a process of income re-concentration through cuts in social spending, corporate tax reductions and increased subsidies to corporates. In almost all nations a parallel development occurred making the rich richer and the poor poorer. Wealth began to concentrate in the hands of a few, creating gross inequality and reduction in the purchasing power of the common man.

Structural Adjustment Policies (SAPs)

The 1970s and the early 1980s have witnessed an explosive growth in the external debt of many developing countries. This trend of increasing debt started, when the OPEC drastically increased the world prices of oil in 1973 and in 1979 (Sikdar 2007: 59). The severe world recession that began in 1981 reduced the demand for exports of many of these countries. The need for more foreign exchange to import oil led to the devaluation of currencies of these countries. Thus, the costs of debt servicing for the loans which they had incurred, increased. This together with the sharp increase in the interest rate forced the countries to borrow for repaying the debt.

To overcome the situation the international financial institutions provided conditional loans to these institutions. Thus the countries were forced to undertake the structural adjustment programmes in the 1980s and 1990s as per the recommendations of these financial institutions. Noted Economist Prabhat Patnaik argues, "apart from the interests of multinational corporations, the structural adjustment regimes imposed on many of the Third World countries by the IMF and the World Bank are in the interests of metropolitan finance capital. The long term interests of these sections have a specific preference for asset acquisition rather than capital accumulation because it enables them to acquire things of a much higher value paying a much lower value" (Rao et al. 1995: 1156).

The economic crisis and the subsequent introduction of the structural adjustment programmes compelled many countries to cut their investment on social sectors. Thus, there occurred a downward spiral in resources available to health sector since the early 1980s (Sonia and Sailesh 2002: 3793).

Governments, particularly of developing countries were unable to deliver free health services as the basic right of the citizens in a traditional manner. User charges and other market mechanisms were introduced in the provision of health care as a result of policy reforms.

Structural Adjustment Policies are economic policies which countries must follow in order to qualify for "new" World Bank and International Monetary Fund (IMF) loans. Although SAPs are designed for individual countries, but they have common guiding principles and features which include: export led growth, privatisation, liberalisation and free market. An implicit belief of the philosophy underlying structural adjustment is that appropriate macro-economic policies are sufficient to reorganise and revitalise the national economy, regardless of its organisational history or institutional character (Orlando and Nelly 2006: 95).

Structural adjustment programs generally proceed in two phases. The first focuses on financial stabilisation, seeking to halt the downward spiral in state solvency by introducing user fees, reducing public sector employment, and removing subsidies. The second focuses on structural adjustment *per se*, seeking to reorganise the economy through devaluation, privatisation, tax reforms, and flexible interest rates (Orlando and Nelly 2006: 96; Rahman and Ali 1996: 4; Briggs and Ian 2001: 20). Using these multiple measures, reformers seek to revive ailing economies and bring them into effective and productive use.

The Conditionalities for SAPs (IMF Conditionality 2007: 1-3; Logan and Kindane 1993: 19) can be numbered as follows:

- Cutting expenditures, also known as Austerity.
- Focusing economic output on direct export and resource extraction.
- Devaluation of currencies.
- Trade liberalisation, or lifting import and export restrictions.
- Increasing the stability of investment (by supplementing foreign direct investment with the opening of domestic stock markets).
- Balancing budgets and not overspending.
- Removing price controls and state subsidies.
- Privatisation or divestiture of all or part of state-owned enterprises.
- Enhancing the rights of foreign investors' viz-a-viz national laws.
- Improving governance and fighting corruption.

Through these conditionalities, Structural Adjustment Programmes generally implement "free market" programmes and policy. These programmes include internal changes (notably privatisation and deregulation) as well as external ones, especially the reduction of trade barriers. Devaluation makes the goods cheaper for foreigners to buy and theoretically makes foreign imports more expensive. Balancing budgets can be done by raising taxes or by cutting government spending, which the IMF recommends. As a result SAPs often results in deep cuts in programmes like education, health and social care and the removal of subsidies designed to control the prices of basics such as food and milk. SAPs hurt the poor most, because they depend heavily on these services and subsidies. Neoliberal policies generally focus on urban areas but inevitably affect rural settings by eliminating agricultural subsidies and overlooking the problems of small farmers and medium-size agricultural producers (Orlando and Nelly 2006: 96).

Impact of SAPs in the Third World

Increased Poverty

Since the 1980s, the social impact of SAPs has been recognised: poverty has increased both in the rural and urban areas; real salaried earnings in many countries have plummeted by more than 60 per cent since the beginning of the 1980s; while the situation is much worse in the informal sector (Hong 2000: 15). In Eastern Europe living standards have fallen between 30 and 80 per cent since the transition to capitalism began. Mexico has seen wage earning income levels plummet to 30 per cent (Petras and Veltmeyer 2001: 78).

In South America, SAPs have rolled back the progress achieved in the 1960s and 70s. The number of people living in poverty rose from 130 million in 1980 to 180 million at the dawn of the 1990s. Income disparities widened with privatisation and deregulation as massive resources were concentrated in the hands of a few. In Mexico the richest 20 per cent received more than 52 per cent of the national income while the income of the poorest 20 per cent had less than five per cent. Bello (1996: 292) notes, "one decade of negative growth only worsened income inequalities, while the cost of adjustment fell on the middle and lower income groups, the top five per cent retained and even increased their living standards."

In Peru the proportion of poor rose to reach 54.1 per cent. SAP resulted in widespread impoverishment, falling wages, lagging prices, and the loss of adequate jobs. These dire trends led to a situation of food insecurity (Orlando and Nelly 2006: 106). In Chile between 1980 and 1990, the proportions of families below 'the line of destitution' rose from 12 to 15 per cent while those below 'the poverty line' (but above the destitution line) from 24 to 26 per cent. Some 40 per cent or 5.2 million people were classified as poor in a country that once boasted of a large middle class. (Bello 1996: 291) This has led to increased hunger and malnutrition.

Social Conditions Worsen

Reforms in the social sector have had dramatic impact on the status of education, health, environment and women and children. The restructuring of the health sector had led to the collapse of both preventive and curative care due to the lack of medical equipment, supplies, poor working conditions, low pay of medical personnel and the resulting low morale. User fees in primary health care and education have led to the exclusion of large sectors of the population from health services as they are unable to pay.

The utilisation of health centres by high risks groups dropped when cost recovery schemes and user financing were introduced. In 1994, medical experts voiced fears that the introduction of user fees, along with SAPs may be contributing to the rapid spread of AIDS in Africa. In the Upper Volta region of Ghana, health care use plummeted by 50 per cent when cost recovery was introduced. In Tanzania, the three public hospitals saw attendance drop by 53.4 per cent in a matter of months in 1994 when user fees were introduced. In Niger, cost recovery measures implemented between 1986 and 1988 led to: a sharp decline in the use of preventive care services; increased exclusion of the most impoverished from care at Niamey Hospital, where outpatients who did not pay for care would wait some 24 days before seeking care while an outpatient who did have to pay for care would wait an average of 51 days (Hong 2000: 17).

Under structural adjustment programmes, women are generally the ones who end up compensating for deficiencies in state and market provisions by increasing the production and supply of food for their families; and it is rural women, in particular, who absorb the greatest costs of social reproduction. Rural women are also vulnerable to increasing violence in the countryside created as transnational corporations (in mining and agro-industry) and local elites use force to dislodge peasants and natives from their traditional lands to gain control of subsoil resources (Orlando and Nelly 2006: 111). There occurred sharp reduction in the enrolment of students in schools especially girls, because of the introduction of charges for registration and monthly fees.

Cuts in public expenditure under SAPs have led to a drastic decline in control and prevention measures. As a result, diseases, once under control or eradicated have made a comeback (Rao *et al.* 1995: 1158). Sub-Saharan Africa records a resurgence of cholera, yellow fever and malaria. In South America the prevalence of malaria and dengue has worsened dramatically since the mid 1980s. The resurgence of communicable diseases particularly malaria, diphtheria, tuberculosis, and cholera all contributed to increased morbidity and mortality amongst children and women (Sonia and Sailesh 2002: 3794). The outbreak of bubonic and pneumonic plague in India in 1994 has been seen 'as the direct consequence of a worsening urban sanitation and public health infrastructure which accompanied the compression of national and municipal budgets under the 1991 IMF-WB, sponsored structural adjustment programme' (Hong 2000: 18).

Globalisation and the Challenges before Bureaucracy

Bureaucracy, being an important instrument of the state to administer its people and manage the affairs of the government, the challenge before bureaucracy owing to globalisation is high. Globalisation advocates an increased role of market and a decreased role of the state. The economic function of the state was limited to as a facilitator and promoter of the market. In such a system, it is quite natural that only the affluent can survive. When the forces of demand and supply determine the price of a commodity, essential commodities too become unaffordable and unreachable to the common man. A vast majority of the population will be destined to starve under such circumstances. Sharp inequality and increased poverty are the features of globalisation of our times. Globalisation is an economic package that takes into account only the aspirations of the economically powerful sections of the society. When this is the case, even though globalisation speaks about a reduced role of the state, in actual sense, it has increased the role and responsibility of every state. Whether every nation state is taking up this increased role or responsibility is a big question? No responsible and "welfare" state can leave its citizens before the avalanche of globalisation, that takes away their culture, livelihoods, values, freedom, environment, commons, peace and prosperity.

It is clear that the Structural Adjustment Policies are not indigenous but outward oriented packages that are based on the needs of the outsiders, especially the global capitalists. Under the SAP there is a shift from production for consumption to production for exports because importance is given to commercial crops than basic goods. Cut back in subsidies, retrenchment, reduced public spending, elimination of tariffs, imposition of user fees etc. provides tough time for the common man. Foreign investments are aimed only at profit and they may withdraw it at any time, just like what happened in South East Asia during 1990s, which worsened the East Asian Crisis. A bubbled economy is not a symbol of progress or development but a warning that it may burst at any moment. So the need of the hour is replacing or countering the outward oriented development packages with indigenous ones that can ensure sufficiency for all before superfluity for some. Civil servants have an important role in this as they are the ones who analyses issues and prepares options for the decision makers.

With the withdrawal of the state, the forces of market entered the scene. As profit is the sole motive behind market transaction, market approach to development will no doubt increase exploitation and oppression. Already there is wide divergence in holding the resources between the rich and the poor. Free market fundamentalism creates a situation that makes the rich richer and poor poorer, a kind of income re-concentration favouring the rich. Moreover market governance has resulted in commodification of the commons. Be it land, water, seed, public spaces, knowledge and other essential services and things, which human beings have access by virtue of being homo sapiens, have been enclosed for private profit. All these will increase inequality in an already iniquitous society. More concentration has to be done in sectors like agriculture, irrigation, education, health care, and other social services to reduce the increasing gulf.

Delicensing has done much damage to the developing societies. A number of multinationals like Enron, Cola, Pepsi, Suez, Vivendi, etc., that won't show least attention to human rights and made the worst human rights violations. Dow Chemicals in Bhopal and Coco-cola in Plachimada played with the life of thousands of innocents and indigenous people, in India. Taming this corporate is an ardours task as they have the support of the World Bank, Globalist Governments and other Financial Institutions. As Ramaswamy (2002: 58) points, "the civil servants have to develop specialised knowledge and skills to have insight into various social, political and economic effects of the policy measures being advocated by multilateral agencies, developed countries and MNCs." It is the duty of the bureaucrats to ensure that the resources of the nation are not plundered by either foreign and national companies or individuals and that the basic rights of the common man are protected.

Civil servants have to chart out better policies, plans and programmes to improve the living conditions of the poor. Together with this they have to enforce the existing rules and regulations, that to a great extend can save the local population and their resources, and can protect the weaker sections from the intrusion of the market. Every attempt should be made to root out corruption and other unfair policies of competition that are stumbles in the path of welfarism. Only a knowledgeable, experienced and neutral bureaucracy can ensure fairness in the market. They have to sensitise the local population about the problems of the unbridled market and organise them in the attempts to counter the same. They have to sprout out the belief that our problems can be solved and development can be achieved through indigenous means.

The global financial crisis has once again proved that more openness is not good for an economy. Crisis anywhere will make its repercussions in domestic economy also. For a developing society with many crippling hands and legs, climbing once again the steps of progress is difficult. So instead of a uni-polar globalisation what is needed is localisation, indigenous policies to suit local needs and local problems. The civil servants have to voice their concerns through serious research. They should educate the local citizens about the harmful effects of globalisation and the ruining nature of consumerist culture. They should develop a safety net that can prevent or minimise the risks associated with the uncertainties of hegemonic globalisation. Co-operation among the bureaucracies is very essential for this and through the transfer of knowledge, experience and expertise, the onslaught of globalisation can be prevented.

All this necessitates a bureaucracy that is patriotic and can rise above their narrow class interest. Everywhere, as Marx says, bureaucracy has a class structure and tries to maintain its status quo and promote its economic interest. Weber's ideal bureaucracy is hard to seen in any society; instead what prevails is the Sala Bureaucracy that gives undue importance to rules, regulations, formalism and personal gains. This often increases chance of corruption and denial of justice to the common man. Lured by the opportunities, salary and other financial packages in the corporate houses, serving bureaucrats and senior retired bureaucrats taking nod for private jobs has become a common thing, especially from the developing world. For example, in India during the last twelve years, i.e., from 2002-2012, more than a century of IAS officers have left their jobs to join big corporate houses. So, to ensure social change, what is needed, is a change in the mind-set of the bureaucrats, to question the inhuman traditions of hierarchy and red tape and to rise above the narrow personal interests for the sake of common good.

References

Alfred, Saad-Filho and Deborah, Johnston (ed) (2005): *Neoliberalism, A Critical Reader*, Pluto Press, London.

Avasthi, Amreshwar and Avasthi, Anand Prakash (2008): *Indian Administration*, Lakshmi Narain Agarwal, Agra.

Bello, Walden (1996): "Structural Adjustment Programs: Success for Whom," in Mander, J. and Goldsmith, E. (eds) *The Case Against The Global Economy,* Sierra Club, San Francisco.

Briggs, John and Ian, Yeboah, E.A. (2001): "Structural Adjustment and the Contemporary Sub-Saharan African City," *Blackwell Publishing* and *The Royal Geographical Society*, 33(1), March, 18-26.

Chopra, J.K. (2009): *Unique Quintessence of Political Science*, Unique Publishers, New Delhi.

Dasgupta, Samir and Kiely, Ray (2006): *Globalisation and After,* Sage, New Delhi.

Harvey, D. (2005): *A Brief History of Neo-liberalism*, Oxford University Press, New York.

Hira, Anil (1998): *Ideas And Economic Policy in Latin America: Regional, National, and Organisational Case Studies*, Praeger Publishers, West Port, USA.

Hong, Evelyne (2000): *Globalisation and the Impact on Health: A Third World View*, Third World Network, Penang.

IMF (2007): *IMF Conditionality*, IMF Fact Sheets, Washington.

Jitha, S.R. (2007): *Higher Bureaucracy and Development*, Kalpaz Publishers, New Delhi.

Logan, Ikubolajeh Bernard and Kidane, Mengisteab (1993): "IMF-World Bank Adjustment and Structural Transformation in Sub-Saharan Africa," *Economic Geography*, 69(1), January, 1-24.

McDonald, David A. and Ruiters, Grey (2005): "Rethinking Privatisation, Towards a Critical Theoretical Perspective," *Public Services Year Book.*

Mittelman, James H. (2000): *The Globalisation Syndrome: Transformation and Resistance*, Princeton University Press, New Jersey.

Orlando, Plaza and Nelly, Stromquist, P. (2006): "Consequences of Structural Adjustment on Economic and Social Domains: Two Decades in the Life of Peru," *Annals of the American Academy of Political and Social Science*, 606, July, 95-115.

Petras, James and Veltmeyer, Henry (2001): *Globalisation Unmasked*, Madhyam Books, New Delhi.

Persky, Joseph; Daniyel, Felzenshtain and Virginia, Carlson (2004): *Does "Trickle Down" Work?*, Institute for Employment Research, Michigam.

Rahman, Rushidan Islam and Ali, Kamar (1996): *Structural Adjustment Policies and Health Care Services*, CIRDAP, Bangladesh.

Ramaswamy, P.R. (2002): "The Challenges of Globalisation for Civil Servants," *IJPA* XLVIII(1), January-March, 50-60.

Rao, Mohan., Nayar, K.R., Rama, Baru V. and Ritu, Priya (1995): "Health and Structural Adjustment, Major Shifts at Policy Level," *Economic and Political Weekly*, 30(20), May 20, 1156-60.

Reinhart Philip (2009): "Economic Development and Social Justice," *Competition Success Review*, XLV(11), May, 48-50.

Ruddar, Dutt (2006): *India's Economy*, S. Chand & Co. Ltd., New Delhi.

Samir, Amin (2009): *The World We Wish to See: Revolutionary Objectives in the Twenty-First Century*, Aakar Books, Delhi.

Sathyanarayana, T. (2003): "Liberalisation, Public Administration and the Public," *IJPA* XLIX(1), January-March, 24-32.

Scholte, Jan Aart (2005): *Globalisation: A Critical Introduction*, Palgrave Macmillan, New York.

Sikdar, Soumyen (2007): *Contemporary Issues in Globalisation*, Oxford University Press, New Delhi.

Sonia, Andrews and Sailesh, Mohan (2002): "User Charges in Health Care: Some Issues," *Economic and Political Weekly*, 37(37), Sept. 14-20, 3793-5.

Steger, Manfred B. and Roy, Ravi, K. (2010): *Neoliberalism: A Very Short Introduction*, Oxford Publishers, New York.

Theodore, Harney MacDonald (2009): *Removing the Barriers to Global Health Equity*, Radcliffe Publishing Ltd., Oxon.

Tony, Schirato and Jen, Webb (2006): *Understanding Globalisation*, Sage Publications, New Delhi.

6

Liberalisation and Development in India

Development has become a key word in the daily discourse and is being used in a variety of connotations, the meaning of which is even opposed to one another. The problem in analysing development is not that it has no meaning, but many meanings. For some, development is an increase in national income, for others it is social development, while some other see it as modernisation. Some consider development as social change when others see it as freedom. So development never can be defined to universal satisfaction, nor is it possible. The uni-dimensional concept of development takes into account only increase in national income or economic growth. Thus, development in its economic dimension is associated with the maximisation of outputs or economic growth. But, any nation including the developed or the developing has to view its agenda of developments in its contexts of social, cultural, political, demographic context. Development thus is a multi-dimensional concept and its goals are not confined to economy merely. This means that development is not only economic but also social and one that touches every aspect of human and social life. It includes economic growth, social progress, political development, nation-building and the like.

The neo-liberal school considers development as one equivalent with increase in GDP (Gross Domestic Product). Foreign Direct Investment (FDI), foreign exchange reserves, and an open market form the means or criteria for development, in such a view point. The distribution of income among the population did not come into picture anywhere. They advocate the *trickle-down* theory which states that the poor are best served by policies that directly improve the welfare of the most prosperous (Persky *et al*. 2004: 70). Under free market capitalism, economic growth and technological change benefit even the poorest countries and people. In such a system development will trickle down to the bottom and for that the welfare of the top must be ensured first. This view of development is one-sided as it takes into account only the increase in national income and not its distribution among the masses. Moreover the freedom of choice in the market can be enjoyed only by a few. There can be seen a partial or one-sided advancement in which the burden of development falls heavily on the other. Such advancement lacks social justice which is an essential element of development.

When development is a process by which a nation improves the economic, political and social well being of the people, development has an intimate relation with social justice, which speaks of a society that offers individuals and groups fair treatment and an impartial share in the benefits of societal development. Social justice encompasses economic justice with its three Principles of – Participation, Distribution and Harmony, which rejects monopolies, special privileges and other exclusionary social barriers to economic self-reliance. If any of these three principles are weakened or missing the system of economic justice and thereby social justice will collapse. So from a policy perspective development can be defined as the efforts to improve the economic well being and quality of life of a community by creating and/or retaining jobs and supporting or growing incomes (Reinhart 2009: 48). This view of development is multi-dimensional and is linked with social change.

The main goal of development is change, a state of change from under-developed to developed one. Development was the top priority of national governments in Third World countries which wanted to get rid of their crippling poverty, hunger, diseases and backwardness. They adopted a number of development packages provided by the west, like the US foreign aid, economic and technical assistance programme, but miserably failed in their attempt. This led a number of scholars especially by those of the Comparative Administrative Group of the United States to analyse the process of development. Their study revealed that the Western development models and concepts of administration are not feasible in developing nations. This in other words means development of the Third World is possible only through indigenous development packages. The outward oriented packages will only increase the dependency of the third world peripheral nations on the developed centre. This, creates an unequal exchange between the centre (core) and the periphery as pointed out by Dependency Theorist Immanuel Wallerstein (1974: 6), which acts as a source of continued dependence of the periphery on the centre. Neo-liberalism is one such package that ensures the dependence of the third world on the developed core. Hence social change is not possible in the neo-liberal development agenda which speaks only about the needs and interests of the affluent sections, be at the national or international level.

Nobel laurite and noted economist Amartya Sen looks upon development as freedom, a process that ends with freedom from poverty and from other social and economic deprivations. In his book *Development as Freedom* he explains: *development can be seen as a process of expanding the real freedoms that people enjoy. These freedoms are both the primary ends and the principal means of development. They include freedom to participate in the economy, which implies access to credit, among other facilities; freedom of political expression and participation; social opportunities, including entitlement to education and health services; transparency guarantees, involving freedom to deal with others openly; and protective security guaranteed by social safety nets, such as unemployment insurance or famine relief.* So, development goes much beyond the accumulation of wealth and the growth of gross national product and other income related variables, to include whole some change. Development includes the ensuring of basic services to the people and freedom to participate in the decision-making process.

For bringing the freedom of development a transformation in the society is needed, a far-reaching transformation of society's economic, social and political structure of dominant organisation of production, distribution and consumption, as Baron pointed out, or a change coupled with growth as Colm and Geiger say (Arora 2010: 13.4). A law of the sea can never bring such a change as it gives undue benefits to the big fish. So, what John Montgomery (1966: 59) calls for is governmental action, when he sees development as an aspect of change that is desirable, broadly predicted or planned or influenced by governmental actions. A controlling actor is essential in the process of designing and implementing development. Market cannot be the controlling actor as the freedom it provides can be enjoyed only by the affluent and powerful. At the same time the state should not be another capitalist or one that promotes the interest of only one section of the society. It should promote with special care the interests of the weaker sections of the society. "The responsibility of the state is to give an atmosphere where development can thrive and allows all stakeholders with equal opportunities to obtain rewards. It should not pile the odds in favour of the powerful and disempower the weak and most vulnerable", says Raju Narayana Swami (IAS) (2011: 12).

Development as social change involves the transformation of an under-developed society to a developed one in its social, political, economic and cultural spheres. Such a transformation is inclusive and accounts the interests of all especially the indigenous population, weaker sections and the marginalised. As the goal is to create a more equitable and just society equitable distribution of income and resources of the nation has prime importance, as it is necessary to ensure the enhancement of the welfare of the deprived. The state should provide proper safety nets to ensure that the needy can stand par with other sections of the society. So welfare functions of the state have more importance and in the market it should be the controller and manager. Enhancement of progress should not be one-sided but multi-faceted covering all walks of life. No society can claim development when a vast majority lives without the basic things of sustenance, when a microscopic minority eats away the resources of the nation such that the burden of development and its benefits are not equitable distributed. In short, development implies change, a change for justice.

Globalisation and Development in India

The dominant development model of our time is 'economic globalisation', a model of economics rooted in the belief that liberal market economics constitute the one and only one choice for the whole world. The advocacy behind globalisation is increased economic development and stability. Capital account liberalisation, interest rate set by the market and flexible exchange regimes created the framework for globalisation. Industries previously closed to Foreign Direct Investment (FDI) have been opened, state properties have been privatised, procedures have been simplified and incentives and concessions (for corporates) have been introduced. The world witnessed the dismantling of state regulations, liberalisation of export-import laws, delicensing, flexible laws including labour laws, corporate tax reductions, increased subsidies to corporates, hegemonious control of employers in hiring, firing, outsourcing, sub-contracting and so on. In short globalisation created an atmosphere free of restrictions, allowing the corporates to have an unbridled play (Reinhart 2009: 48, 2007: 99).

Addressing the 56th National Development Council Meeting held on 22nd October 2011, Dr. Manmohan Singh, the honourable Prime Minister of India, called for a rapid, inclusive and sustainable growth, portraying them as the goals for the 12th Five Year Plans (2012-17). Echoing that our aim has always been inclusive growth, the Prime Minister accepted that we have not done nearly well on inclusiveness (*Yojana* 2012: 6). It is a fact that even though we have delivered high growth it couldn't ensure broad spread of benefits to all sections of our population, particularly the Scheduled Castes, Scheduled Tribes, the Other Backward Classes and other marginalised groups. At the outset of the speech itself the Prime Minister attributed a very large role to the government in the process of development. Stress was also given to development in the agricultural sector, which he now sees as relevant for inclusiveness. This is a clear withdrawal from the stand he adopted in the wave of economic globalisation in India, i.e. 1991.

Globalisation, an important element in the reforms package intends to integrate Indian economy with the world economy. Economic reforms in India were introduced by Rajiv Gandhi (1985) but it was Narasimha Rao Government (1991-1996) which gave a definite shape and start to the new economic reforms of globalisation by announcing the New Industrial Policy (NIP) of 1991. It was the unprecedented balance of payment crisis in 1990-91 that forced India into the path of liberalisation. Besides this the economic reforms initiated by Rajiv Gandhi caused foreign liability for India. Rajiv Gandhi Government under the persuasion of neo-liberal economists, borrowed extensively from multinational banks to finance developmental programmes and this resulted in the explosion of external debt of India (Mathew 2007: 10). India responded with a reform trinity popularly referred to as "Liberalisation, Privatisation and Globalisation." India accepted the SAP package of IMF and opened the doors of the economy for liberalisation.

The NIP marked a sharp departure from the earlier Industrial Policy of 1956. The main aims of the NIP were:

- To introduce liberalisation with a view to integrate Indian economy with the world economy.
- To remove restrictions on Foreign Direct Investment (FDI).
- To shed the load of public enterprises incurring losses.

The NIP led the government to take serious initiatives in respect of policies in areas like: (a) Industrial Licensing; (b) Foreign Investment; (c) Foreign Technology Policy; (d) Public Sector Policy; and (e) MRTP Act. Industrial licensing was abolished for all industries except 18 (now 8) that included coal, petroleum, motorcars, cigars, hazardous chemicals, pharmaceuticals, luxury items etc. The number of industries reserved for public sector has been brought down to six. The list now includes - arms and ammunition, atomic energy, mineral oils, railway transport and atomic minerals. In case of foreign investment it was decided to approve 51 per cent foreign equity in high priority industries. Today 100 per cent FDI is permitted in Pharmaceuticals, 74 per cent in Telecom, 49 per cent in banking, 50-100 per cent in Tourism, 100 per cent in development of townships, 26 per cent in defense and so on (Sikdar 2007: 96-7). The government also decided to disinvest public enterprises working in loss. The giant leap towards disinvestment was made by the NDA government that appointed a Minister exclusively for this purpose and made a target of 12,000 crores for 2003 by way of disinvestments. The MRTP Act was amended and the working of MRTP Commission was first restricted to controlling and regulating monopolistic restrictive and unfair trade practices and later replaced with a Competitive Commission.

All these measures brought out a number of changes in the economy. India became an investment destination of number of firms because of its unexplored and at the same time large market. Economic reforms to one extent have ended the scarcity of capital that plagued Indian business. This offered a boost to Indian economy. The GDP rate accelerated from 5.6 per cent (1980-90) to 8.7 per cent by 2007-08, after then it began to decline under the influence of the financial crisis and clocked to 6.9 per cent in 2011-12 The foreign exchange reserves currently stands at $200 billion as against less than $I billion during 1990-91. In the inflow of FDI India became the fourth largest recipient touching at $44 billion in 2009. The rapid progress in science and technology has transferred the pace of means of transport and communication. It increased the production manifold. Modern amenities of life including furniture, electronic items, consumer durables and almost all foreign goods and eatables became available in Indian market at more or less equivalent prices. The boom in IT and other sectors generated millions of job opportunities. This is the one aspect of globalisation.

The other aspect is that the policy of globalisation is not a free lunch. The neo-liberal development agenda had adversely affected India's indigenous development strategy that ensured basic minimum for all. The march of globalisation destroyed agriculture, the backbone of Indian economy. Agriculture still continues to be a key sector in India and about 58.2 per cent of the population is dependent on agriculture for their livelihood (India 2012: 71). Its contribution to the nations GDP was 13.9 per cent during 2011-2012. The contribution of agriculture and allied sectors to the nation's GDP has been declining since 1950-51 (53.1 per cent). But the rate of decline has augmented since 1990-91. Within a period of 20 years there occurred a decline of 15.7 per cent, i.e. from 29.6 per cent in 1990-91 to 22.3 per cent in 2000-01 and from there a steep decline to 13.9 per cent in 2011-12 (Economy 2012: 40). Agriculture growth slowed from 4.69 pe rcent in 1991 to 2.6 per cent in 1997 and to 1.1 per cent in 2002-03 (Pohare 2011: 18). The growth of GDP in agriculture, forestry and fishery together was only 1 per cent during 2002-05 and by 2010 it became just 0.2 per cent (Agricultural Statistics 2010).

The rate of growth of food grains declined to two per cent by 2006 as against four per cent in the pre-reforms period. The fluctuating food grains production in India witnessed a steep fall in 2002-03 when the decline in food grains production is apprehended to be anywhere between 13-14 per cent (Business Leads, 2003). It is a known fact that Indian agriculture depends upon the gambling of monsoon. Climatic factors have to a great extend affected our food grain production. The decline in production together with the fall in prices made agriculture an unprofitable business for many. The annual rate of growth of employment in agricultural sector declined to 0.66 per cent by 1993-2000 as against 2.73 per cent in 1987. As many as 8 million people quit farming between the two censuses of 1991 and 2001 (ISIS 2010). The rate of people leaving farming has been rising and on an average, close to 2,000 people a day abandon farming in the country. The decline in agriculture sector shows that the fate of about 58.2 per cent of the population is in a precarious position.

The decline of agriculture resulted in increased unemployment and farmer's suicide. Many small scale agriculturists were forced to abandon their profession and migrate to south Indian states of Kerala, Tamil Nadu and Pondicherry (UT), especially in the construction sector. Working hours ranging from 08:00 am to 06:00 pm and unhygienic conditions of stay make their life a core. First hand information from the migrant workers in Pondicherry (from Bengal, Bihar and Orissa) reveals that many are fed up with the hefty work in the construction sector that too under the hot sun. Not only they were underpaid but also denied basic human rights. They have to live in temporary sheds made up of aluminium sheets. One who knows the climate of Pondicherry can understand how difficult it will be to stay in such camps during the severe hot months. There are no better facilities for cooking, washing, bathing and other primary needs. It won't be an exaggeration if one says that cattle sheds are even better than the camps of migrant workers. Many are with their family, both husband and wife working and children helping in domestic works. These children are quite naturally denied opportunities for education. The conditions of this workers is pathetic, as they cannot go back until their debts are repaid; even if repaid they have to continue as migrant workers so long as agriculture becomes profitable.

P. Sainath, Rural Affairs editor of *The Hindu,* points that within 10 years from 1991, the number of Indian farm households in debt almost doubled from 26 per cent to 48.6 per cent (Sainath 2010). The mounting dept shot up farmer's suicide in India. According to the National Crime Records Bureau (NCRB) data, more than 2,16,000 farmers have committed suicide in India since 1997. More than 17,000 farmers committed suicide in 2009, the worst since 2004. That takes the total number of recorded farmer suicides since 1997 to 216,500 (Rupashree 2011). Nearly two-thirds occurred in five states, Maharashtra, Karnataka, Andhra Pradesh, Madhya Pradesh and Chhattisgarh, with one-third of the country's population. In the period 1997-2002, farm suicides in the five Big States accounted for roughly one out of every 12 of all suicides in the country. In 2003-08, they accounted for nearly one out of every 10 (Sainath 2009). Dr. Nagaraj has repeatedly pointed out; the suicides appear concentrated in regions of high commercialisation of agriculture and very high peasant debt. Cash crop farmers seemed far more vulnerable to suicide than those growing food crops. The suicide of cotton cultivators of Vidharba region of Maharashtra substantiates the above said argument.

Predatory commercialisation of the countryside; a massive decline in investment in agriculture; the withdrawal of bank credit at a time of soaring input prices; the crash in farm incomes combined with an explosion of cultivation costs; the shifting of millions from food crop to cash crop cultivation with all its risks; the corporate hijack of every major sector of agriculture including, and especially, seed; growing water stress and moves towards privatisation of that resource; land grabbing in the name of SEZs are the main reasons pointed for the huge crisis in agricultural sector. Large tracts of lands including prime agricultural lands have been acquired for the projects, forcing thousands out of their livelihood in West Bengal, Orissa, Bihar, Uttar Pradesh, Andra Pradesh, and Maharashtra. The irrational land acquisition even without providing adequate compensation and rehabilitation package is threatening the food security of the nation and this is dangerous. In Bhatta Parsual, Greater Noida (UP), about 6000 acres of land is being acquired by infrastructure company Jaiprakash Associates to build luxury townships and sports facilities, including a Formula 1 racetrack, in the guise of building the Yamuna Expressway (Vandana Siva 2011).

Indigenous, cottage and small-scale industries also suffered heavily. As a result unemployment and poverty steeped up. The proportion of unemployed to the total labour force has been increasing from 2.62 per cent (1993-94) to 2.70 per cent (1999-2000) and 3.6 per cent (2004-05) (Sezhiyan 2007: 9). Ruddar Dutt (2008: 254) points, "The employment situation in India has worsened in the era of globalisation. The rate of growth of employment which was of the order of 2.04 per cent per year during 1983-94 declined to a low level of 0.98 per cent during the period 1994-2000." As a result of 1687 closures a total of 1.20 lakh workers lost their jobs. Production units have resorted to layoff to cut down labour costs. During the seven year post-reform period a total of 4.91 lakh workers were laid off. On the plea of redundancy, a total of 20,720 workers were retrenched during 1991-97. The total employment in the organised sector declined from 273.7 lakhs in 1994 to 264.4 lakhs in 2004 and to 250 lakhs in 2007, an average negative growth rate of 0.38 per cent (Dutt 2007: 10).

The persons below poverty line, is a matter of controversy as a number game is going on in fixing the line. Instead of reducing poverty all attempts are going on to remove many from the below poverty line. As per the Tendulkar Committee (Appointed by the Government of India) Report around 37.2 per cent of the total population are under the below poverty line, 41.8 per cent in rural areas and 25.7 per cent in urban areas (2004-05 Estimates). But the Planning Commission, on 19th March 2012, reduced the poverty line to Rs. 28.65 per capita daily consumption in cities and Rs. 22.42 in rural areas, scaling down India's poverty ratio to 29.8 per cent in 2009-10 (The Hindu 2012a: 14). At the same time the Government of India (in its affidavit to the Supreme Court) came with a benchmark of Rs. 32 in urban areas and Rs. 26 in rural areas, to define those who are to be treated as being below or above the poverty line (The Hindu 2012b: 10). The gravity of the problem can be identified when we compare the above said figures with the findings of the Arjun Sengupta Committee on Unorganised Sector, that 85 per cent of the country's unorganised workforce lives on Rs. 20 a day (Chronicle 2012: 113).

Income inequality in India is on the rise since globalisation. The Planning commission admits that income inequality in both rural and urban areas are increasing. Under the Gini Coefficient used, there was a marginal increase in inequality in rural areas from 0.27 per cent during 2004-05 to 0.28 per cent during 2009-10. In urban areas, the situation deteriorated more sharply, from 0.35 per cent to 0.37 per cent (The Hindu 2012a: 14). The 66th round of NSSO on income and expenditure carried out in between July 2009 and June 2010 reveals that 50 per cent of the population in rural India lives on less than Rs.35 a day and as many in the city population lives on Rs. 66 a day. The survey also finds that the poorest 10 per cent of the population lives on Rs.15 a day in rural areas and Rs.20 a day in urban areas (Express News 2012: 10). The average all-India monthly per capita expenditure (MPCE) is Rs.1053.64 in rural areas and Rs.1984.66 in urban areas, but for the poorest 10 per cent it is Rs.453 in rural areas and Rs. 599 in urban areas (Ashwani 2011: 10). When the top 10 per cent of the population owns 52.9 per cent of the total wealth i.e., more than half of the nation's wealth (Manas 2010), an overwhelming 836 million people or 77 per cent of the total population live on a per capita consumption of less than Rupees Twenty a day (Arjun Sengupta 2007). This means that money was (is) concentrated in few hands and this is the main reason for the paradox of increase in GDP coupled with increase in poverty.

The growth of slum population is another fall out. Of its 13 million populations Mumbai has 54 per cent in slums. Similar is the case of Delhi where about 45 per cent in slums (Sezhiyan 2007: 10). According to "Slums in India – A Statistical Compendium 2011," published by the Union Government, every eighth urban child in India in the age group of 0-6 years stays in slums. The total number of children living in slums is about 7.6 million, and this constitutes 13.1 per cent of total child population of the urban areas. Maharashtra has the highest slum child population with around 1.7 million children staying in slums. Even in progressive state of Kerala more than 10 per cent of the child population stays in slums. Chandigarh has the highest proportion of slum child population.

The quality of life especially in rural areas declined sharply, with a secular decline in social services, mainly in education and health. Even though the literacy rate in India has gone up from 65.38 per cent in 2001 to 74.04 per cent in 2011, fact remains that 34 per cent of the world's illiterate adults are residing in India and India has the largest number of illiterates in the world. Even today there are many children who cannot attend schools. The commonly reported reason for dropout is 'costs too much' for both boys and girls, followed by 'required for outside work for payment in cash or kind' for boys and 'required for household work' for girls (NFHS 2005-06: 34). About children at work the survey (p. 47) states that nearly one in every eight (12 per cent) children of the age group 5-14 years works either for their own household or for somebody else. Two per cent of children are engaged in paid work, three per cent are engaged in unpaid work for someone who is not a member of their household, three per cent are engaged in household chores for 28 or more hours in a week, and five per cent are engaged in work in a family business.

The HUNGaMA (Hunger and Malnutrition) Survey Report, by the Naandi Foundation, released on January 11, 2012, says that child malnutrition is widespread across states and districts (of focus ones). In the 100 focus districts[1], 42 per cent of the children under-five are underweight and 59 per cent are stunted (HUNGaMA 2012: 8). The survey found that of the stunted children about half are severely stunted and about half of all children are underweight or stunted by the time they are two years. As per the study the prevalence of malnutrition is significantly higher among children from low-income families. Children from households identifying as Muslim, Scheduled Castes or Scheduled Tribes generally have worsen nutrition (p. 9). The survey also finds that the rate of child underweight and stunning is significantly higher among mothers with low levels of education (66 per cent). The report was so shocking that the Prime Minister, while releasing the same, described it as a "national shame" (Aarati 2012: 1). The only positive thing out of the survey is that there is a decline in the prevalence of underweight children from 53 per cent in 2004 to 42 per cent in 2011. But while comparing the impressive GDP from 2004 the level of under-nutrition is unacceptable.

The Global Hunger Index (GHI) 2011, places India in a low performing rank of 67 out of 81. The GHI is prepared on the basis of three equally weighted indicators of the proportion of undernourished, prevalence of underweight children and mortality rate. In case of Global Prosperity Index 2011, India has slipped three places to rank 91 out of 110 countries. As per the Index, India ranks low on access to education and health (Wizard 2012: 185, 186). The NFHS Report (2005-06) reveals that 56 per cent of married women in the age group 15-45 years were found anaemic. Among married men in the age group 15-49 years, 24.3 were found to be anaemic (NFHS 2005-06: 291, 310, 312). The rate of infant mortality in India is 55 (Census 2011b: 12) as against Sri Lanka (13), China (30) and Vietnam (19) (UNICEF 2008). As per the UNICEF figures of 2008, one out of every four children in the world who die under the age of five is an Indian. The rate of maternal mortality rate is 212 (2011b: 5) as against Sri Lanka (92), China (56) and Vietnam (130). UNICEF report states, "Every five minutes an Indian dies from complications related to pregnancy and childbirth, adding up to approximately 1,30,000 women deaths per year" (Teena 2006: 1). Of the 5.36 lakh women who died during pregnancy or after child birth in 2005 globally, India accounted for 1.17 lakh (Kounteya 2007).

The new census (2011a) data, released on March 13, 2012, shows that though half of Indian's do not have a toilet at home, over half own a telephone. In case of basic facilities, 67.2 per cent households have electricity – 92.7 per cent in urban areas and 55.3 per cent in rural areas. Piped drinking water (from treated source) is available to only 32 per cent of total population

– 62 per cent in urban and only 17.9 per cent in rural areas. 17 per cent still fetch water from a source located more than 500 metres in rural areas or 100 metres in urban centres. Only 46.9 per cent of the total 246.6 million households have toilet facilities, 81.4 per cent in urban areas and 30.7 in rural areas. 3.2 per cent use public toilets and the rest 49.8 per cent ease in public. In stark contrast 63.2 per cent of the households own a telephone connection – 53.2 per cent of mobile phones. Even though we have more access to electricity and have televisions (47.2 per cent), women are forced to rely on traditional smoky fuels to cook, 49.0 per cent – 20.1 in urban and 62.5 in rural. LPG for cooking was available to only 11.4 per cent of the rural households while it is 65 per cent in urban households. Around 37.1 per cent of the total households are having one room households – 32.1 in urban and 39.4 in rural.

The new economic policy, which entails liberalisation, privatisation and globalisation, are redefining the role of state and administration to suit the foreign capital. The withdrawal of the state from essential services allowed big corporates to monopolise the market. The disinvestment policy made many public sector undertakings (PSUs) partially or totally under the control of big corporates. These include Bharat Aluminium Corporation (BALCO), National Aluminium Corporation (NALCO), Computer Maintenance Corporation (CMC), Indian Petroleum Corporation Limited (IPCL), Videsh Sanchar Nigam Limited (VSNL), Indian Tourism Development Corporation (ITDC), Gas Authority of India Limited (GAII), and National Thermal Power Corporation (NTPC) etc. Moreover some of the profits making public sector undertakings were also disinvested. They are Bharat Heavy Electricals Limited (BHEL), Maruti, ITDC and Modern Foods. Many of them went into the hands of multinational corporations while others fallen fatally like FACT (Ruddar 2006: 242). Having lost the key sectors the government is not in a position to intervene in the market fruitfully. All these have seriously affected our financial security and are the stumbling blocks in curbing inflation and other problems. Not satisfied with the disinvestment of profit making PSUs, the liberal government now eyes on the reserves of the public sector companies which is estimated to be more than Rs. 2.5 lakh crore. The economist Prime Minister is of the view that when the government is facing fiscal deficit it is not advisable to keep this much money with the PSUs (Kerala Kaumudi 2012a: 4). Such an action no doubt curbs the wings of the profit making PSUs and ensures the private sector an advantage over them.

A number of initiatives were done in the last two decades to liberalise the market. Together with de-licensing, price de-control was also facilitated to promote the corporate business interest. The pricing of petrol, diesel, cooking gas, medicines were de-controlled, allowing the market forces to determine its price, there by taking away the role of the state in fixing the prices. The price of essential commodities went up like anything when the subsidies on a number of items like diesel were taken away. The spiralling cost of petrol and diesel has the cascading effect of increasing the price of almost all the essential commodities. At the same time subsidies and concessions for the corporate sector has increased. While the corporate concession was nearly Rs. 35,000 crore in the 2009-10 budget, it increased to around Rs. 88,000 crore in 2010-11 (Sainath 2011). The total revenue foregone by means of concessions in corporate income tax, personal income tax, excise duty and customs duty was Rs. 5,11,630 crore in 2010-11 (Rukmini 2011), it further rose to Rs. 5,29,432 crore in 2012-13 budget. Normally, write-offs under the three heads of Corporate Income Tax, Excise Duty and Customs Duty largely benefits the big institutions, in 2012-13 it stood at an estimated Rs. 4,87,112 crore (Sruthisagar 2012). It is an irony that the concession to the corporates is on the rise when the Prime Minister states that subsidies to the common man are a burden and needs to be taken away to avoid the increase in fiscal deficit. It needed a general election to waive the debt of farmers in India but no such thing was needed to bail out the corporates when the financial crisis stepped in.

Privatisation has become a watch word and symbol of development in India. The state is withdrawing itself from many areas and privatised many of the services. Attempts to privatise Railways have already begun and the central government is pressuring states to privatise the energy sector, despite the fact that such a move increases the rate of electricity manifold. The Draft Water Policy 2012 has echoed the need for privatisation in the immediate future. All there are by pointing the financial crunch of the nation, while sitting on the heap of wealth. It is sad that the Oxford Economist Prime Minister Dr. Manmohan Singh who knows that "money does not grow in trees" (TOI 2012) doesn't know that through the prudent allocation of resources of the nation and by curbing corruption money can be mobilised within the nation. Instead of doing the same the soft government is interested in inviting FDI even in retail sector which highly detrimental to the interest of the farmers and consumers. From the CAG report on coal allocation it is clear that the nation lost Rs. 1,86,000 crore and by slamming the levy at the Delhi airport an amount of Rs.3,415 was given out (Express News 2012: 1). When the loss in 2G (Rs.1,76,000 crore), potential loss in the leasing of land in the Delhi airport (Rs. 1,63,557 crore) and the corporate subsidy in the 2012-13 budget (Rs. 4,87,112 crore) is added up, it becomes a handsome sum of Rs. 10,16,084 crore which is more than enough to remove poverty in India.

The new development strategy has familiarised a new concept "developmental terrorism" – terror for development. In the name of development innocent thousands, tribals, women, children and peasants, are being displaced of their land and livelihood. The rise of Special Economic Zones further aggravated the situation with cold blooded murders, forcible eviction, police firing, lathi-charges and other gruesome practices in a number of states. In Special Economic Zones we can see the culmination of all the neo-liberal principles of dismantling of state regulations, liberalisation of export-import laws, delicensing, flexible laws including labour laws, corporate tax reduction, increased subsidies to corporates, hegemonious control of employers in hiring, firing, outsourcing, subcontracting and so on. Through massive displacements in the name of development what the governments are doing is pauperisation of the local population by taking away their only practical source of income to ensure further prosperity of large business corporates (Reinhart 2007: 105). Day-in and day-out, many are being washed out to be have-nots in the lop-sided development strategy.

Two decades are over since India embraced liberalisation and this period is enough to analyse the impact of such a policy. The advocates of globalisation used the twin theme of economic development and stability in the furtherance of their principle. But experience shows that the development during this period was one sided and devoid of human face or in other words exclusive development (Jitha and Reinhart 2012: 56). The policy of liberalisation created decline in agriculture, small scale, cottage and indigenous industries. There also occurred a secular decline in the standard of social services especially in education and health. The inequality is to such a level that when the top 10 per cent of the population owns 52.9 per cent of the total wealth i.e. more than half of the nation's wealth (Manas 2010), the poorest 10 per cent of the population lives on Rs.15 a day in rural areas and Rs. 20 a day in urban areas (Express News 2012: 10). The impressive GDP together with the increasing poverty shows that the *trickle down theory of development* advocated by the agents of globalisation is a folly. India's experience with liberalisation shows that it is not *trickling down* that works but *sucking up. Free market fundamentalism acts like a syringe that sucks up the resources of the poor and injects down that to the rich.*

Liberalisation also raises a big question about *whose interest the government is protecting?* Normally state is there to protect the interests of its citizens and take care of the poor and disadvantaged. But under liberalisation we can see the government as a batsman for the corporates, many-a-times. When taxing the common man heavily on each and every item the state doesn't have any reluctance in granting huge concessions to the corporate houses. Those who are stumbles in the path for this are simply wiped out. That is the case with former Petroleum Minister Jaipal Reddy. When he tried to prevent the loss of Rs. 33,500 crore to the exchequer by putting the Reliance under pressure, a cabinet reshuffle was made to throw him out of the petroleum ministry (Kerala Kaumudi 2012b: 5; The Hindu 2012c: 1). Reddy not only rejected the proposal of Reliance to raise the price of natural gas that it supplies but also rejected the geographical reasons suggested by reliance to reduce the production of natural gas from the Krishna-Godavari basin. He was shifted to the Science and Technology ministry after the reshuffle.

Neo-liberalism has totally shattered the concept of development. The rise in billionaires and the booming middle class with fancy apartments and flats, corporate houses with rich neighbourhoods, glittering shopping malls and other modern luxuries have became the symbol of development. Quoting the words of Dr. Manmohan Singh, the Prime Minister of India, "I think our nation has prospered as a result of that (liberalisation). If you look at the list of top 100 firms today you will find a sea change in that list today. New entrepreneurs have come into the list. These are some of the gains of liberalisation which we must cherish, we must nurse and we must develop" (MIB 2011: 5). Nowhere is the sound of the common man, helpless peasants committing suicide, dispossessed tribals, anemic women, underfed children and other marginalized folks in the slums and ghettos of metro cities, when it comes to the debate of development, to the Prime Minister who always boast of the benefits of liberalisation in India. To the neo-liberalists India is only a market, not a nation, and to the neo-liberal rulers the inhabitants are not citizens but mere consumers.

Neo-liberalism is not the right model of development. Globalisation has destroyed India's indigenous development and with the New Economic Policy of 1991 began the unbalanced phase of Indian economic development. It resulted in the concentration of wealth in the hands of a few, keeping the majority out of the benefits of development. Rich became richer and the poor poorer. While the rich and educated benefited, new risks cropped up for the poor and downtrodden. It is clear that social justice, the essential ingredient of development is absent in neo-liberalism. Development to be meaningful and fruitful should be capable of removing tears from the eyes of the poor and for that the exogenous packages should go. The need of the hour is indigenous packages that can ensure each and everyone - basic things for sustenance, equal opportunities and equitable (minimum) distribution of wealth. Social equality and social rights could be enjoyed by all. Exploitation of man by man should end and no one should be deprived of those social conditions which are essential for his development. The benefits of development must reach the poor and it should be capable of removing the hurdles in the path of their emancipation. Development to be complete and just requires "sufficiency for all before superfluity for some."

Notes

1. The 100 focus districts come from six states: Bihar, Jharkhand, Madhya Pradesh, Orissa, Rajasthan and Uttar Pradesh.

References

Anil Kumar, Jain and Parul, Gupta (2008): "Globalisation: The Indian Experience," *Mainstream*, XLVI(8), Feb. 8-14, 15-20.

Arora N. D. (2010): *Political Science*, McGraw Hill Education, New Delhi.

Ashwini, Kumar (2011): "90 pc Rural India Surviving on Rs.50 a Day: Survey," *The New Indian Express*, Kochi, September 28, 10.

Business Leads (2003): "Macro-economic Overview of India: Agriculture," *Business Leads*, April 30.

Census (2011a): *Census of India's Houselisting and House Census Data Highlights – 2011*, Office of the Registar General and Census Commissioner, Ministry of Home Affairs, Government of India.

—— (2011b): *Maternal and Child Mortality and Total Fertility Rates*, Office of the Registrar General and Census Commissioner, Ministry of Home Affairs, Government of India. July 7.

Dutt, Ruddar (2007): "India as an Economic Superpower, Myth and Reality," *Mainstream*, XLV(30), July 13-19, 7-11.

Dutt, Ruddar and Sundharam K.P.M. (2008): *Indian Economy*, S. Chand & Company, New Delhi.

Economy (2012): "Economic Survey 2011-12," *Dhankar Publications*, New Delhi.

Express News (2012): "Mother of All Scams: Rs. 3.78 Lakh Crore," *The New Indian Express*, Kochi, August 19, 1.

HUNGaMA (2012): *The HUNGaMA Survey Report – 2011*, Naandi Foundation, Hyderabad.

IIPS and Macro International (2007): *National Family Health Survey (NFHS-3)* 2005-06, Vol. 1, IIPS, Mumbai.

India (2012): *India Year Book*, Publications Division, Government of India, New Delhi.

ISIS (2010): *Farmer Suicides and Bt Cotton Nightmare Unfolding in India*, Institute of Science in Society, January 6.

Jitha, S.R. and Reinhart, Philip (2012): "Higher Bureaucracy, Liberalisation and Social Change," *South Asian Journal of Socio Political Studies*, XII(2), Jan.-June, 53-6.

John, Montgomery (1966): "A Royal Invitation: Variation on Three Classic Themes," in Montgomery and William Siffin (eds.) *Approaches to Development: Politics, Administration and Change*, Mc Graw-Hill, New York.

Kerala Kaumudi (2012a): "Adutha Lakshyam Pothumekhala Companykalude Karuthal Dhanashekaram," *Kerala Kaumudi*, November 4, 4.

—— (2012b): "33,500 Kodi Nashtapedathe Nokkiyappol Vakuppu Mattam," *Kerala Kaumudi*, October 31, 5.

Kounteya, Sinha (2007): "India Reports Maximum Number of Child Birth Deaths," *Times of India*, October 16.

Mathew, Aerthayil (2008): "Agrarian Crisis in India is a Creation of the Policy of Globalisation," *Mainstream*, XLVI(13), March 14-20, 8-11.

Mathew, Kurian V. (2007): "Financial Liberalisation and the Third World: A Study with Reference to India," *Mainstream*, XLV(11), March 2-8, 7-10.

MIB (2011): "Interaction with Newspaper Editors," *Ministry of Information and Broadcasting*, Government of New Delhi.

Raju, Narayana Swami (2011): "Land Acquisition and Development-Induced Displacement: A Case Study from Kerala," *Pragathi*, 5(115), 5-22.

Reinhart, Philip (2009): "Economic Development and Social Justice," *Competition Success Review*, XLV(11), May, 48-50.

Reinhart, Philip (2007): "Special Economic Zones, Neo-Liberalism and an Exclusive Development Process in India: A Critique," *Holistic Thought,* VI(1 and 2), 99-108.

Rukmini, Shrinivasan (2011): "Revenue Foregone, But Not Forgiven," *The Times of India,* March 5, http://blogs.timesofindia.indiatimes.com/developmentdialogue/entry/revenu e-foregone-but-not-forgiven accessed on 30-01-2013.

Rupashree Nanda (2011): "Farmer Suicide Increase at an Alarming Rate," http://ibnlive.in.com/news/farmer-suicides-increase-at-an-alarming-rate/140746-3.html accessed on 20-04-2011.

Pohare, P.V. (2011): "Impact of Globalisation on Indian Agriculture," *International Research Journal*, II(26), March.

Sainath, P. (2011): "From Questionable Social Subsidies to Unquestioned Corporate Welfare," *Daktre,* September 18, http://www.daktre.com/2011/09/sainath-talk/ accessed on 30-01-2013.

—— (2010): "Farm Suicides: A 12-Year Saga," *The Hindu,* January 25.

——(2009): "Neo-liberal Terrorism in India: The Largest Wave of Suicides in History," *Counterpunch*, February 12.

Sezhiyan, Era (2007): "Globalisation of Indian Economy, Globe for the Rich-Zero for the Poor,'' *Mainstream,* XLV(20), May 4-10, 7-11.

Sikdar, Soumyen (2007): *Contemporary Issues in Globalisation,* Oxford University Press, New Delhi.

Sruthisagar, Yamunan (2012): "This Revenues Forgone, But Not Forgotten,"IBN http://ibnlive.in.com/news/this-revenues-forgone-but-not-forgotten/239984-60-120. html accessed on 30-01-2013.

Sujay, Mehdudia (2012): "Now, Coal Burns Rs.186,000-crore Hole in Exchequer," *The Hindu,* Thiruvananthapuram, August 18, 1.

Teena, Tatcher (2006): *"UNICEF: India Slips on MMR, Unlikely to Meet 2015 Target,"* Indian Express, December 23.

The Hindu (2012a): "Inequality has gone up, notwithstanding dip in Poverty," *The Hindu,* March 21, 14.

—— (2012b): "A Different Poverty Trap," *The Hindu,* March 22, 10.

—— (2012c): "Prime Minister Owes an Explanation on Shifting Jaipal Reddy: BJP, SP," *The Hindu,* October 30, 1.

TOI (2012): "We Need to Contain Subsidies, Money Doesn't Grow on Trees, Manmohan Singh Says," *The Times of India,* September 12, http://articles.timesofindia.india times.com/2012-09-21/india/34001615_1_diesel-price-hard-decisions-fiscal-deficit accessed on 12-10-2012.

UNDP (2009): *Human Development Report* 2009, Palgrave Macmillion, New York.

UNICEF (2008): *Statistics and Monitoring,* UNICEF.

Vandana Siva (2011): "The Great Land Grab: India's War on Farmers," *Al Jazeera,* http://english.aljazeera.net/indepth/opinion/2011/06/2011671175667987.html accessed on 07-06-2011.

Wizard (2012): *Wizard Current Affairs* 2012, Career Classics, New Delhi.

Yojana (2012): "Towards Rapid, Inclusive and Sustainable Growth," *Yojana,* Special Issue, Approach to 12th Five Year Plan, January.

7

Bureaucracy in the Post-Liberalised India

Since 1991, the context of administration has been changing under the impact of the New Economic Policy. The concepts of Liberalisation, Privatisation and Globalisation have gained wider currency indicating the more openness of the government to international competition, deregulation and dismantling of series of government control and downsizing of bureaucracy by handing over selected activities to the private sector and by encouraging the non-governmental organisations to work more and more in the social development sector particularly in sectors like health, education, water supply etc. This new administrative environment that emphasises public-private partnership and market-friendly strategies, demands a reorientation and attitudinal change on the part of higher bureaucracy. The policies of LPG are designed to minimise the role of a welfare state by reducing expenditure in many essential areas and allow market forces to take over. This will increase inequality and uneven distribution of national resources and will sharpen the existing contradiction in the Indian society.

In actual practice, free market economy has increased the responsibility of the politicians and administrators and the challenge before them is to uplift their people from poverty, malnutrition, illiteracy and deprivation. It is their duty to ensure social justice, equity, self-reliance and sustainable development (Jitha and Reinhart 2012: 54). Without state intervention social equity cannot take place and without control over national economic and productive resources implementation of welfare programmes like food security, job security etc. is not possible. This necessitates the creation of a cadre of professionally trained and dedicated administrators as well as moral and just politicians who can stand against the forces of corruption and unscrupulous commercial and business interests (Dwivedi 1998: 62). Bureaucracy being the powerful and competent should take the initiative and they should become the agents of rapid socio-economic change. Bureaucracy, especially higher bureaucracy is the only group that has been untouched in the wave of globalisation. Though, expected to save the society from the harmful effects of globalisation, the bureaucracy have not offered any creative actions to solve the burning problems of the society. Instead they were interested in exploring the possibilities of globalisation for themselves, such as posting abroad, career mobility, employment in international agencies, and reemployment after retirement in these agencies.

The role of training especially foreign training as a catalyst for bringing the bureaucrats into the path of liberalisation is readily accepted by all. A study of privatisation of water reveals that the large private firms have actively sought contracts around the world by flying bureaucrats to visit privatised concessions in other countries, hosting workshops and sponsoring pro-privatisation research (McDonald and Ruiters 2005: 16). Together with this we have to read that foreign training was made compulsory for the IAS personnels and they need the stamp of the stipulated foreign universities to move on to the next rank. International exposure of bureaucrats is good if it is for solving collective problems or for sophisticated training in solving the existing or the new generation problems. But the rationality behind the classes being handled by the capitalist agents like World Bank, IMF and MNCs is skeptical as the trio has the track record of deliberately forcing the neo-liberal policies on the developing nations. It is assumed that the agenda of the government is to give them training to implement the liberalisation polices through civil service, whichever be the government in power (Jitha 2011: 145). During the years 2010, 2011 and 2012 a total of 367 IAS officers, 112, 120 and 135 respectively have been send for foreign training, incurring an expenditure of Rs. 1,03,97,109, Rs. 98,44,446 and Rs.1,34,75,607 respectively (LBSNAA RTI 2013).

It seems that the higher bureaucracy of India has learned to reap the benefits of globalisation, for their aggrandisement. Many of the higher bureaucrats are lured by the opportunities in the private sector. So, mid-career officers who abandoned their official stardoms to jump onto the private sector bandwagon are increasing in India. An RTI reply received from the Department of Personnel and Training reveals that 153 IAS officers from different cadres opted for voluntary retirement between 2000 and 2012 (DoPT RTI 2013a). Their cadre-wise 'drop out' includes 18 each from Karnataka and Maharashtra, 15 from Gujarat, 12 each from Bihar and Uttar Pradesh, 9 from Andhra Pradesh,

8 from West Bengal, 7 from Uttarakhand, 6 each from Chhattisgarh, Himachal Pradesh and Kerala, 4 each from Rajasthan and Haryana, 3 from Punjab, and 1 from Jammu and Kashmir (Kumar 2012). The nestling ground for many who sought private employment includes: IDFC, World Bank, DLF, IT firm Cisco Systems, Ramky Group, Reliance Industries, L&T, PricewaterhouseCoopers, Infrastructure Leasing and Financial Services and banking divisions of ICICI and HSBC.

As per Rule 16(2) of the All India Service (DCRB) Rules, 1958, any officer of all India service after completing 50 years of age or 20 years of service becomes eligible for the voluntary retirement. The State Government can accept the voluntary retirement of those who complete 30 years of service and for those, who completed less than 30 years of service, approval of the Union Government is a must [Rule 16(2A)]. For accepting employment after retirement, the previous sanction of the Central Government is necessary (Rule 26). The state government can under Rule 26(1) give previous sanction for officers below the rank of secretary and has not worked under the Central Government during the preceding three years prior to his/her retirement from the service, but the final decision resides with the central government. Normally, there is a cooling-off period of one year after retirement to take up a commercial employment. But there is a queue of officers at all times, before the Department of Personnel and Training (DoPT), the cadre controlling authority of the IAS in India, seeking permission to join private companies after retirement without completing the mandatory cooling-off period from the date of retirement. The mandatory cooling-off period was two years until January 1, 2007 but it was reduced to one year, no doubt by the hectic lobbying of IAS officers. The pensioner for the purpose of employment after retirement has to submit an application under Schedule L of the All India Service (DCRB) Rules, 1958 to the Central Government, and in granting or refusing permission the pensioner's privy to sensitive or strategic information in the last three years of his service which is directly related to the areas of interest or work of the organisation which he proposes to join or the areas in which he proposes to practice/ consult is taken into consideration.

The list of "quitters" is long comprising mid-career officers like Rajiv Talwar, who resigned from the post of Additional Director-General in the Tourism Ministry to join the realty major DLF; Prakash Kumar, who left the post of Secretary in the Delhi Government to join the IT firm Cisco Systems; O.P. Agarwal, an Assam cadre officer who joined IDFC; Dhiraj Mathur, an MP cadre officer who joined PWC; Rajkamal, a Chhattisgarh cadre officer who joined McKinsey; Jayant Parimal, a Gujarat-cadre IAS officer who joined Reliance Industries and Ravi Kant, a West Bengal cadre officer who joined the Ramky Group (Kumar 2012). The reasons stated for disenchantment includes political interference, handsome pay at the corporate houses, professional reasons and freedom in the private sector. *India Today* (2012) reports a serving IAS officer pointing political interference as the reason why IAS officers were leaving their jobs. "In Gujarat, many IAS officers left their jobs mainly because of this reason. After 2001, when CM Narendra Modi took over, around 10 officers left as they were not comfortable with the political system," the officer has stated.

With regard to better payment in the private sector, *Hindustan Times* (2007) reports a senior officer saying "Senior IAS officers have started realising that they are not being paid in the services as per their capabilities that is why officers across the country have started quitting the service." As far as salary is concerned, the officers get five times better pay in the private sector. According to reports, these IAS officers are getting salaries between Rs. 10,000 per sitting as director or have been hired for pay packages of Rs.50 lakh to Rs 5 crore per year. Ravi Kant, a 1985-batch officer who holds a degree in civil engineering from IIT Roorkee and a Master's degree in economics from the University of Manchester is said to have quit for professional reasons (Kumar 2012). To, officers like Rohit Modi, who joined as CEO of L&T; O.P Agarwal, who joined as CEO of Urban Mass Transit Co.; and Shailesh Pathak, who joined as Director (Investments) at ICICI Venture, the private sector offers more freedom. Speaking about the freedom in the private sector Mr. Agarwal, former Urban Development Joint Secretary (Assam Cadre Officer) states that: "If you need to go somewhere or if you want to take a decision on a particular expenditure, you just go ahead. If you commit something, you don't need any approvals. That's what I am liking about the private sector" (Shantanu 2008).

Whatever may be the reason stated for quitting the service, the post retirement activities of this officials reveals that majority are motivated by the financial benefit from corporate employment, for seeking voluntary retirement. The IAS drain is occurring at a time when the nation is facing an acute shortage of 1,777 IAS officers. The current strength of IAS officers in the country is 4,377 as against the sanctioned strength of 6,154 (DoPT RTI 2013; Vishwa 2012). This drain causes huge financial loss to the exchequer too as around Rs. 4 lakh are spent by the government to train one IAS officer. In 2007, Rs. 13.8 crore was spent on the midcareer training programme of 320 IAS officers and in 2008 and 2009, the expenditure per trainee was Rs. 3.8 lakh and Rs 4.08 lakh respectively (India Today 2012). The information received under RTI shows that during the years 2010, 2011 and 2012 the government spend an amount of Rs. 1.03 crore, Rs. 98.44 and Rs. 1.34 crore respectively for the IAS Phase II Foreign Visit alone. The expenditure per trainee for this foreign exposure visits to Singapore and Vietnam were Rs. 92,831, Rs. 82,037 and Rs. 99,819 respectively for the corresponding years. The Mid Career Training Programme during these years incurred an expenditure of Rs. 3.32 crore, Rs. 3.20 crore and Rs. 1.55 crore for 252, 399 and 300 trainees respectively for the corresponding years (DoPT RTI 2013b).

Voluntary retirement of officials and the rush for central posting is very much affecting the state cadre. Of the current strength of 4,377 IAS officers in the nation, one out of every six, i.e. 678 are currently posted in different central ministries in Delhi. The highest number of IAS officers (78) who are posted in Delhi belongs to the Uttar Pradesh cadre, followed by 41 from Madhya Pradesh, 40 from Kerala, 38 from Tamil Nadu, 35 from West Bengal, 32 from Odisha, 28 each from Bihar and Rajasthan, 25 each from Karnataka and Himachal Pradesh, 24 from Haryana and 21 from Gujarat (Vishwa 2012). The rush for central service is not a secret in India, but now-a-days with the rush to the Capital, reluctance in coming back to the respective cadre after the tenure is also increasing. When the cream of its officers gets parked at the capital the respective states runs short of officials. Kerala is the worst affected as 40 of its 158 babus are posted in Delhi. Twelve states including Assam, Chhattisgarh, Gujarat, Himachal Pradesh, Jharkhand, Kerala, Maharashtra, Manipur, Mizoram, Odisha, Punjab and UP have written to the Union Government in 2012, asking for repatriation of their IAS officers.

Private sector has been a pasturing ground for the retired senior bureaucrats, from long back. But recent years have witnessed a renewed surge in the appetite to take private employment. In the year 2011, seven IAS officers including five senior officers sought permission of the Department of Personnel and Training (DoPT) to take up private jobs during post-retirement. The senior most bureaucrats includes former Finance and Revenue Secretary Sunil Mitra, former Civil Aviation Secretary M. Madhavan Nambiar and former Home Secretary G.K. Pillai. The RTI application filed to the DoPT shows that Mitra received permission to join Infrastructure Professionals Enterprise, New Delhi as an Independent and Non-Executive Director on 30/09/2011. His other four applications to join as Non-Executive Director in the Board of Taxo Rail & Engineering Ltd. and as Advisor to RP-Sanjiv Goenka Group of Companies, M/s EMTA Coal Ltd. and M/s Patton International Ltd. were not granted permission by the DoPT (DoPT RTI 2013a). Mitra was an officer of West Bengal cadre who retired on June 30, 2011 and was the disinvestment secretary before handling finance and revenue. Indian Express (2012) reports, as per his application, Mitra will get "sitting fee of Rs. 10,000 per board/committee meeting attended, air passage, hotel stay and local transport for board/committee meetings" in case of Infrastructure Professionals. Madhavan Nambiar and G.K Pillai were granted permission to join as Independent Member on the Board of Independent Infrastructure Company (by L & T) and as Chair of the Board of Advisors of the IvyCap Trust Fund, respectively with respect to their application (DoPT RTI 2013a).

A dam majority of officers (IAS) after retirement, be it through VRS or otherwise, were able to get government sanction and exemption from the cooling-off period for joining commercial employment, with in an average span of 5-8 months from the date of their application. G.K. Pillai, the former

Home Secretary who retired from service on June 30, 2011 got permission on August 18, 2011 to join as Chair in the IvyCap, i.e., within 49 days. Ashok Mohan Chakraborty, who retired as Chief Secretary of West Bengal on April 30, 2010 was allowed to join as Resident Director of the Essar Group on October 7, 2010. Similarly, Anil Baijal, a 1969 batch Union Territory cadre IAS officer who retired as Secretary, Ministry of Urban Development on October 31, 2006 was allowed to join the IDFC as Adviser and Chairman of its PPP initiative on June 22, 2007. Turning down the exemption application is very few and as per information available through the RTI, of the applications received from 112 IAS officers in between 2000 to 2011, only seven were not granted permission by the Central Government (DoPT RTI 2013a). This is the case with other services also. For example only two applications were turned down in 2011 one is that of an Indian Revenue Service officer who got consultancy offers from two private firms, each paying Rs. 30 lakh per month and other that of an officer who retired from the Urban Development Ministry and had a job offer from a construction firm. In case of the latter officer it was found that the firm he intended to join had been awarded contracts by the ministry during the officer's tenure (Parimal 2011). Instances are there where officers want to join companies that they had interacted with. This includes a former NHAI (National Highway Authority of India) Chairman who applied to join a construction company (permission was refused in his case); former TRAI (Telecom Regulatory Authority of India) Chairman, Pradip Baijal who joined PR Consultant and lobbyist Nira Radia's Vaishnavi Corporate Communications.

Retired senior officials even associated themselves with corporate lobbying firms, directly or indirectly after demitting office. The bureaucrats in question include former TRAI Chairman and Disinvestment Secretary Pradip Baijal, Ex-economic Affairs Secretary C.M. Vasudev, former Industrial Policy and Promotion Secretary Ajay Dua and Ex-Trai Member D.P.S. Seth, for their association with Radia firms including Vaishanavi Communications, Noesis strategic Consulting Services, Vitcom Consulting and NeUCom Consulting. Baijal, the former TRAI Chairman joined Vaishnavi Corporate Communications after retirement and partnered Radia to set up Noesis Consultants. Battling with series of scams, especially after 2G Spectrum scam that involved the cozy relationship between the PR Consultant and lobbyist Nira Radia and four former bureaucrats mentioned above; the DoPT is looking at increasing the cooling-off period to three years, in order to break these kinds of associations. Hinting this V. Narayanaswami, the Minister of State, Home, who is in charge of the DoPT (2011), has stated that "there is always a possibility of vested interests, which we want to stop. We are thinking of going back to the three year cooling-off period that was changed seven or eight years ago"(Parimal 2011).

Facts and figures make it clear that a handful of bureaucrats are very much interested in serving the corporate sector. They are no longer motivated by national interest while in-service, but by the cosy sinecures after retirement. When liberalisation and globalisation opened up new pastures for the civil servants, IAS has become a gateway for corporate employment. The problem and danger is that those officials who want to have post retirement jobs in private firms will engage in unofficial supports and contracts for the firms, like Baijal. Some will mourn like T. Balakrishnan, former Principal Secretary, Industries Department, Government of Kerala. Addressing a seminar organised by the Industrial Development Corporation he expressed his sadness as the Coco-Cola factory at Plachimada, known for its worst human rights violations, can't be saved (Indian Express 2010: 1). He is also badly known for supporting the Tata Group (Kerala Kaumudi, May 25, 2010. P. 1) and irregularities involved in handing over acres of wetland for the corporate giant Reliance and KGS group for the controversial Aranmula Airport Project (Janayugam 2012: 7). When officers like Balakrishnan were in the plum posts common man won't get justice at least in words. When self interest supersedes national interest the chance of corruption will increase. That is why there are officials like R.K Srivastava, an IAS officer of the 1984 Arunachal Pradesh-Goa-Mizoram-Union Territories cadre, with 35 cases of corruption; and Vinod Kumar, an Odisha cadre officer of 1989 with 20 sanctions for prosecution against him. Srivastava is accused of corruption in the Rs. 4,000-crore cooperative group housing scheme scam in Delhi that came to light in 2004 and Vinod Kumar is charged with misappropriating funds during his tenure as the MD of the Orissa Rural Housing Development Corporation. Of the 89 sanctions okayed for the prosecution of IAS officers during the last five years, from 2011, under the Prevention of Corruption Act, 1988, 55 were against this two officers who have multiple cases against them (Gangadhar 2012).

On the other hand India has bureaucrats of impregnable integrity who are totally dedicated to their profession and is compassionate to the problems of the common man. In this line comes IAS officers like Vinod Rai, V.J. Kurien, P.H. Kurien and Dr. Raju Narayana Swami (all Kerala cadre); Ashok Khemka (Haryana); Darpan Jain, Subodh Yadav and Salma K. Fahim and Shalini Rajneesh (Karnataka); K. Nagarajan, U. Sagayam, Gagandeep Singh Bedi and Sheela Rani (Tamil Nadu); Alex Paul Menon (Sukma District Collector, Chhattisgarh); S. Suresh Kumar, Dr. G. Vani Mohan and Vakati Karuna (Andhra Pradesh), Vikas Kharge (Maharashtra) and number of others whose faces are no frequently covered by the media. Steel boned IPS officers but soft to the problems of the common man, like P. Vijayan (Kerala), Manoje Nath and Shivdeep Waman Lande (Bihar), N.C Asthana (IG of CoBRA), Asra Garg and P. Kannappan (Tamil Nadu), Archana Ramasundaram (ADGP Training), Damayanti Sen (West Bengal) also adds to this list.

CAG Vinod Rai, a Kerala cadre officer is at the top in the list of officials who had given and is giving relentless service to the nation. Ignoring political-bureaucratic-corporate pressures, enticement and persuasion he exposed a series of corruption, including mismanagement of public fund, be it in the allocation of 2G Spectrum, the ISRO Devas-Antrix Deal, the allocation of coal blocks, modernisation of Delhi airport, implementation of JNNURM and on Ultra Mega Power Projects. Vinod Rai and the office of CAG (Comptroller and Auditor General of India) first attracted the wrath of the government (Congress led UPA) and the ruling parties in November 2010 with its report on 2G Spectrum allocation that estimated a loss of staggering Rs.1.76 lakh crore. The ruling party and their ministers let lose a bundle of allegations against the CAG and his report. But matters got an upside down when the honourable Supreme Court of India took account of the CAG's report seriously which ultimately culminated in the cancellation of 122 2G licences allotted by former Telecom Minister A Raja, without auctioning (Vishwas 2012: 9; Kerala Kaumudi 2012: 1). The CAG embarrassed the ruling UPA again in August 2012, with the revelations on coal block allocation, airport modernisation and power projects. The report finds that the allocation of coal blocks in between 2005 and 2009 were without any bidding and this resulted in financial gains to the private beneficiaries of the coal blocks up to an amount of Rs. 1,86 lakh crore (Sunday Express 2012: 1). Prime Minister Dr. Manmohan Singh who had earlier told the bureaucrats to take bold decisions openly came against the CAG taming its report on coal as "misleading" and "flawed" (Express News 2012a: 1). While inaugurating the 7th Civil Service Day on April 21, 2012 the Prime Minister asked civil servants to take bold decisions and expressing the government's 'commitment' to protect the honest he assured "no witch hunting" against officers taking bold action (Sunday Express 2012a: 7).

With regard to modernisation of the Delhi airport, the CAG report says that the violation of bid conditions has given a monetary benefit of Rs.3,415 crore to the operator. The report also mentioned that the government policy of leasing out airport land at throw-away price missed an opportunity to potentially earn Rs. 1.63 lakh crore, over a sixty year period with an investment of Rs. 2,450 crore (Sujay 2012: 1) or just 1.50 per cent of the amount that can be earned. Besides reporting the diversion of funds totally nearly Rs. 115 crore in the Jawaharlal Nehru Urban Renewal Mission (JNNURM) (Express News 2012b: 7), the UPA's flagship urban infrastructure scheme and the post-bidding concessions to the Reliance Power Limited for its 4000 MW Sasan mega power project to the tune of Rs. 29,033 crore (Sujay 2012a: 1), the CAG asked the Petroleum Ministry to withhold approvals for the Mukesh Ambani owned company for their repeated failure in submitting audit records and information relating to the Krishan Godavari D6 block and for the British Gas as it failed to submit information and records relating to the Panna-Mukta-

Tapti gas fields (Sujay 2012b: 1). The CAG also pulled up the DRDO for its irregularities. In its report tabled before the Parliament on November 29, 2012, the CAG pointed out deficiencies and procedural irregularities relating to misleading nomenclature of sanction issuing authority, absence of data base of sanctions and splitting of sanctions in the DRDO (Express News 2012c: 7). The CAG's report underscores that the efforts of the Ministry of Defence to bring in transparency and objectivity in functioning of its department remains unachieved.

The report of the CAG on the above mentioned things reveals multi-dimensional aspects:

1. It points out the boldness of Vinod Rai, as an officer. Without his boldness this much information about corruption wouldn't have pictured out;
2. It exposed the gross mismanagement of public money, rampant corruption and the unholy corporate-bureaucratic-political nexus in the country;
3. The reports empirically prove that liberalisation or de-licensing increases the chance of corruption. Economic reforms in India increased the intensity and quantity of corruption as against its propagators advocacy of diminishing corruption;
4. The 2G report germinated the rise of new generation popular struggles against corruption that brought the students and youngsters to the fore front, that too voluntarily. All these struggles got welcome in every nook and corner of the nation and showed the apathy and anger of the younger generation towards the corrupt.
5. Rejects the neo-liberal hypothesis that "the state doesn't have adequate finance to run all activities, hence privatise." For example, as per the Budget Document 2012-13 of the Government of India, what the Finance Ministry proposes to raise through disinvestment of public enterprises is Rs. 30,000 crore, during the year 2012-13. But the loss to the exchequer from the 2G scam is more than five times this amount. If the government had auctioned the 2G it could have got Rs. 1.76 lakh crore. Disinvestment could have been avoided and with the balance amount four MNREGA like projects (Allocation for MNREGA in 2012-13 Budget is Rs. 33,000 crore) could have been implemented.

The office of CAG under Vinod Rai played the role of an activist and a loyal watch dog of the public finance of the nation. It is because of this activism and loyalty, the common man in India and round the world came to know that in India there is an office of Comptroller and Auditor General, which is a constitutional body.

The outstanding leadership provided by V.J. Kurien, a Kerala cadre IAS officer is behind the success of the country's first Public-Private-Participation airport in Kochi. CIAL (Cochin International Airport Limited) under its MD V.J. Kurien made a profit of Rs.100 crore in 2011, without any user charges. The airport was built at a cost of Rs. 300 crore and is now one of the leading international airports in India (Srivasta 2012). For this success Kurien had to attract the wrath of many senior politicians, bureaucrats and business houses. One the wake of the airport being redeveloped in 2007 he was offered a bribe of one crore rupees to choose the second lowest bidder for the contract to build the airport runway (Sharell 2012). Even though Kurien was transferred for not succumbing to pressures, the Government was forced to call him back within two years, as the airport began to make losses. Another efficient IAS officer is P.H. Kurien, who in his capacity as the Controller General of Patents granted the country's first compulsory licence to Nacto Pharma, to produce and market an anti-cancer drug Sorafenib, the patent for which is held by the German Pharmaceutical giant Bayer. The licence will enable the Nacto to produce generic versions of Sorafenib, which will reduce the cost of a month's dosage (120-200 mg tabs) to Rs. 8,800 while the same is priced at Rs. 2.8 lakh by Bayer under the brand name Nexavar (Chandrasekar 2012: 10). Another upright officer is Raju Narayana Swami, for whom the problems of common man are more important than personal considerations.

Transfers were nothing new to Ashok Khemka, senior IAS officer of Haryana, because this officer with a reputation of integrity has been transferred 43 times in his career spanning two decades (The Hindu 2012: 1), all because of his uncompromising stand towards corruption and cent per cent responsibility towards duty. Khemka hit the news again when he ordered a probe into the alleged undervaluation of properties registered by Robert Vadra, son-in-law of Mrs. Sonia Gandhi or his companies as vendor or vendee across four districts, on October 8, 2012. On the third day of his ordering the probe Khemka was issued transfer order to the post of Haryana Seed Development Corporation, a post that was held by an officer 12 years his junior. This kind of humiliation was familiar to Khemka as together with the post of Director-General of Land Consolidation and Land Records-cum-Inspector General of Registration, he was given additional charge of Special Collector, a charge held by him below his rank and the appellate for which lay with officers who were junior to him in service (The Hindu 2012: 1). When he found irregularities in the deal (Vadra-DLF), on his last day in office as the Inspector General of Registration, Government of Haryana, i.e., on October 15, 2012, he cancelled the sale of 3.531 acres of land in Manesar by Robert Vadra to realty giant DLF. Khemka's transfer comes only after three months in his assignment as Inspector General of Registration, where he became an eye sore to the corrupt political bureaucratic hierarchy, because besides probing the Vadra deals, he has uncovered massive fraud in the transfer of panchayat lands to relater companies and some powerful bureaucrats and politicians. Khemka himself sees the transfer as a "deliberated and malafide action to punish him due to some vested elements in the political bureaucratic hierarchy affected by the exposure of the scam in consolidation under the garb of exercise of powers" (The Hindu 2012a: 10).

For U. Sagayam IAS nothing threatens or prevents him from taking action even against MNCs. As District Revenue Officer of the Kanchipuram District of Tamil Nadu in 1999, he took on a powerful MNC by sealing its plant for selling contaminated soft drinks. He also banned the sale of the soft drink throughout the district (Nardeep 2012: 2). There, he took on the sand mafia, ordering them to stop dredging sand from the Palar riverbed where large-scale dredging had made the area flood-prone. He stands up against corruption not only by hanging a board citing *'Lanjam Thavirtthu, Nenjam Namartthu'* (Reject bribes, hold your head high), above his seat, but also by taking strict action against the defaulters. As district collector of Namakkal, he voluntarily declared his assets: a bank balance of Rs. 7,172 and a house in Madurai worth Rs. 9 lakh (Pushpa 2011). Sagayam was an officer with a humble heart. He brought out the benefits of welfare measures to the poor and strengthened the Village Administrative Officer (VAO) system, to better the lot of villagers. Sagayam was so dear to the villagers that why when the errant VAOs ganged up with the help of politicians to get him transferred the villages came in support for him, forcing the politicians to withdraw. He not only sanctioned old-age pension for the abandoned but also took action against children who don't take care of their aging parents. He was a role model for all IAS office to follow. While with one hand he stood strictly against corruption and with the other he proliferated the benefits of development to all under his jurisdiction.

Like Sagayam, Sidhanta Singh is a fearless bureaucrat and a one-man army against pollution in Odisha. This 1982 batch IFS officer, in his capacity as the Member Secretary of the Odisha Pollution Control Board, imposed a penalty of Rs. 13.77 crore on Hindalco Industries owned by the Aditya Birla Group, for unauthorised sale for unauthorised sale of anode butts containing fluoride, a highly polluting material, from its smelter (Ashutosh 2012). The penalty is in tune with the "Polluter Pays" principle as there had been violation of environmental laws. Earlier in June 2011, he ordered the closure of 31-sponge iron plants for not adhering to environmental norms. Subodh Yadav was another powerful IAS officer. Though he got only seven months as Deputy Commissioner in Mangalore, he detected severe tax evasion worth hundreds of crores. Within this time he did much welfare measures like reserving 200 acres of land for the rehabilitation of Malekudiya tribe and a cleanliness drive in Mangalore (Nardeep 2012: 1). These officers through their bold actions revealed that if the higher bureaucrats are determined, no power of corporates can bend them and it is hard to purchase them also.

Salini Rajneesh was the other do-gooder bureaucrat and in her stint as the Secretary of Hyderabad Karnataka Development in Gulbarga Hills she showed what a people friendly bureaucracy should be like. Her accessibility, efforts at developing infrastructure at Gulbarge, initiative to restore water tanks at Belgaum etc. made her one of the best known bureaucrats in the nation. Such was Gagandeep Bedi's popularity that the local residents of Cuddalore District asked the Tamil Nadu Chief Minister to make him the "permanent collector." His actions including the rescue operation in the aftermath of the Tsunami, in which he personally rescued a group of stranded fishermen, made him a demi-god to the public. Sheela Rani was known for her pro-activeness in every department she has worked. Her role in literacy movement as Collector of Pudukottai, in eliminating infanticide as the Health and Family Welfare Secretary and eco-friendly initiatives as the head of Tamil Nadu Pollution Control Board were highly appreciative and remarkable. Salini, Gagamdeep and Sheela in their official made change in the society. It is their self-motivated and dedicated actions that made them people-friendly bureaucrats.

It was Rentala Chandrashekhar, J. Satyanarayana and their team of IAS officers who pioneered e-governance in the country. This initiative is now benefiting millions of people. As Srivatsa Krishna (2012) says, "if today millions of Indians are able to pay their electricity bills online or transact on their property easily, without paying bribes to anyone, the credit goes, not to 'Lokpal' watching over every single government servant, but to these IAS officers." Another officer in this regard is Vikas Kharge, to whom well-being of the public is the top concern. He realised the potential of the e-File, an innovative software developed by the National Informatics Centre, Mussoorie (April 2011) and used this to clear 360 files while on a 21 days election duty in Uttar Pradesh. He was serving as Commissioner for Family Welfare and Director of National Rural Health Mission in Maharashtra at that time. Vikas Kharge is an exemption to those officers who have a number of excuses for the pending files in their desk. He proved that physical presence of an officer is not necessary to do with files, a mind that can understand the needs and problems of the common man is enough, the rest will come in its way.

Vakati Karuna, in her capacity as the Joint Collector of Warrangal proved that one civil servant can make difference with simple handfuls. She introduced a scheme known as *Guppedu Biyyam*, under which Self-help Groups collect a handful of rice once a week from every household from selected for distribution among the destitute. The scheme has now spread to more than 23 grama panchayats. It was the personal initiative of S. Suresh Kumar, Medak District Collector that led to the renovation of government hostels in the district. He went beyond the call of duty to raise Rs. 1.31 crore for improving government hostels. Salma Fahim was another IAS officer who brought change. Her efforts as the Project Director for the Karnataka State Aids Prevention Society reduced the prevalence of AIDS in the state to 0.67 per cent in 2012 as against 1.76 in 2011. She is also known as a passionate propagator of women empowerment. The success of Vakati, Suresh Kumar and Salma shows that initiatives is more important than finance in the success of any scheme. They raised the finance with popular support and personally monitored the scheme to ensure its success. They did all this when many departments and officers are lapsing lion share of the funds allotted to them for different development and welfare projects.

Dr. G. Vani Mohan is one of the most popular IAS officers in the nation. In her capacity as the District Collector of West Godavari District of Andhra Pradesh she initiated a series of welfare programmes to improve the quality of life of the poor and needy. She launched *Abhilasha* on June 8, 2011, trust registered for bringing changes in the areas of health, welfare hostels, veterinary medicine and welfare of the disabled. The programme aims at providing artificial limbs, tricycles, wheelchairs, hearing aids, crutches, walking sticks, braille slates, blood storage units, ultrasound equipments, ventilators, incubators, oxygen cylinders and surgical equipments in the Primary and Community Health Centres and artificial insemination facilities in dispensaries (Abhilasha 2013). The scheme has become so popular that it is now receiving support from various sources. Dr. Vani says "When I started the project, I had virtually no money. Now, support is pouring in from different sections of society" (Nagaraja 2012: 120). MPs, MLAs, Public Sector Enterprises and individuals are now contributing to this project. The programme has so far mobilized Rs. 8.86 crores and spends Rs. 7.36 crores (Abhilasha 2013). Education and health care are the main focus of the scheme. Abhilasha aims at improving basic amenities and comforts in the hostels by providing water filters, toilets, bathroom blocks, drainage facilities, fans and so on, together with ensuring quality education. Other initiatives include bringing prisoners to the mainstream by promoting skill development, milk mission and protein rich food to below poverty line families.

Within one year of its implementation Abhilasha wrote a new history in the welfare activities of the West Godavari district. Nearly 3,733 disabled persons were identified during the conduct of health camps to supply the requisite aids and appliances to them. Nearly 100 polio surgeries were done for the benefit of the polio affected persons. Plastic surgery was performed to 93 cleft-lip, cleft-palate and skin burnt persons under the programme (Sampath 2012; Abhilasha 2013). 300 Tricycles and 15 wheel chairs were distributed to needy disabled persons. The other services in the health sector includes: IRCS components blood bank at District hospital, Eluru; Blood storage centre in Area hospital, Jangareddigudem; Blood storage center in CHC, Palakol; two Ambulances were provided to Polavaram and Buttaigudem PHCs in Tribal area and safe drinking water to hospitals (Abhilasha 2013). The district administration has renovated as many as 99 welfare hostel buildings. Water purifiers were fitted to 43 hostels to ensure safe drinking water to the students and solar water heating systems were also installed at 12 hostels (Sampath 2012). Many other projects are in the pipeline. This much success within a single year is not a small thing and shows Dr. Vani as a successful bureaucrat. Her *Asaraya* initiative in 2010 as Additional Commissioner of Greater Hyderabad Municipal Corporation bagged national award from the Ministry of Social Justice, Government of India. Through her initiatives what Dr. Vani says is rather than going through the routine file administration a bureaucrat should do something sensitive to ensure the uplift of the poor and needy. She also pictures out how a District Collector can change the face of his/her district.

Under the economic reforms there is a vigorous call to downsize the bureaucracy. Neo-liberalism that calls for increased role of the market and decreased role of the state demands a bureaucracy that is less in size. This is because the new economic policy incurs a shift from state centred model of development to market model of development. Because of the Structural Adjustment Policies there occurred a marked decrease in the public spending for welfare measures on areas like education, health care, sanitation etc. This resulted in massive layoffs in countries where government is the largest employer. Together with the promotion of foreign investment, the governments are resorting to public sector disinvestments and total sale of public sector undertakings. Closures have been used as a device to reduce the component of permanent workers. In India alone, as a result of 1687 closures a total of 1.20 lakh workers lost their jobs. Production units have resorted to layoff to cut down labour costs. During the seven year post-reform period a total of 4.91 lakh workers were laid off and on the plea of redundancy, a total of 20,720 workers were retrenched during 1991-97 (Dutt 2007: 10).

The reality is that many of the nations of the third world is running short of an adequately sized bureaucracy. News paper report reveals that India has only a fifth as many public servants as United States, relative to population. India has 1,622.8 government servants for every 100,000 residents. In stark contrast, the U.S. has 7,681. The Central government, with 3.1 million employees has 257 serving every 100,000 population, against the U.S. Federal Government's 840. We all know that Indian Railways accounts for 44.81 per cent of the entire central government workforce, so when their numbers (1,394,418) are removed there are only about 125 central employees serving every 100,000 people. The Group C and D comprise respectively 59.69 per cent and 29.37 per cent of the public servants. This, points out the acute shortage of skilled staff and administrators in service who comprise only less than 10.94 per cent (Praveen 2012:1).

Considering the rise in population in the country, the numbers of government servants are not increasing. India's population was 1028.7 million (102.87 crores) in 2001. By the 2011 census it marked a growth of 17.64

per cent to reach 1210.2 million, i.e., an increase of 181.5 million (Census 2011: 8). But figures show a marginal decline of 0.13 per cent in the size of the Central government employees in 2008 from 2006 (Praveen 2012: 1). This is not the case with central government alone, state governments are also facing this crisis. For example, in the State of Kerala, the number of government employees including teachers were 5,26,428 in 2002 (Jitha 2007: 106) but by 2013 it came down to 5,02,675 (Josprakash 2013: 6). There occurred a decline of 23,735 employees. Of the 5,02,673 employees, teachers constitute 2,46,976, nearly half of the total state government employees. At the same time Kerala's population increased from 31.84 million (3.18 crore) in 2001 to 33.38 million in 2011, a decadal increase of 4.86 per cent, or in numbers an increase of 1.54 million (Census 2011: 23). So when the population roughly increased, decadal by 4.86 per cent, the number of employees declined by 4.51 per cent, from 2001 to 2011. India's relatively backward States have low numbers of public servants. Bihar has just 457.60 per 100,000, Madhya Pradesh 826.47, Uttar Pradesh has 801.67, Orissa 1,191.97 and Chhattisgarh 1,174.62 (Praveen 2012: 1). This means that staff members are not available for the provision of education, health and social services needed to address the worst kinds of poverty.

The police forces of the nation too are daunted with shortage of personnel. As per the information provided by the Union Home Secretary R.K. Singh to the Parliamentary Standing Committee in April 2012, there is a shortage of 1,327 IPS officers (Vishwa 2012). The actual strength of IPS in the country is 3,393, against the sanctioned strength of 4,720. Key organisations such as the Intelligence Bureau (I.B.), the Central Reserve Police Force (CRPF), the Border Security Force (BSF), the Indo-Tibetan Border Police (ITBP), the Central Industrial Security Force (CISF), the Sashastra Seema Bal (SSB) and the National Security Guard (NSG) have been facing a serious shortage of IPS officers. Similar is the case with states grappling with problems like Maoism, terrorism and insurgency (Purnima 2010). Coming to police personnels, India has about 1.13 million policemen. China has 1.7 million and the US, which is one-quarter of India's size in terms of population is having 8,00,000 policemen. The ratio of policemen to population in India is 0.95, lower than that of Papua New Guinea, Sri Lanka, Jamaica, Estonia, Moldova, Slovenia, Kyrgyzstan and Lithuania. In a list of 48 countries, India's rank is 47th in terms of the policemen to population ratio (TOI 2010). When the nation is facing severe law and order problems, including those by the banned maoist groups, the nation should have adequate personnels to keep up the situation. The terrorist attack on Mumbai in November 2008 taught us several things about law and order and emergency management, to avoid repetition of history, India needs enough policemen, both officers and other ranks.

The march of globalisation has strengthened Private Bureaucracy, a feature of modern capitalist society and the public bureaucracy has now become the sponsors of private bureaucracy. Private bureaucracy simply refers to the employees of the corporate houses and more specifically it means the top officials or executives who are engaged in steering the wheel of its administration. Increasing the profit and fame of the company, expanding its market and securing its monopoly are their important duties. While the public bureaucracy is funded by taxing the population, private bureaucracy is funded by sales revenue and careful investment of profits. Unrestricted competition is leading to the absolute rule of the private bureaucracies over the whole world and dismembering of the public bureaucracy. Day-by-day serving bureaucrats and retired ones are migrating to be a part of the private bureaucracy. This is because there are great opportunities to make money in the private sector than in government. The entry of highly experienced public bureaucrats strengthens the private bureaucracy and provides the companies new vigour and avenues for profit making. The unaccountable private bureaucracy, whose sole function is to maximise the profit of the corporate, is the one making maximum damage to human rights.

References

Abhilasha (2013): Abhilasha Website, http://210.212.211.3/abhilasha/about.html.

Ashutosh, Mishra (2012): "Hindalco Fined by Green Body," *The Telegraph*, Calcutta, February 28, http://www.telegraphindia. com/1120228/jsp/odisha/story_15187317. jsp#.UQIV-8knrv8 accessed on 15-01-2013.

Census (2011): *Census 2011 Provisional Population Totals*, Office of the Registrar General and Census Commissioner, India, Ministry of Home Affairs, March 31, 8.

Chandrasekhar, C.P. (2012): "A Big Step Forward," *Frontline*, 29(8), May 4, 10-2.

DoPT (2013a): *List of Members Who Retired Voluntarily From Service, 2000-2012; List of IAS Officers Who have Taken Voluntary Retirement and were Granted Permission to Join Post Commercial Employment, 2008-till date; List of Cases in Which Previous Sanction of the Central Government has been Granted, 2000-till date*, Ministry of Personnel, PG and Pensions, Department of Personnel and Training, Government of India, New Delhi, RTI Dated 08-02-2013.

—— (2013b): *Cadre Strength of Indian Administrative Service (As on 01-01-2012)*, Ministry of Personnel, PG and Pensions, Department of Personnel and Training, Government of India, New Delhi, RTI Dated 16-01-2013.

Dutt, Ruddar (2007): "India as an Economic Superpower, Myth and Reality," *Mainstream*, XLV(30), July 13-19, 7-11.

Dwivedi, O.P. (1998): "Development Administration: An Overview," in Chaturvedi, T.N (ed.), *Fifty Years of Indian Administration: Retrospect and Prospects*, Indian Institute of Public Administration, New Delhi.

DCRB (1958): *All India Services (Death-Cum-Retirement Benefits) Rules, 1958*, Government of India.

Express News (2012a): "PM 'Throws' Coal at CAG," *The New Indian Express*, Kochi, August 28.

——(2012b): "Gross Lapses in JNNURM: CAG," *The New Indian Express*, Kochi, November 30.

—— (2012c): "CAG Pulls up DRDO for Irregularities," *The New Indian Express*, Kochi, November 30.

Gangadhar, Patil (2012): "Of 89 Sanctions to Prosecute IAS Officers, 55 Just Against 2," *Daily News and Analysis*, November 12, http://www.dnaindia.com/india/report_of-89-sanctions-to-prosecute-ias-officers-55-just-against-2_1763466 accessed on 14-12-2012.

Hindustan Times (2007): "IAS Officer May Quit for MNC," *The Hindustan Times*, January 14, http://www.hindustantimes.com/News-Feed/NM21/IAS-officer-may-quit-for-MNC/Article1-199686.aspx accessed on 10-12-2012.

Jitha, S.R. (2007): *Higher Bureaucracy and Development*, Kalpaz Publications, New Delhi.

——(2011): "Bureaucracy and Human Rights Under Liberalisation," in P. Sukumaran Nair (ed.), *Human Rights in a Changing World*, Kalpaz Publications, New Delhi, 141-9.

Jitha, S.R. and Reinhart, Philip (2012): "Higher Bureaucracy, Liberalisation and Social Change," *South Asian Journal of Socio Political Studies*, XII(2), Jan-June, 53-56.

Josprakash, C.R. (2013): "Panimudakkunnathu Enthinu Vendi," *Kerala Kaumudi*, Kochi, January 6,6.

Kerala Kaumudi (2012): "2G: 122 Licensukal Supremekodahi Radhakki," *Kerala Kaumudi*, Kochi, February 3.

Kumar, Vikram (2012): "IAS Officers Make A Beeline for Greener Pastures in Private Sector," *India Today*, June 15, http://indiatoday.intoday.in/story/ias-officers-private-sector-big-corporate-houses/1/200738.html accessed on 15-12-2102.

LBSNAA (2013): *Details of Expenditure Incurred on IAS Officers in Connection with Their Foreign Exposure Visit During 2010-2012 IAS Phase-II*, Lal Bahadur Shastri National Academy of Administration, Government of India, Mussoorie, RTI Dated 04-02-2-13.

McDonald, David A. and Ruiters, Grey (2005): "Rethinking Privatisation, Towards a Critical Theoretical Perspective," *Public Services Year Book*, 9-20.

Nagaraja, G. (2012): "Welfare Mission," *Frontline*, 29(8), May 4, 120-2.

Nardeep Singh, Dahiya (2012): "Stainless Steel," *The New Sunday Express* (Magazine), Kochi, May 6, 1-2.

Parimal, Peeuyush (2011): "Conflict of Interest," *The Sunday Indian*, December 10, http://www. thesundayindian. com/en/story/conflict-of-interest/268/26965/ accessed on 14-12-2012.

Praveen, Swami (2012): "Figures Bust Myth India's Bureaucracy is *Bloated*," *The Hindu*, Thiruvananthapuram, January 30, 1.

Purnima, S. Tripathi (2010): "Recruitment Now," *Frontline*, 27(14), July 16.

Pushpa, Iyengar (2011): "Under a Dangerous Motto," *Outlook India.com*, August 22, http://www.outlookindia.com/article.aspx?277990 accessed on 24-12-2012.

Sampat, G. Samritan (2012): "Abhilasha to Help Hostels, Hospitals," *The Deccan*

Chronicle, December 13, http://www.deccanchronicle.com/121213/news-current-affairs/article/abhilasha-help-hostels-hospitals accessed on 15-01-2013.

Sharell (2010): "Why It is so Easy to Become Corrupt in India," *Inspirational India*, September 10, http://www.whiteindianhousewife.com/2010/09/why-its-so-easy-to-become-corrupt-in-india/ accessed on 20-01-2013.

Shantanu, Nandan Sharma (2008): "IAS Officers Enjoy the Freedom in the Private Sector," *The Economic Times*, Feb. 17, http://articles.economictimes.indiatimes.com/2008-02-17/news/28446038_1_ias-officers-private-sector-freedom accessed on 10-12-2012.

Shyamlal Yadav (2012): "Senior Retired IAS Officers Take Nod for Private Jobs," *The New Indian Express*, April 9, http://www.indianexpress.com/news/senior-retired-ias-officers-take-nod-for-private-jobs/934257 accessed on 10-12-2012.

Srivatsa, Krishna (2012): "Is Indian Bureaucracy the Worst?," *The Economic Times*, January 16.

Sujay, Mehdudia (2012): "Levy of Airport Development Fee Slammed," *The Hindu*, Thiruvananthapuram, August 18.

——(2012a): "Now, Coal Burns Rs. 186,000-crore Hole in Exchequer," *The Hindu*, Thiruvananthapuram, August 18.

——(2012b): "CAG Hits Back at RIL, British Gas," *The Hindu*, Thiruvananthapuram, November 17.

Sunday Express (2012): "Mother of all Scams: Rs. 3.78 Lakh Crore," *The New Sunday Express*, Kochi, August 19.

——(2012a): "Take Bold Decisions: PM to Babus," *The New Sunday Express*, Kochi, August 28.

The Hindu (2012): "Khemka Refutes Haryana Government Claims, Says Transfer Mala Fide," *The Hindu*, October 17.

The Hindu (2012a) "Senior Official Probing Vadra-DLF Land Deal Shunted Out," *The Hindu*, October 16.

TOI (2010): "Less Rules, More Bureaucracy, Please," *Times of India*, January 26, http://articles.timesofindia. indiatimes.com/2010-06-26/edit-page/28306609_1_ias-officers-bureaucracy-corrupt-bureaucrats accessed on 10-12-2012.

Vishwa, Mohan (2012): "Central Posting Continues Lures Bureaucrats," *Times of India*, September 7, http://articles.timesofindia.indiatimes.com/2012-09-07/delhi/33676521_1_ias-officers-state-cadres-figures-show accessed on 10-12-2012.

Vishwas, Kumar (2012): "Judgement Vindicate CAG Report," *The New Indian Express*, Kochi, February.

8

Bureaucracy and Corruption

Corruption is a malady that has penetrated into the deeper roots of every society and its pervasiveness is such that no society developed, developing and under developed is free from it. Be it society or culture, politics or economy corruption is making its vital presence felt in all walks of the life. In developing societies corruption is institutionalised and out of control, posing impediment to development. While corruption at the higher level damages the economy and the country, corruption at the lower level makes the life of the people miserable. In India corruption no longer surprises anyone as it has become a part of the administrative and political culture. The report of Transparency International reveals that about 62 per cent of people have the first hand experience of paying bribe or "using a contact" to get a job done in public office (ICS 2005:1). A day seldom passes in India without the press reporting cases of corruption. So, it is not an exaggeration that India is ranked 95 out of 180 nations in Transparency International's Corruption Precipitation Index 2011 (CPI 2011).

Scandals like the Bofors, Sugar, Fodder and Uniform in Bihar, Urea, Telecom, Coal in Tamil Nadu and the recent Spectrum (2G), Commonwealth Games (CWG), Adarsh, ISRO (Devas Antrix Deal), Coal, Tetra Truck and the VVIP Chopper have shown the widespread tentacles of corruption in India. Of this 2G, ISRO and Coal forms the new generation scams and is part of the multi-billion dollar club. When big scams are of big news value, the real evil is the silent pervasive corruption in which even the slum-dwellers were not exempted. In these cases, the amount paid will include paltry sum of Rs. 5

also. One would wonder when he/she hears about the story of a five rupees bribe. But it is one that has been paid by a slum-dweller in Kolkata to get monthly ration (Express News 2012a: 9). When a nurse or attender in a public health institution asks a couple of notes for giving care or to move the stretcher and when the doctor asks something to provide 'free surgery' out of millions received from the government, the poor are directly affected than the mega scams. These scandalous attempts divert whatever the state spends for the welfare of the targeted groups (Express News 2011: 8). But this doesn't means that mega scams have nothing related to the common man, as it is the national wealth for the welfare schemes that are going into private pockets. Be it mega or not, corruption forms a part of human rights violations, either directly or indirectly.

Corruption is one of those phenomena that are easier to identify than to define. Corruption hardly requires any narration or explanation as many are exposed sufficiently enough to various forms of corruption and also to all sorts of methodologies relating to corruption. Simply put corruption implies amassing wealth or anything which actually does not belong to the person who had usurped it. In India the basic law that deals with corruption is the Prevention of Corruption Act 1947. The Act includes in its ambit, the scope of corruption as – criminal misconduct by public servant in the discharge of official duty, habitual taking of illegal gratifications to influence a public servant, possession of wealth disproportionate to the known source of income and attempt to misappropriate property entrusted to one as a public servant. Infinite are the modes of corruption. Corruption need not be monetary and as a general term it covers the misuse of authority. In contemporary usage corruption means the betrayal of public trust for individual or group gains.

Corruption is not a new phenomenon. Turning back the pages of history, helps find instances of corruption during times of Ramayan, Mahabharat and Mauryan Empire. Kautilya in Arthashastra says, "Just as it is impossible not to taste the honey that find itself at the top of the tongue, so it is impossible for a government official not to eat up at least a bit of King's revenue" (Ramesh and Rajni 2011: 595). Corruption was also rampant during the Sultanate and Mughal periods. But during the ancient and mediaeval times the scope of corruption was limited because the scope of public administration too was limited. Corruption in India got a good nurture under the patronage of British Administration. Though corruption among higher bureaucrats were rare the lower echelons of service were more corrupt especially in departments like the police, revenue, excise, that were commonly known to be the corrupt departments. Scarcity of essential commodities, immense war effort involving expenditure of thousands of crores of rupees over various war supplies and contracts, etc., provided opportunities for amassing wealth, bribery, corruption and favouratism (Avasti and Avasti 2008: 497). This tendency was further aggravated by the post-war flush of money.

After independence India adopted a socialist pattern and this resulted in placing a number of restrictions on private initiative and enterprises, in the name of preventing monopolies and protecting broader national interest. Licence, Quota and Permit Raj system came into being. The launching of developmental programmes increased government spending and the government entered into all kinds of economic and trading activities. All these opened the flood gates of political and bureaucratic corruption and provided ample opportunities for the corruption-prone ministers and public servants at all levels to amass illegal gains by abusing their offices and powers. The working of many of the departments of the government like customs, central excise, railways, etc., were dilatory. This has encouraged the growth of "speed money" and "influence peddlers' who act as contact men on commission basis. Whatever may be the reasons for corruption, corruption has reached to such an extent that in the year 1990 alone, the CBI registered 1116 cases in all, 930 against public servants and 186 against private person's firms. 640 cases were registered against gazetted officers in which 943 were involved and the percentage of cases involving gazetted officers being 57:4 (Avasti and Avasti 2008: 501).

Corruption operates at various levels in public sphere which influences political and administrative behaviour. The general mode of corruption in the modern states are extravagant expenditure of public money, provision of employment for kith and kins, friends and supporters, getting of speed money for doing a work, entering within transactions with government by giving some percentage of the officials, placing the governmental machinery at the disposal of conditionality for winning the elections, delaying the functions for bribe money, favouring the functions for having money or things etc.

The Central Vigilance Commission has listed around 25 modes or forms of corruption. Such as:

1. Acceptance of substandard stores of works.
2. Misappropriation of public money.
3. Showing favours to contractors and firms.
4. Claiming false travelling allowance, house rent etc.
5. Possessing assets disproportionate to income.
6. Misuse of Government employees for personal work.
7. Borrowing money from contractors and firms having official dealings with officers.
8. Causing loss to the Government by negligence or otherwise.
9. Abe of official position or powers.

10. Acceptance of illegal gratification in recruitment, posting, transfers and promotion etc. are some of them.
11. Purchase of immovable property without prior sanction.
12. Production of forged certificate of date of birth or marriage.
13. Irregularities in reservation of seats, by rail or air.
14. Non-delivery of money orders, insured covers.
15. Replacement of new postage stamps by used ones.
16. Irregularity in grant of import and export license.
17. Irregularity in grant of telephone connection.
18. Moral turpitude.
19. Under assessment of income tax.
20. Acceptance of gift.
21. Misuse of advance sanctioned for the purchase of scooters or cars.
22. Abnormal delay in settlement of compensation claims to displaced persons.
23. Cheating in connection with sale and purchase of plots for residential purpose.
24. Unauthorised occupation and subletting of government quarters.
25. Incurring pecuniary obligation of persons to whom the public servants have official obligation.

Corruption in Indian bureaucracy has now come to be accepted as a part of the machinery that governs India. Neither rules nor regulations come on the way and without face or shame illegal qualifications are openly demanded. At the same time fact cannot be undermined that the civil servants take their cues from the politicians, who rank amongst the world's most corrupt. If political environment gets corrupted, administrative environment is bound to be get polluted. There is a nexus between bureaucrats and politicians in corruption cases (Jitha 2007: 100). In such a relationship both gain and protect each other. The lower level operates as agents of higher-level passing up to shares in the bribes received at the operational level. Bureaucratic corruption has corrupted the public as well. People have accordingly learned to live with corrupt administrative set up. They habitually step a couple of hundred or thousand rupee notes into the hands of politicians, the railway clerks, telephone staff, road transport officials, police officials etc. (Guham and Samuel 2001: 246).

The spread of corruption in India are totally pictured in the studies of Transparency International's – India Corruption Study 2005 and TII-CMS India Corruption Study 2007. India Corruption Study 2005 is the largest corruption survey ever undertaken in the country, covering 11 Public Services including police, judiciary, land administration, municipal services, government hospitals, electricity, public distribution system (PDS), income tax, water supply, schools and rural financial institutions. The study estimates the bribe paid by the common citizens of the country while availing one or more of the eleven public services in a year as Rs. 21608 crore (TII-CMS 2005a: 1). Police stands out high on the corruption index (Rs. 3899 crore), lower judiciary (Rs. 2630 crore) and land administration (Rs. 3126 crore) are rated next to police. When Kerala stands out as the least corrupt state, Bihar ranks as the most corrupt state. The study reveals that tax payers are harassed by corrupt officials and the value of petty corruption in Income Tax Department in the country is estimated to be Rs.496 crore per annum (TII-CMS 2005b: 1). While 47 per cent paid bribe directly, 28 per cent had used Chartered Accountants as intermediary to give bribe to the officials. The study also found higher perception and experience of corruption in low income States as compared to high income States, which goes against the popular belief that higher income tax provides greater scope/avenues for corruption. Officials create hurdles so that the tax-payer is fed up and forced to pay bribe to avail services.

India Corruption Study 2007 reveals the most shameful face of corruption in India that even the poorer sections are not spared by the corrupted administrators and politicians. The study which focused on BPL (Below Poverty Line) households found that about one-third of below poverty line households in the country bribed officials to avail a total of 11 services - from police, PDS, banking, housing, forest, land records, NREGS, water supply, electricity, school education and hospital. According to the survey which covered 22,728 households in all states and Union Territories, Rs. 883 crore in all was estimated to be paid as bribe by BPL households (TII-CMS 2008: 8). Among the 11 services covered in the study, Police and Land Records/ Registration services stand out for their "alarming level" of corruption; and School Education (up to class XII) and Banking Service (including postal service) comes out with "moderate level" of corruption. Around 7.5 per cent of the participants had experience of paying a bribe and another 7.5 per cent had used a contact for matters related to the National Rural Employment Guarantee Scheme (NREGS) which includes registration, to get selected, issuance of job card and wage payment, 4.4 per cent did not take the service because they were asked for bribe. The study also points that more than half of the eligible households in North Eastern States did not have a BPL card on reasons that they could not pay bribe or have a "contact" to influence.

The survey brings out a wide gap between the levels of perception and experience of BPL households about corruption. This indicates that for the common man majority of the public officials are corrupt and it is with this intention in mind they are approaching them. This perception is, as per the study, relatively high in police, land records and housing. Citizens have to make a number of visits to get a particular service. The survey says, "The number of visits one has to make is an indirect indicator for "seeking bribe" in that service". Repeated visits will no doubt add to the perception about that office or official as corrupt. As regards the relative position of States on corruption, in availing the 11 public services by BPL households, Assam, J & K, Bihar, Madhya Pradesh and Uttar Pradesh have an "alarming level" of corruption, while Himachal Pradesh, Uttaranchal, Delhi and Punjab have "moderate level". Other striking thing in the survey is that when Kerala is ranked as the least corrupt state in the India Corruption Study 2005 (TII-CMS 2005a: 11), when it comes to corruption involving BPL population it is ranked as "high" (TII-CMS 2008: 8) in the four points scale of - alarming, very high, high and moderate level of corruption.

When the TII-CMS India Corruption Study 2005 and 2007 reveals the spread of corruption in India, the CMS-India Corruption Study 2012 portrays the degraded and de-humane face of corruption in India. Because, the study shows that the public servants were not ashamed of in taking bribe from the slum-dwellers that have nothing to sell but their skins. So it has come to such a stage that many of the public officials didn't even have the prick of conscience while denying basic services to the very poor. The survey recorded the paltry sum of Rs. 5 paid by one slum dweller in Kolkata for getting monthly ration. The most often paid amount among various services was highest in police, which is Rs. 100. Over 60 per cent of the slum-dwellers opined that corruption has increased in the past one year (Express News 2012a: 9). The CMS- India Corruption Study 2012 was conducted among the slum-dwellers in the cities of Ahmedabad, Bangalore, Bhubaneswar, Chennai, Delhi, Hyderabad, Goa, Kolkata and Mumbai. The report of the survey was released on December 7, 2012.

The common men are denied of basic justice in the hands of corrupt officials. Neither rules nor regulations come on the way and illegal and impermissible transactions are carried out quickly (Jitha 2007: 232). Because of corruption the common man are the most suffocated. Each day they have to wait on the *verandas* of the government offices. To avoid this they have to someway satisfy the officials. Corruption reduces the net income of the poor and wreaks programmes related to the basic needs, from sanitation to education to health care. Shocking is the news that, in Bihar more than 80 per cent of the subsidised food aid to the poor is stolen. Corruption results in the misallocation of resources to the detriment of poverty reduction programmes. The only reason for many of our poverty reduction programmes leaping in darkness is corruption. It is also corruption that promotes or fosters black money, which if unchecked may destabilise the nation's economy.

For a student on Public Administration the study about corruption in India is something interesting. There is politics, sociology, economics, culture and all these makes the study inter-disciplinary or multi-disciplinary. Though not inbuilt, corruption in India works on the basis of some generally 'accepted' principles and has some unique characters or features that are as follows:

- **Corruption has become a part of the common sense culture in India** and it no longer surprises any one. Only an honest or upright officer surprises everyone now-a-days and the common man will look him with sympathy and someone will go to the extent of saying that he/she does not know how to make money. In hegemonising corruption as a part of common culture both the public officials (including politicians) and citizens have their role. Many public officials see corruption as their prerogative right and to the 'jobless' politician it is their sole source of income. Being a 'right' these officials will not hesitate in asking bribes openly[1]. So, the ecology of administration has got corrupted and polluted. In this ecology of administration, people too have accepted their destiny to be exploited by them. They remain as the silent spectators of corruption and this increases the chance of corruption.

- **Corruption has got institutionalised in our system and society**. Now-a-days corruption has become a regular source of income for many officials like the monthly salary. Each work is assigned with a specific charge or amount and in Kerala it is known as *padi*, say Rs.100, Rs. 200 which goes on depending upon the work. This is for the ones who are not the *regular visitors* of various departments. For the *regular customers* it is monthly, known in Kerala as *masapadi*. Usually this is for the police, excise, sales tax and customs and is paid quiet often by liquor barrens, mafias including land-sand-forest and those who engage in any sort of illegal and immoral activities. Industrialists and business persons too pay this for the licensing authorities, checking inspectors of departments concerned, regulating authorities like pollution control boards (unit levels) and even to local politicians, such that their *business* will not get interrupted. *The rate of payment is based on the rank of the receiver or status of the payee.* When one goes up the bureaucratic ladder the amount will also increase. So the equation is *the higher the rank of the officer the higher the rate of payment.* When it is a couple of thousand rupees or ten thousands for the lower bureaucrats, when it comes to the Deputy Director, it is lakhs. The CBI on January 16, 2013 arrested a deputy director of the Ministry of Environment and Forest (MoEF), for allegedly accepting a bribe of Rs.7 lakhs for procuring environmental clearance for an Orissa-based power and steel company (Rahul 2013). In case of ministers it will go crores as in the 2G.

As this monthly payment is many times than their official salary they were not to part with this. So when an upright officer takes charge, to say an honest collector or commissioner, the corrupt will form a cartel or join together to evict the upright officer. They will use political influence and when it does not work they will go for physically removing that officer. Attempt for that occurred in Kerala, in Calicut against the District Collector K.V. Mohankumar IAS and in Kollam against City Police Commissioner, Debesh Kumar Behera

IPS, when they became a headache to the sand mafias. The Collector had to encounter two hostile gangs in separate incidents in and around a place known as Feroke in Calicut within a gap of one hour, while leading a squad of police and revenue officials to check smuggling of sand (The Hindu 2012a: 1). In case of the City Police Commissioner the police-politician-sand mafia nexus hatched out plans to murder him by running over with a truck (The Poineer 2012). Behera is known for his relentless fight against the sand mafia.

- **Corruption in India quite often includes the principles of *ability-to-pay, willingness-to-pay and mutual-trust.*** Exemptions are there where the mixture of two or sometimes these three principles can be seen. The first principle, i.e., the ability-to-pay is applicable with regard to basic services where the target population of the corrupted person is the common man or one below the middle class. Here the amount of bribe depends upon one's ability to pay the "specific amount" or income of the person. Normally it will be couple of hundreds or thousands. The slum dweller paying Rs. 5 is the best example of this principle (Express News 2012a: 9). Kind, instead of cash is also accepted under this principle[2]. There may not be any room for bargaining in this case.

The second principle, ***willingness-to-pay*** is often seen in case of award of contracts, appointments and the like. The amount of bribe or the equivalent depends upon the willingness of the 'needy' and this principle works like the sale of offices prevailed in France, where the office goes to the higher bidder. In case of willingness-to-pay the bargaining power of the corrupted person is so high because in most cases the needy will be ready to pay whatever the corrupt asks. Usually unqualified and less qualified firms and persons will go for this principle. This principle can be better explained with the help of an example. *Suppose there are* 8 *licences in a Circle and the number of firms competing for it is 20. Let the general rule of allocation is one firm one licence. Then, those who have offered the first eight amounts in the descending order of arrangement (say, Rs.* 20 *lakh,* 19 *lakh,* 18 *lakh....... 15 lakh) will get the licence, as per this principle. If more than 8 firms are ready to pay highest amount cited as* Rs. 20 *lakh, there works the bargaining power of the corrupted one (the one who allots the licence). In such a race those who offered less than* Rs.20 *lakh will be eliminated from the scene and the game will be between those who offered above* Rs. 20 *lakh. Finally, the licence will go to the highest bidders.* Willingness to pay cannot work in cases where the number of applicants is less than the number of posts. The most important problem associated with this principle is the sabotage of merit and its potential to create maximum damage to the society.

In **mutual-trust** both gains, to a great extend alike. Here there is no bargaining, everything goes in a friendly-manner. A favour from one side gives its reciprocal on the other side. *When you close your eyes towards something, you will be rewarded either with a promotion or a handsome purse.* Mutual understanding is the basis on which this principle works. One may come voluntarily to help you and you may need to give only what you like. It will create a long standing friendship to the benefit of both. Bureaucratic-politician-business-mafia nexus generally works on the basis of this principle. While working in a nexus setup the corrupted always have to retain the confidence of his fellow partners, otherwise the chance of eliminating him/her will be high. This is because nexuses work like chains where the actions of one can trap others also. As any revelation, either voluntarily or through force affects the all group no one will be ready to take a risk.

- **There can be seen corruption with damage and without damage.** No doubt corruption involves damage to the society but some have direct and sudden effect while that of the other is indirect and long run. Take the case of an unqualified firm. It will obtain the licence by the exchange of bribe. But it will create negative externalities in the society, to say, in the form of pollution. Its repercussions affect a large section of the society. Similarly an unqualified person in a post damages its dignity and quiet often he will be interested in making money as much as possible to balance what he has given. Such a person perpetuates corruption in society and it goes as a chain reaction. In both these cases the **damage is direct and immediate.** Corruptions with damage can most be seen under the operation of willingness-to-pay principle. Corruption **without damage** involves the case of meritorious, desired and qualified that are forced to bribe, to get what they deserve. In such cases there won't be much damage to the society because of their qualification. A qualified firm with green technology will not create pollution and will maintain the criteria's needed for its working. Such a firm will not cause pollution or any other externalities to the society. It is circumstances that forced them to offer bribe and such a large majority won't perpetuate corruption under their initiative. So direct immediate damage to the society is not there in the case of qualified ones. The first case involves corruption with theft and the second case involves corruption without theft, as explained by Mikhal Drugor (2009: 4).

- **Corruption has got personified and public office has become a persona of corruption.** This is to such an extent that when someone uses corruption as a synonym of public office or official one cannot say it is wrong. *Instances are there where all officers of a single office have been netted by the Vigilance and Anti-Corruption Bureau.* Back in 2009, May 12, six employees of the Mining and Geology Department of Alappuzha District Office in Kerala, including the Office Head Tomson, Mineral Revenue Inspector Sakthidharan, UD Typist Amrutavalli, LD Clerk Manju, Driver Madhusoodanan Nair and the Night Watchman Naser Haneef were caught by the vigilance while taking bribe for issuing a licence. Vigilance and Anti-corruption officials also recovered Rs.17,300 from their possession. Medical test also proved that three men among them were under the influence of alcohol while on duty (TOI 2009). As all the members got arrested the

Alappuzha District Office of the Mining and Geology remained closed on that day (The Hindu 2009: 3). Incidents like this will increase the perception of the common man that all or majority of the public officials are corrupt.

There is always the problem to identify the corrupt as observed by Kautilya, "just as one cannot observe fish drinking water, so it is impossible not to find employees having revenue positions indulging in embezzling money" (Ramesh and Rajni 2011: 595). No doubt the person who gives the bribe can know who is the corrupt but there may be chain of officials or persons involved and in such cases one can know only a single chain, others continue in anonymity. Thanks to the modern medias that catches the corruption of politicians and bureaucrats lively. Only after the corruption is caught up, the public can understand who else are involved in and how much is the damage. Till then in the perception of common man all there are corrupt and that is what reflected in the India Corruption Study 2007 of the Transparency International. The study conducted among BPL households finds huge difference in the levels of perception and experiences of corruption (TII-CMS 2008: 10). When 54 per cent of the respondents perceive services in PDS to be corrupt, the actual experience is only 8 per cent. For school education it is 28 per cent and 5 per cent, water supply 42 per cent and 12 per cent, hospital 46 per cent and 11 per cent, electricity 44 per cent and 11 per cent, NREGS 47 and 11 per cent, banking 26 per cent and 7 per cent and in forest it is 36 per cent and 11 per cent. The levels of perceptions are thus three to eight times higher than the actual experiences of corruption. The increase in levels of perception is dangerous as it will in the long run *sanskritises* corruption.

- **Corruption in India has a degrading, inhumane and barbaric face.** It is this nature that makes corruption a human rights violation. Corruption becomes inhumane, when even the poorest of the poor were not excluded from it. When a doctor in a government hospital asks for bribe for performing a surgery it is quite inhumane. The government gives the doctor a fixed salary and provides all facilities, so there is no need of pocket expenditure for the part of the doctor in performing the surgery. By refusing to perform the surgery a doctor is violating not only his official duty but also the moral principle that a physician should uphold. We know that in a country like India it is the poor who normally depends on the government hospitals. When such is the case the above said actions none other than barbaric in nature.

Corruption becomes degrading when merit is compromised or sacrificed. This degrades the society as the unqualified will be corrupt all times. He will engage in all sort of corrupt activities. More than that, the society loses the service of the talented. Just imagine the case of a 'doctor' who failed in most of the subjects, but somehow 'managed' to pass the exam and finally with the influence of his in-laws became an assistant professor in a government medical college. Think about the condition of the patients who come in front of him!!

Sometimes corrupt officials act as puppets in the hands of others to tarnish the image of someone. By accepting bribe from someone charging malafide cases against the other is the most common form and is practiced by the police. Criminal charges have been framed against many social and human rights activists due to the reason that they are raising their voice against the different forms of evils in the society. Not only police, other officials also do the same, but in a different way. Day-in and day-out the media is bringing to light similar incidents. In a number of cases the victims may not even get justice. This is a nasty nature of corruption in India.

The termination of whistle blowers is the another inhumane and barbaric face of corruption in India. A number of whistle blowers including government servants and civil rights activists have been assassinated for the reason of exposing corruption. This is something scaring to the whistle blowers in the country. The latest of those murders include one in Mumbai and the other in Bangalore during the last week of November 2012. While the RTI activist in Mumbai was stabbed 27 times, the one in Bangalore was shot dead from close range (TOI 2012b). In between January 2010 and September 2011, around 16 RTI activists have been killed for revealing corruption, 40 others have been beaten or attacked after filing requests. But the interesting thing is that no official numbers are there (Mehul and Andrew 2011). Unfortunately, the whistle blowers were not provided adequate protection in practice.

- **There is a nexus between bureaucrats and politicians in corruption.** In this unholy nexus one supports and protects the other. *Many bureaucrats act as conscience keepers of the politicians and such bureaucrats will be rewarded with plum posts. They will do their level best to ensure the interest of their political masters and these political masters will in return provide protection.* The Adarsh Housing scam involving the politicians, bureaucrats and defence personnel's is the best example of this nexus. The trio appropriated flats intended for the widows of the Kargil warriors (Anupama 2010: 28). All news papers, reports such a case that has become controversial in the State of Kerala related to the upcoming Kochi Metro Project. Much after shifted from the post of MD, Kochi Metro Rail Limited (KMRL), the Ex-MD wrote a letter to the Union Urban Development Secretary seeking a clarification on DMRC (Delhi Metro Rail Corporation) Principal Advisor E. Sreedharan's role in the Kochi Metro. The Ex-MD did this totally out of his official capacity and got up controversial as attempts have been there from unknown sources to scuttle DMRC's involvement in the Kochi Metro Project[3] (The Hindu 2012b: 4). As Kochi Metro is one of dream projects of Kerala it cannot be let lose by the state, in the name of technicalities. But the action against this Ex-MD ended in just seeking a clarification letter from him (The Hindu 2012c: 1; Express News 2012b: 1). So, it is clear beyond doubt that *someone powerful* is there to protect this IAS officer, otherwise he would have at least served with a suspension, because he did what he is not entrusted to do, or in other words not in official capacity.

The nexus will expand with the inclusion of various kinds of mafias, say land, sand, mining etc. The laws of protection will apply to them also. In the 2G Spectrum case, Commonwealth scam, Adarsh Flat scam, Coal etc. we can see this nexus. It is this nexus that makes the ministers bat for the private telecom companies even when the CAG finds huge loss to the exchequer in the Spectrum allocation and Supreme Court validates the same (The Hindu 2012d: 1, 10). To some ministers actions against the corrupt by putting them behind bars will hamper investments in the country. Such a remark came from the Union Minister Salman Kurshid when the Supreme Court barred many businessmen involved the mega 1.76 lakh crore 2G scandal by refusing bail (Prabhakar 2011: 1). To the then Law Minister it was a matter of great concern that the corrupt were not granted bail by the court. At the same time, nowhere is recorded his concern for the hundreds who were kept in prison without any trial. When an upright officer takes stringent stand against any mafias an MP may come from any quarter to save him.[4]

- **The upright officers will be removed from the posts as they act as a stumble in the path of corruption.** Raju Narayana Swami IAS of the Kerala cadre is the best example. The latest incident is that he has been removed from the post of Civil Supplies Commissioner for not succumbing to the interest of the minister. *Malayala Manorama* reports (2013: 13) Raju Narayana Swami as saying "I co-operated with all the activities of the ministry, but started un-attending the meeting called by the minister when his recommendations have crossed the limit. I cannot issue an order in the morning for one party and another for the other in the afternoon, with regard to the same matter. If court summons me then I will provide the truth." This IAS topper had to face much hardship including suspension from service due to political pressure. He was transferred from the post of Thrissur District Collector by a simple fax message when he stood firm on revenue recovery. Later he was transferred from the post of Kasargod Collector to Employment Director when he did not write a favourable report for obtaining a paramedical course in a hospital without facilities, which belongs to a Minister's daughter (Jitha 2007: 210, 211). Ashok Khemka IAS of Haryana, who got 43 transfers with in a service of 23 years (The Hindu 2012e: 1) and U. Sagayam IAS of the Tamil Nadu cadre who has been transferred 18 times (Pushpa 2011) in the last 22 years for not accepting bribery are the other examples.

With regard to honest investigating officers there life is at risk in many cases. All sorts of pressures will be made on them to get the corrupted saved. This occurred on the ongoing 2G case where a series of allegations came against the Rajeshwar, the senior Enforcement Directorate (ED) Officer probing the scam. When the Uttar Pradesh Government moved to take action against this officer the Supreme Court came for his support observing that the allegations against Rajeshwar were being made *to prevent him from conducting the probe in the scam fearlessly*. While staying the government's action against the ED officer the bench of Justice G.S Singhvi and Justice Radhakrishnan made a remark that supports the present argument - "God has been very kind to Rajeshwar. He is still alive and is surviving" (Express News 2012c: 10).

In Madhya Pradesh, the mining mafia crushed a young IPS officer named Narendrakumar under the wheels of a tractor troller while attempting to stop the vehicle carrying coal. Narendrakumar, was a threat to the mining mafia as he has taken tough stand against the mafia. The mafia also has assassinated senior journalist Chandrika Kumar Rai and his family for reporting the illegal quarrying in the Moraina District. He also exposed the nexus between the politicians and the mining mafia (Kerala Kaumudi 2012: 9).

- **Corruption isolates and marginalises the honest and efficient officers.** Usually those who won't support corruption will be isolated in service. The political masters will exclude them from key positions. After retirement too there services won't be taken. At the same time those who are known as more flexible and/or corrupt while in service will get plum post after retirement in government agencies. In many cases it is seen that the honest officers even won't get the support of the co-cadres. The lashing out at Ashok Khemka IAS by his fellow cadre officer P.C. Gupta, the Head of Haryana Town and Country Planning is the best example. Gupta in his letter to the Chief Secretary challenged the actions of Khemka cancelling the mutation[5] of land in the controversial Vadra-DLF deal (Express News 2012d: 1). M.N Vijayakumar is another officer who has been isolated for his relentless fight against corruption. From September 2006 to February 2007 he has been transferred six times in six months apparently because he had reported serious corrupt practices by senior officers. When the persons against whom question marks are there were allowed to continue, Vijayakumar was frequently transfered to see that it becomes difficult for him to pursue against the corrupt actions of his senior officials. He was even labeled as disobedient (TWB 2012).

But instances are there where the public supported the honest officers. This happened when many village administrative officers in the district of Namakkal ganged up with politicians to get U. Sagayam IAS, the Collector, transferred. Over 5,000 villagers protested, saying they wouldn't let Sagayam go. So politicians had to retreat (Pushpa 2011). In case of Gagandeep S. Bedi IAS, the district population requested the Tamil Nadu Chief Minister to make him the permanent Collector of Cuddalore (Nardeep 2012: 1). When the upright officers are kept out of key posts the loss is to the society, because only these officers can make change in the system.

- **Corruption has a bargaining power in politics.** This explains why many governments even though they are minority they won't come down from power. Especially such bargaining power is high in case of coalition politics. If the holder of the balance has some files against some party leaders the power centre can use the sword of CBI investigation to get their vote favoured in the house or at least can get them abstained from voting. A review of the national politics in India during these days shows the working of this principle. With regard to the FDI vote in Parliament, the UPA had all the chance of failure. But the opposition motion against FDI in the Parliament got defeated with the abstention of BSP and SP members. Both had earlier vehemently opposed the FDI in retail sector in the course of the debate in Lok Sabha (Vinay and Balaji 2012: 1). Mulayam Singh and Mayavati, leaders of the SP and BSP respectively, are having a number of CBI investigations over their head and the chance of more is likely. When the regional political parties become more and more corrupt, the power of the one at the centre increases. The same law applies in state politics also. This is because the existence of many sub-regional parties depends upon their access to power. Their insignificant numerical strength forces them to be a part of coalition. If the party leaders are corrupt then the majority party can easily tune these small parties to their interests. They cannot go out of the coalition as it equals parting their existence.

- **Corruption in India gets the shield of politics, religion and caste.** It is a totally disappointing fact that the corrupt uses religion, caste and politics to wipe away the taint of their actions and many often they succeeds in that attempt. The Political Party A will make a roar when some from Party B gets involved in corruption. But when some allegations came against its members suddenly Party A will defend them by putting the blame on Party B's attempt to tarnish them. This is the case with Party B also. Actually both parties gain here as the charge of corruption will get faded and it just becomes a political issue. For example, when *India Against Corruption* activist Arvind Kejriwal came with the Robert Vadra-DLF land deal BJP made a hue and cry in the nation against the Congress. But when the same Kejriwal alleged that the BJP President Nitin Gaddkari took undue favours from the Maharashtra government in allotment of land acquired from Vidarbha farmers for a public purpose, in 2005, the allegations became "false and baseless" for BJP (Gargi 2012: 1; The Hindu 2012e: 10). Similarly for Sonia Gandhi, the Congress President, corruption is rampant in BJP-rules states (The Hindu 2012f: 12), but she sees no corruption in 2G, CWG, Coal or with related to her son-in-law Robert Vadra in the DLF deal, where the value of a property went up from Rs. 7.5 crore to Rs. 58 crore in just 65 days (The Hindu 2012g: 1; Express News 2012d: 7).

Caste and religion are the other shields for corruption. For being corrupt, there is no religion, no caste and no moral principles of the great religious teachings bar them from such a practice. But when caught up for corruption, all on a sudden religion and caste comes up and they will argue that it is an attempt to tarnish their community or that they are been victimised as they belong to a particular community. Suddenly caste and communal feelings will sprang up, sentiments of many gets hurted and then the issue of corruption vanishes somewhere in thin air. Corruption is corruption and it needs to be looked upon like that, not in the colour of caste or religion, and one should treat the corrupt as anti-national and anti-social.

- **Corruption is something that affects the economic security of the nation.** Corruption is a dragon eating the resources of the nation in a slow and steady but alarming rate. Large scale tax evasions reduce the revenue of the state in dangerous proportions. In such cases, to meet the development needs the state will be forced to depend on foreign loans. This affects the economic sovereignty and there by indirectly political sovereignty of a state as it has to apply the conditions of the donor agency or the state. Besides this, corruption delays developmental activities, discourages investments and drops poverty reduction programmes. It also increases the circulation of unaccountable money in the economy and affects anti-inflationary and anti-deflationary measures of the government. Day by day corruption is adding to the unaccountable money or black money that has now become half of our GDP, as estimated by the Global Financial Integrity in 2011. The problem with this money is that now-a-days they are being used for illicit trade of drugs, arms and even terrorist activities (Dhiraj and Sandheep 2011: 21). So, the economic security in one sense is affecting the physical security of the nation also.

Corruption at all levels need to be checked out, otherwise it will derail the democratic set up. Besides being a moral necessity, fight against corruption is also an economic necessity because the nation is aspiring to emerge as an important global player. Numerous are the reasons for increasing corruptions in India. Main reasons are lack of transparency and accountability in the system, lack of effective corruption reporting mechanism, clumsy handling of corruption cases, administrative delays, ineffective judicial system and political causes. The administrative procedure is so complicated and cumbersome and this often increases chances of corruption. Laws for the common man and short cuts for the influential is the accepted norm in India. For the common man each file has to move up and down in the bureaucratic ladder. The lop-sided administrative structure and low salaries to middle and junior level officers also increases the chance of corruption. Lastly, liberalisation with all its openness provided a cool temperature for the spread of and speedy growth of corruption in India.

End Notes

1. On December, 2012 two women *Havildars*, Minimol Pathros and Aniamma John of the air customs wing at the Cochin International Airport Ltd (CIAL) were caught on live camera by Asianet, a news channel in Kerala while taking bribe from a person who had sent the unaccompanied baggage from the UAE. The channel showed the clear video records of these *havildars* asking a bribe

of Rs. 1200, and saying that no 'reduction can be made in the amount'. Both were suspended from service pending enquiry (TOI, 2012).

2. Such a case has been reported by the media some years back when the vigilance raided out *prawn* and *pearl spot* from the freezer of a medical unit of the Kottayam Medical College, alleged to be given as bribe to a senior doctor.
3. P. Rajeev, M.P. from Kerala in a press meet arranged at Kochi criticised the actions of the Ex-MD of KMRL and alleged it as an attempt to scuttle DMRC's involvement in the Kochi Metro Project (The Hindu 2012b: 4). Attempts have been there to avoid DMRC from the Kochi Metro for some vested interests "hiding back".
4. This is what happened in Valapattanam of Kannur District in Kerala when the Sub-Inspector of Police caught some members of the sand mafia (Deccan Chronicle 2012).
5. Mutation is the legal term for substitution of the name of one person by the name of another in the record showing right or title to the property.

References

Anupama, Katakam (2010): "House of Scandal," *India Today*, 27(24), July 14-27, December 3, 28-32.

Avasthi, Amreshwar and Avasthi, Anand Prakash (2008): *Indian Administration*, Lakshmi Narain Agarwal, Agra.

CPI (2011): *Corruption Perception Index 2011*, Transparency International.

Deccan Chronicle (2012): "Caught in Quicksand," *Deccan Chronicle*, November 17, http://www.deccanchronicle.com/121117/news-current-affairs/article/caught-quicksand accessed on 10-12-2012.

Dhiraj, Nayyar and Sandheep, Unnithan (2011): "The Great Indian Robbery," *India Today*, XXXVI(5), January 31, 18-24.

Express News (2012a): "Corruption in Public Services Shoots Up, Says Study," *The New Indian Express*, Kochi, December.

—— (2012b): "Tom Jose Faces Metro Music," *The New Indian Express*, Kochi, October 23.1.

—— (2012c): "SC Stays Action Against ED Officer in 2G Case," *The New Indian Express*, Kochi, November.

——(2012d): "Vadra-DLF Land Deal Gets Murkier," *The New Indian Express*, Kochi, October.

—— (2012d): "Transferred Haryana Official Cancels DLF-Vadra Deal," *The New Indian Express*, Kochi, October.

——(2011): "Big Scams are Big News but Silent, Pervasive Corruption is Real Evil," *The New Sunday Express* (Magazine), Kochi, November.

Gargi, Parsai (2012): "Kejriwal Targets Gadkari," *The Hindu*, Thiruvananthapuram October.

Guham, S. and Samuel, Paul (2001): "Corruption in India," in S. Subramonian (ed.) *India's Developmental Experience*, Oxford University Press, New Delhi.

ICS (2005): *India Corruption Study 2005 Vol. I*, Transparency International India, New Delhi, June 30.

Jitha, S.R. (2007): *Higher Bureaucracy and Development*, Kalpaz Publications, New Delhi.

Kerala Kaumudi (2012): "IPS Officer-ea Tracter Kayatti Konnu," *Kerala Kaumudi*, Kochi, March.

Manorama (2013): "Anoop Casil Kodathi Vilichal Sathyam Bhodippikkum," *Malayala Manorama*, Thiruvananthapuram, January.

Mehul, Srivastava and Andrew, MacAskill (2011): "In India, Whistle-Blowers Pay with Their Lives," *Businessweek Magazine*, October 20, http://www.businessweek.com /magazine/in-india-whistleblowers-pay-with-their-lives-10202011.html accessed on 28-01-2013.

Mikhal, Drugor (2009): "Competition in Bureaucracy and Corruption." *Department of Economics, University of Oxford*, January, 1-25.

Nardeep Singh, Dahiya (2012): "Stainless Steel," *The New Sunday Express* (Magazine), Kochi, May 6, 1-2.

Pushpa, Iyengar (2011): "Under a Dangerous Motto," *Outlook India.com*, August 22, http://www.outlookindia.com/article.aspx?277990 accessed on 24-12-2012.

Rahul, Tripathi (2013): "MoEF Deputy Director Held for Taking Bribe, Rs. 1 Cr. Seized," *Indian Express*, January 17, http://www.indianexpress.com/news/moef-deputy-director-held-for-taking-bribe-rs-1-cr-seized/1060898/ accessed on 20-01-2013.

Ramesh, K. Arora and Rajni, Goyal (2011): *Indian Public Administration*, New Age International, New Delhi.

The Hindu (2012a): "Kozhikode Collector Escapes Attack," *The Hindu*, Thiruvananthapuram, December.

—— (2012b): "Clarify on Letter by Tom Jose: MP," *The Hindu*, Thiruvananthapuram, October.

—— (2012c): "Principal Secretary Tom Jose Has Some Explaining to Do Now," *The Hindu*, Thiruvananthapuram, October.

—— (2012d): "After Failed Auction, Congress Mocks CAG," *The Hindu*, November 16.

—— (2012e): "Khemka Refutes Haryana Government Claims, Says Transfer Mala Fide," *The Hindu*, Thiruvananthapuram, October.

—— (2012f): "Corruption Rampant in BJP-ruled States: Sonia," *The Hindu*, Thiruvananthapuram, October.

—— (2012g): "Senior Official Probing Vadra-DLF Land Deal Shunted Out," *The Hindu*, Thiruvananthapuram, October.

—— (2009): "Bribery Accused to be Suspended," *The Hindu*, Thiruvananthapuram, May.

The Pioneer (2012): "Police-mafia Nexus Strong in Kerala," *The Pioneer*, November 10, http://www.dailypioneer.com/state-editions/kochi/108086-police-mafia-nexus-strong-in-kerala.html accessed on 15-11-2012.

TOI (2012a): "Two Customs Staff in the Dock on Bribery Charges," *The Times of India*, December 4, http://articles.timesofindia.indiatimes.com/2012-12-04/kochi/35593835 _1_customs-staff-customs-officials-unaccompanied-baggage accessed on 26-01-2013.

—— (2012a): "Whistleblowers Face Death Threats, But Cops Cool," *The Times of India*, November 26, http://articles.timesofindia.indiatimes.com/2012-11-26/hyderabad /35366434_1_rti-activists-death-threats-illegal-sand accessed on 28-01-2013.

—— (2009): "All 6 Staffers of a Govt. Office Held for Bribery," *The Times of India*, May 13, http://timesofindia.indiatimes.com/Cities/All-6-staffers-of-a-govt-office-held-for-bribery/articleshow/4522764.cms accesses on 13-05-2009.

TII-CMS (2008): *India Corruption Study 2007, With Focus on BPL Households*, Transparency International India and Centre for Media Studies, New Delhi, June.

—— (2005a): *India Corruption Study – 2005*, Transparency International India and Centre for Media Studies, New Delhi, June 30.

—— (2005b): *India Corruption Study – 2005, Vol. II, Corruption in Income Tax*, Transparency International India and Centre for Media Studies, New Delhi.

Vinay, Kumar and Balaji, J. (2012): "Manmohan Wins FDI Vote," *The Hindu*, Thiruvananthapuram, December 6.

9

Liberalisation and Corruption

Liberalisation is quite often cited as a solution for corruption. The argument is that it is the licence permit raj system that promotes corruption and liberalisation through the process of deregulation reduces the chance of corruption. But actual experiences show that corruption has increased not only quantitatively but also qualitatively. Corruption spread like anything and it penetrated into many areas that were previously untouched by it. Corruption with regard to privatisation of water supply is the best example. Together with the number of corruption the so-called amount involved in it also made a dramatic rise under the patronage of globalisation. The number of actors in an unregulated economy is more than a regulated one and this forms the basic reason for the increased number of corruption. Other thing with related to corruption under liberalisation is corruption-with-damage which is basically high, compared to the pre-liberalised period.

The march of liberalisation provided a comfortable climate for the spread of corruption. During the monopoly regime it was core for an unqualified firm to obtain a licence. As the file seeking permission to obtain the licence has to move up and down a number of bureaucratic ladders of many departments, the chance of any negatives getting concealed is very low. If so obtained, the number of such firms will be very few in number as while granting the licence the required qualification is a must. Together with this, the chance of the licence getting cancelled for any violation of conditions, in the later stage is also high in a monopoly regime. This will force the firms to comply with the quality norms. Exemptions are there but in majority of cases this is the accepted rule. More than that, a qualified firm pays only lower bribe than an unqualified one. Corruption-with-damage is comparatively very low in a monopoly regime as the number of unqualified firms obtaining licence is negligible.

In a liberalised regime, it is quite easy for an unqualified firm to obtain a licence. Globalisation usually advocates single window clearances instead of multi-departmental clearances. So, it is easy to bribe and get the licence cleared. But if the officer is honest and efficient single window can curb corruption. Usually in single window clearances it may not be possible to take into account all aspects of the impact of the specific project. Take the case of Coca-Cola company in Plachimada, Kerala. It came through a single window clearance where no ecological study of the impact of ground water extortion was made. Many SEZ (Special Economic Zones) clearances were through single window. Experiences show that SEZ in India proved to be one of the biggest land grab in its history. Data available from the website of the Ministry of Commerce shows that there exists vast difference between the projected benefits and actual benefits from SEZs.

The actors in a globalised economy are more compared to the pre-globalised era. In the monopoly regime many services were under the total control of the government or government directly provided those services. When the number of services reserved for the government decreased more private players entered the scene. The number of private players further increased when Foreign Direct Investment and Foreign Institutional Investment were allowed. Private sectors are now the main actors in telecommunications, infrastructure development, tourism, development of townships etc. In defence sector too private actors now play a major role. A vast market like India lures everyone so whatever can be done will be done to catch up that market. It is this that made US retail giant Walmart spend $25 million over four years for various lobbying activities, including for gaining access to Indian markets (Express News 2012a: 1). Under globalisation, the competition is between the numerically large numbers of firms and less number of opportunities. This always increases corruption.

It can also be noted that the increase in the number of players haven't benefitted the population in many cases. The normal rule is that when the number of firms selling similar products increases, it creates acute competition in the market which in turn produces quality product at competitive price. But this has been limited to a few cases. In case of pharma companies it was the cost of medicines that increased under competition. A kind of cartel formation can also be seen in the market[1]. Cartels anywhere protect their interest by reducing competition through entering into mutual beneficial agreements. In the urge for profit the companies will engage in activities like wage reduction, more working hours, reduction in safety standards and the like. Usually, it is seen that many firms or industries won't run their waste treatment plants on account of the high cost associated with its operation. They will normally run the waste water and solid waste either to the nearby water body or dump it in nearby fields. Indulging in such a practice in majority of cases needs the support of the local bureaucracy especially the staffs of the pollution control board. There lies the chance of corruption, corruption-with-damage. When the number of such practices increases the rate of corruption also increases.

Taking the case of 2G scam, India's one of the biggest scams in history, around 46 companies were in the race for obtaining the spectrum licence. The 122 licences in the 22 circles were allotted in the year 2008 on a first-come-first-serve basis at a price pegged at 2001. This itself was to foster corruption because India's telecom market was at its height in 2008 with a staggering of above 35 crore mobile phone connections. As the demand for spectrum was higher than the supply, an auction could have collected a much higher price when the companies compete with themselves to catch the market. Without taking into account all these realities the telecom ministry under A. Raja decided to allocate spectrum on the first-come basis that too at a rate of 2001, ignoring the advice of TRAI, Law Ministry and Finance Ministry. The then Telecom Secretary and Member (Finance) also questioned the allocation of spectrum at a throw away price (Kerala Kaumudi 2012a: 6). Even the note of the Cabinet Secretary K.M. Chandrashekar, the senior most bureaucrat of the nation, recommending an entry fee of Rs. 36,000 crore for the spectrum was also struck down. Raja set aside all these to help the two private companies Swan Telecom Pvt. Ltd. and Unitech Wireless Ltd. to get the spectrum at a much lower cost. The CBI court also found prima facie evidence for A. Raja, (former telecom minister), Siddharth Behuria (former telecom secretary) and R.K. Chandolia (Raja's former personal secretary) conspiring to allocate spectrum to the two private companies Swan and Unitech, in violation of law to cause wrongful gain to the companies (Vishwas 2011: 1).

In spectrum what we can see is for the profit of the private companies especially Swan and Unitech, competitive bidding was avoided. Both got licence without any prior telecom experience. Swan even didn't meet the eligibility criteria. After getting the licence Swan sold 45 per cent of their stake to Etisalat of UAE and Unitech sold their stake to 60 per cent of their stake to Telinore of Norway. Another company Tata Teleservice sold their stake to Docomo. So the number of players in the race increased. For getting the licence of 13 circles Swan gave only 1537 crores but for the 45 per cent stake they sold to Etisalat they secured Rs 4500 crore. Similar is the case with Unitech which bought the licences of 22 circles with Rs 1651 crore got Rs 6150 crore when it sold 60 per cent of the stakes to Telinore (Kerala Kaumudi 2012a: 6). The loss to the exchequer was a whooping sum which has been estimated by the Comptroller and Auditor General of India (CAG) as Rs 1.76 lakh crore. Whatever may be the controversy regarding the report of the CAG, the vindication of its report by the Supreme Court pinpoints the corruption involved in spectrum allocation. The Supreme Court also cancelled the 122 licences allotted to various companies (The Hindu 2012a: 1; Kerala Kaumudi 2012b: 1; Vishwas 2012: 9). So, it is clear that the increase in the number of firms won't decrease corruption but can augment the same. With the entry of foreign companies whose motto is wholesome exploitation of the periphery, the looting of resources has increased.

The allocation of coal blocks showcases other instances of corruption. When it was the monopoly of government companies, corruption was less but with the entry of private companies the number and amount increased. Undue favours were given to the private firms including Jindals, Tatas, Rungtas, Birlas in the form of under-pricing. Financial gain to the private beneficiaries of coal block is Rs 1.86 lakh crore. So in allocating coal blocks by avoiding competitive bidding made the loss of Rs 1.86 lakh crore (Sunday Express 2012: 1) to the government. It is clear that under-pricing was made to ensure profit to these private firms. A look at the 'donation' given by some of the firms that got coal blocks to the political parties proves this argument. The information collected by the Association of Democratic Reforms through RTI shows that the Jindal Steel and Power Limited which got 12 coal blocks has given the congress party a donation of Rs 1.5 crore, in between 2004 and 2009. The Starlight Energy Ltd. that had got coal blocks in Odisha has given one crore in 2004-05 and another Rs five crore in 2009-10 to the congress party. The Madras Aluminium Limited, a sister concern of the Starlight gave the BJP Rs 3.5 crore as donation. When the Congress got Rs nine crore from Tata, BJP got Rs 6.8 crore and the Samajwadi Party (SP) got Rs 1.58 crore as donations (Sanakan 2012: 5).

So the post-liberalisation era has made not only the businessman millionares but also the political parties. Congress became the richest party followed by the BJP. The information collected by the Association of Democratic Reforms and National Election Watch through RTI shows that during the last seven years starting from the financial year 2004-05, and 2010-11, the Indian National Congress grew richer by Rs 2008 crore and the BJP earned Rs 994 crore. This is followed by BSP with Rs 484 crore, CPM Rs 417 crore, SP Rs 279 crore, AIADMK Rs 60 crore, TDP Rs 54 crore, DMK Rs 44 crore and TRS Rs. 10 crore, during the same period. There is also an increase in the bottom-line of the income of the political parties. When the Congress and the BJP increased their bottom-line income from Rs. 232 crore in 2004-05 to Rs. 307 crore in 2010-11 and Rs. 104 crore to Rs. 168 crore respectively, the BSP made a whooping improvement of Rs. 115.7 crore in 2010-11 from the Rs. 4.4 crore of 2004-05 (Express News 2012b: 1). The increase in the income of BSP is around 2629.54 per cent compared to with that in 2004-05. The tax free income of the main ten political parties during the five years period between 2007-08 and 2011-12 touches Rs. 2490 crore. The Congress and the BJP account for around 80 per cent of the exempted amount (Express News 2012c: 11).

Normally, political parties are exempted from the payment of taxes but they have to maintain a book of account for donations or income above Rs 20,000. The above said income includes only those above Rs. 20,000. It is a clear fact that the majority of Indians who lives on half a dollar per day cannot pay a sum of above Rs 20,000 to the political parties. The biggest contributors to the political parties are the corporate giants like Reliance, Tatas, Jindal, Bharti, Torrent etc. It can also be noted that many organisations contributing to the top parties. For example, The General Electoral Trust and Torrent Power Limited form the biggest donors to the big parties, Congress and the BJP. Their share to Congress was Rs 36.41 crore and 14.15 crore respectively and to BJP Rs 26.07 crore and Rs13 crore respectively. Bharti Electoral Trust with Rs11 crore is the third biggest donor to Congress while Asianet Holding Private Limited with Rs 10 crore is the third biggest donor for BJP (Express News 2012b: 1). The Election Commission of India has come across instances of suspected violations of the Foreign Contribution Regulation Act by the Congress and BJP. Both had accepted donations of Rs five crore each from the subsidiaries of multi-national firm Vedanta group, Sterlite Industries and Sesa Goa Group. Vedanta Group, according to its annual report 2011-12, had paid $5.69 million to various political parties in India in the last three years (Express News 2012d: 7)

So, the main source of donation is private corporates and their donation is not for improving the well being of the rest of the population, but as a token for the benefits they have got or to get from the government in various forms including exemptions in laws, regulations and tax. The post-bidding concessions to the Reliance Power Limited for its 4000 MW Sasan mega power project was to the tune of Rs 29,033 crore. Reliance was allotted an additional coal block, Chhatrasal by pointing that the two blocks allocated initially were not adequate for the project. Further it was allowed to use surplus coal from the initially allocated two blocks Moher and Moher-Amlohri. Chhatrasal was given to Reliance by de-allocating it from the Public Sector NTPC (Sujay 2012: 1). If there is nothing to hide in the contributions being received by the political parties they wouldn't have gone for engaging top lawyers at the hearing of the Chief Information Commissioner, in order to resist attempts to give out information on IT returns (Express News 2012b: 1).

The post-liberalisation government officers have realised that their decisions can make others rich (Jitha 2011: 50). Their logic is "If greedy Indian business man can evade taxes, influence policies and make money through devious means, the government officer who moves the file can have a share of the booty." This increased the number of corruption. Corruption is now corroding the steel frame of Indian administration. The number of corruption cases in which IAS officers are getting involved is on the rise. Instances are there where one officer is having multiple charges like that of the 1984 Arunachal Pradesh-Goa-Mizoram-Union Territories cadre IAS officer R.K. Srivastava with 35 cases of corruption and Vinod Kumar, an Odisha cadre officer of 1989 with 20 sanction for prosecution against him (Gangadhar 2012). The corruption at the higher levels induces the lower ones to get engaged in it. Their logic is "If the higher officials can engage in fishing the sharks in the high seas, why they can't fish in the waters under their claim." This has penetrated corruption as a normal right to the bottom level. The living style of higher officials or the rich, entices many to have a life of luxury. This together with the high consumerism under liberalisation prompts for corrupt practices. So under liberalisation a *dropping-down* of corruption can be seen. Instead of the benefits of development trickling down, it was corruption that trickled down in all spheres of life, known as *Dropping-down of Corruption*.

The allure of consumerism is one that fosters corruption. Liberalisation has increased the choice of one through the increased imports. It brought variety of goods and services in the market. Almost all foreign goods became available in Indian market at more or less equivalent prices. Modern amenities of life like TV, refrigerator, washing machine, VCR etc. reached the market in any numbers. The glittering shopping malls and enchanting tourist destinations provided new avenues of shopping and refreshments. The choice of the consumer has thus widely increased under liberalisation. Availability of more products increases the marginal utility of the consumer income, given that they have a taste for variety (Baksi *et al.* 2009: 215). Similarly, the marginal utility of bribe income also increased. There are a number of items or services on which the income can be utilised. This increases corruption by increasing the incentive to be corrupt. Thus, liberalisation while increasing the allure of consumerism strengthens the prospects of officials to be corrupt.

The Adarsh Housing Scandal is the best example of the allure of consumerism and corruption. The housing society was originally meant for Kargil War widows, but appropriated by the relatives and in-laws of the Chief Minister, top bureaucrats and defence personnel (Anupama 2010: 28). The scam also highlights the unholy nexus between the political class, bureaucracy and the army officials. When Maharashtra Chief Minister Ashok Chavan lost his chair, CBI charge-sheeted and later arrested the IAS bands, Ramanand Tiwari, then Principal Secretary, Urban Development; Subash Lala, then Principal Secretary to the Chief Minister, Pradeep Vyas, the Mumbai Collector in 2004; Jairaj Pathak, former Munincipal Commissioner (Express News 2012e: 11). The defence personnel's charge-sheeted by the CBI includes A.R. Kumar, then GOC, Mumbai, M.M. Wanchoo, Romesh Sharma, both retired Brigadiers; T.K. Sinha, then Colonel in the MG & G area and Tej Kishan Kaul, retired Major General. Either these persons or their near relatives own flats in the building. Tiwari and Lala were allegedly conspired to transfer floor space index and misguided the Mumbai

Metropolitan Region Development Authority on issues relating to Adarsh. When Jairaj Phatak allowed the building's height to be increased without referring the matter to the high-rise committee, Pradeep Vyas, the then Collector accepted false documentation on incomes and allowed several memberships to go through on the basis of it. The other person in question is the Deputy Secretary P.V. Deshmukh, who conspired with the other guilty higher bureaucrats and cleared the building proposal (Anupama 2012: 24).

In response to an RTI query in 2011, the Department of Personnel and Training (DoPT) released a list of 13 corrupt babus. The officers include Karan Bir Singh Sidhu (Punjab), R.K. Shrivastava (Arunachal Pradesh, Goa, Mizoram and Union Territory - AGMUT), Kavaddi Narsimha (AGMUT), J.S.L. Vasava (Assam-Manipur), R.S. Shrivastava (Rajasthan), L.V. Subramaniam (Andhra Pradesh), Mandeep Singh (Punjab), Sanjeev Kumar (Haryana) and Subhash Chand Ahluwalia (Himachal Pradesh), Rakesh Mohan (AGMUT), Prafulla Chandra Mishra (Odisha), Sudhir Prasad (Jharkhand) and Vinod Kumar (Odisha) (Express News 2012e: 11). R.K. Shrivastava and Vinod Kumar had multiple charges against them. The year 2011 also saw a number of IAS officers either charge-sheeted by any investigating offices or being under scanner. A record number of have been investigated by the CBI in corruption cases between January 2011 and March 2012 and a number of officers, IAS and IPS officers, both serving and retired, have been arrested and jailed in states all over the nation like Maharashtra, Odisha, Andhra Pradesh, Nagaland and Delhi.

The scams in Andhra Pradesh felled two powerful IAS officers – Y. Srilakshmi and B.P. Acharya. Srilakshmi is regarded as one of the most powerful IAS officers in the state and she was charged with helping mining tycoon and former Karnataka minister Gali Janardhan Reddy in the illegal mining of iron ore through his Obulapuram Mining Company (OMC). The IAS officer had been instrumental in issuing the controversial GO that helped Janardhan to export the iron ore from the Obulapuram mines, which were supposed to be captive mines for his proposed Brahmani steel plant in Kadapa (Srinivasa 2011). The CBI also alleges she demanded a huge bribe, running into crores of rupees, from an applicant C. Shashi Kumar to grant a Prospecting Licence (Express News 2012e: 11). Charged under Section 120-B read with 409 of IPC and Section 13 (2) read with 13 (1) (d) of Prevention of Corruption Act, 1988, besides the Mines Act and Forest Act she was arrested on November 28, 2011 and lodged in the Central Prison for Women, Chanchalguda. Srilakshmi is the first serving bureaucrat to be arrested by the CBI in any corruption case in the state and she was named accused No. 3 in the case.

B.P. Acharya was the second officer to be toppled in the scam in Andhra Pradesh. This 1983 batch IAS officer was the accused No. 1 in the APIIC-

Emaar property scam. Acharya was serving as the Principal Secretary (Home) when he was arrested for corruption. He was the Managing Director of AP Industrial Infrastructure Corporation (APIIC) when the alleged irregularities leading to the dilution of APIIC's equity in the joint venture with Emaar properties, the Emaar Hills Township Private Limited (EHTPL), took place. The Corporations equity diluted from 49 per cent to 26 per cent and then to 6.5 per cent in the township developed by the Emmar Group (Sunday Indian 2012). The CBI alleges he played a key role in the APIIC deal with Emaar Properties and the subsequent dilution of the government's stake in the project that caused a huge loss of revenue to the state exchequer. Acharya was arrested on January 30, 2012 and charged under Sections 120-B read with 420, 409 477-A of IPC and Section 13 (2) read with 13 (1) (c) and (d) of Prevention of Corruption Act (Express News 2012e: 11). L.V Subramanyam, Accharya's batch mate is under scanner in the Emmar-MGF scam.

The Commonwealth Games scam sacked top officials including its chairman Suresh Kalmadi, a Congress MP. He was charge-sheeted on alleged foreign exchange violations in the Queen's Baton Relay held in 2009 in London and for allegedly handing out contracts to a Swiss time-keeping company that provided equipment and services at exorbitant rates, causing huge loss to the government. The arrested officials includes Prasar Bharati CEO B.S. Lalli and Doordarshan Director-General Aruna Sharma and the CBI registered cases against them for colluding with the UK-based broadcast firm SIS LIVE during the Commonwealth Games 2010 that resulted in a loss of Rs135 crore. The High Level Shunglu Panel, appointed by the Prime Minister, which went into alleged financial irregularities in the Commonwealth Games, has strongly indicted B.S. Lalli and Aruna Sharma, accusing them of "collusion" with the UK-based firm which benefitted Rs 135 crore in the broadcast deal. The panel recommended action against the two officials saying "they cannot be rescued from the acts of omission and commission which facilitated this wrong-doing" (Outlook 2011). The CBI also booked a serving IAS officer, Vijay Kumar Gautam, in connection with alleged irregularities in awarding consultancy works related to Commonwealth Games to a Switzerland-based firm, on August 2012. Gautam is a 1987 batch IAS officer from the Maharashtra cadre and was chief operating officer of the Commonwealth Games Organising Committee. He was booked along with sacked Organising Committee (OC) Chairman Suresh Kalmadi, CEO of Swiss firm Event Knowledge Services Craig Gordon, former OC Secretary General Lalit Bhanot, former OC Treasurer A.K. Mattoo and other unknown persons (TOI 2012a). Another officer booked in by the CBI in connection with the CWG scam is Parimal Rai, for the alleged irregularities in the construction of a convention centre, which resulted in a loss of Rs 15 crore. This 1985-batch IAS officer was the chairman of NDMC at the time of the CWG (Rahul 2012).

The other IAS officers arrested during the periods 2010, 2011 and 2012 were Ravi Inder Singh, Pradeep Kumar, Pradeep Shukla, Debaditya Chakraborty and O. Ravi. Ravi Inder Singh was arrested by the Delhi Police and jailed for passing on sensitive information to business houses in exchange for cash and sexual favours (Express News 2012e: 11). Singh, a 1994-batch officer was working as Director in the sensitive Internal Security Division in the home ministry and he was under surveillance of Delhi Police's Special Cell before being arrested (India Today 2010). The Internal Security Division is considered to be the most sensitive wing and handles all crucial issues related to the country's security. Pradeep Kumar is a 1991-batch officer of the Jharkhand cadre and was the Health Secretary there when the Rs 130 crore National Rural Health Mission scam took place. He allegedly accepted a bribe of Rs 4.85 lakh and acquired disproportionate assets (Express News 2012e: 11). Pradeep Shukla was another senior IAS officer and was arrested by the CBI on May 10, 2012 for alleged involvement in the NRHM scam in Uttar Pradesh. He was named in the first case registered in NRHM scam in which it was alleged that officials of Uttar Pradesh Health Department entered into criminal conspiracy with officers of UP Processing and Construction Cooperative Federation Ltd. (PACCFED) and Directors of three private firms based at Moradabad and Gajraula, in the contract of upgradation of 89 district level hospitals involving an amount of Rs 89 crore. The estimated loss to government exchequer was pegged at around Rs 25 lakh per hospital thereby resulting in loss of Rs 22.5 crore. He has also been booked for other two cases making the total cost running up to Rs 250 crore (PTI 2012a). Senior IAS officer S.P. Ram, former Director General of Family Welfare, who is accused of pre-deciding the vendor for awarding the contract of medical equipment through Uttar Pradesh Small Industries Corporation (UPSIC) to two firms based in Moradabad which resulted in a loss of Rs 1.5 crore to the exchequer, is under scanner of the CBI in the same case (Express News 2012e: 11).

Debaditya Chakraborty, the 1976-batch IAS officer of the West Bengal cadre was arrested for his alleged involvement in an Rs 125 crore scam, in Kolkata. He was arrested on February 1, 2012, along with R.M. Jamir, a retired IAS officer who was the Director of the West Bengal Essential Commodities Services Corporation (WBECSC), during the scam and Chakraborty its managing director. The PSU was entrusted with the export of iron ore to a Chinese firm in a joint venture with Bharat Inmate, a private exporter. In the subsequent fiasco, the PSU suffered a loss of 125 crore (TOI 2012b). So the duo was accused of misappropriating funds in the iron ore export deal. O. RAVI is a 1983 batch Gujarat cadre IAS officer arrested by the CBI on 2010 after being charged with an excise duty evasion scandal of Rs 340 crore and for bribery. He allegedly took a bribe of Rs 25 lakh to get the Daman Administrator transferred and the favours shown to the Royal distilleries in Daman resulted in a loss of Rs340 crore to the exchequer (DNA 2010). He was posted as Joint Secretary in the Union Home Ministry before his arrest (Rahul 2012). In 2010, Neera Yadav, a 1971-batch IAS officer of Uttar Pradesh was sentenced to four years imprisonment after the CBI court found her guilty of violating rules to help Flex Industries get an industrial plot in Noida in 1995, when she was the chairman of the New Okhla Industrial Development Authority (Noida). She is the first Chief Secretary to be jailed for corruption. The first bureaucrat to be jailed in independent India was Union Industries and Commerce Secretary S.A. Venkatraman in 1951, in a cycle parts import scam (Express News 2012e: 11).

The officers under scanner of the investigating agencies includes K.Suresh Kumar, a 1982-batch, Madhya Pradesh-cadre IAS officer; B.V. Selvaraj, a 1981-batch, UT-cadre IAS officer; Abrahum Varickamackal, a 1998-batch UT-cadre IAS officer; Sada Kant, a 1983-batch Uttar Pradesh-cadre IAS officer; Manoj Kumar Aggarwal, a 1990-batch West Bengal-cadre IAS officer; Rakesh Mohan, 1978-batch UT-cadre IAS officer and Shiv Shankar Sharma, 1981-batch Bihar-cadre IAS officer (Financial Express 2012: 10; Rahul 2012). Kumar has been booked for allegedly allowing the berthing of a foreign vessel, which neither had valid papers nor crew on board, in violation of rules in 2007. By allowing it to dock and not collecting payments, including additional berth hire charges, demurrage and legal expenses, a loss of over Rs 20 crore was allegedly caused to the government. The CBI seized Rs 2.36 crore during raids on Kumar's home. The charge against Varickamackal was that he allegedly abused his official position between 2006 and 2009 and without authorisation awarded contracts to one Kassim for supply of river sand and granite chips from the mainland to the islands of Lakshadweep. Sada Kant was under the scanner for his alleged role in the award of a contract involving a high-altitude road in Leh (Indian Express 2011). Selvaraj and Rakesh Mohan allegedly took bribe for awarding contracts in Lakshadweep and Delhi respectively. Manoj Kumar and Shiv Shankar were under scanner for having disproportional assets, beyond their known source of income (Rahul 2012). The Haryana multi-crore forestry scam is also likely to hit many IAS and IFS (Forest) officers.

Many IAS officers have wealth disproportionate to their known source of income. Nitish Janardhan Thakur was one such officer and the Anti-Corruption Bureau of Maharashtra on March 14, 2012 unearthed assets worth over Rs118.39 crore allegedly belonging to him. He was posted as Deputy Collector of the Raigad district, adjacent to Mumbai, from 1988-2010 and was suspended in 2010 following charges of corruption (PTI 2012b). The CBI in November 2011 charge-sheeted K. Dhanalakshmi Gowda, an Uttar Pradesh cadre 2001 batch IAS officer, who was serving as Director in the Ministry of Social Justice, for allegedly possessing disproportionate assets of Rs 3.15 crore. She is alleged to have benami properties in the name of her mother who abetted her to acquire the assets in her name, as per the CBI sources (Express

News 2012e: 11). One of the main reasons for not stating income or filing asset information is the presence of disproportionate income. As per the information made public by the DoPT on November 12, 2012, 70, IAS officers out of the total cadre strength of 4,377 didn't submit the immoveable property returns (IPR) (Yadish 2012: 7). According to the AIS rules 1968, every officer needs to submit IPR latest by January 31 of every year. The Press Note by the Vigilance Director, Kerala State on February 11, 2012 shows that investigations were going on against 1,100 government servants for having income disproportionate to the known sources. This includes that of 30 IAS and IPS officers having multiple charges. A total of 375 investigations were on against various IAS, IPS, IFS (Forest) and several departmental heads in the state (Mathrubhumi 2013: 5).

The Enforcement Directorate (ED) has so far attached the property of many IAS officers in excess of their known source of income. In November 2011, the ED attached property worth Rs 350 crore belonging to the suspended Madhya Pradesh IAS officer couples Arvind and Tinu Joshi, disproportionate to their known source of income. This is known to be the biggest amount of ill-gotten money probably detected from any IAS officer in the country and was unearthed following several Income Tax raids on the premises of the duo. The raids were carried out following complaints that the officers had allegedly made huge investments in an insurance company. Both Arvind and Tinu, are 1979-batch IAS Officers of the Madhya Pradesh Cadre, and have held important positions in the Centre since the late 80s. Tinu served as Deputy Secretary in the PMO from July 1, 1988 to January 1, 1990 while Arvind was Joint Secretary in the Defence Ministry during the 1999 Kargil hostilities. In the report to the Madhya Pradesh Chief Secretary, Avni Vaish and Lokayukta P.V. Naolekar, the ED has given details of investments made including the Joshis purchase of agricultural or non-agricultural land at a number of places, 25 flats of which 18 are in Guwahati, six in Bhopal and one in New Delhi and seven plots at Patel Nagar. The report also claimed that Arvind Joshi had allegedly indulged in speculative trading in shares, futures and options to the tune of Rs 270 crore in the last three years, from 2010 (Deccan Herald 2011).

The unaccountable money because of corruption in various forms is creating a parallel economy in the nation, which if unchecked may destabilise the development and economy of the nation. Even though numerous revelations are there from various sources regarding the tax-evaded money of Indians in various foreign banks, little attempt has been made by the Government to recover the same. No official data exists regarding the quantum of black money in India. Even the "economist" Prime Minister, Dr. Manmohan Singh does not have the calculation or the basis of calculation. In the Prime Minister's address at the "Interaction with Newspaper Editors" on June 29, 2011, regarding black money, he said "4 lakh crores or whatever the figures or black money being mentioned... I do not know what is the basis of those calculations..." (MIB 2011: 4). According to Global Financial Integrity (GFI), a programme of the Washington-based Center for International Policy the outflow of illicit money from India during 2002-06 was estimated to be \$137.5 billion (Rs 6.88 lakh crore) (Gurumurthy 2009).

There is no official count of the size and the growth of the parallel economy. The last such study was by the National Institute of Public Finance and Policy (NIPFP) in 1985. It estimated the size of the parallel economy at between Rs31,500 crore and Rs 36,786 crore in 1983-84. This amounted to about 20 per cent of India's GDP that year. To the Indira Gandhi Institute of Development Research (IGIDR) which estimated the amount of black money in its India Development Report 1999-2000, the quantum of black money is at Rs 3,54,000 crore in 1999, equaling 20 per cent of the GDP (Priya 2008). By 2008 the quantum of black money in India escalated to half of India's GDP or \$500 billion i.e. Rs 22.5 lakh crore in Indian rupees. This was the key findings of the comprehensive study on *Drivers and Dynamics of Illicit Financial Flows From India: 1948-2008* conducted by the Global Financial Integrity (Dhiraj and Sandheep 2011: 19). To the CBI Director, A.P. Singh, Indians have a black money deposit of Rs 24.5 lakh crore in foreign banks, lion share of which is in Swiss Banks (Kerala Kaumudi 2012c: 1).

The transfer of illicit money is mainly to foreign banks and the most popular destinations are Switzerland, Luxembourg, Channel Islands and the Bahamas. Normally black money are kickbacks for arms deals, bribes for contracts and skimming of profit by corporate and diverting them into foreign accounts for evading taxes. This not only violates the tax codes but a number of civil and criminal codes including customs regulations, VAT assessments, banking regulations and regarding money laundering. Most of the black money comes back for anti-national activities including terrorism. But the soft governments in India are providing the culprits to have safe heavens in foreign countries. Economic liberalisation has only increased the outflow of illicit money from the country. Corruption has got liberalised paying the way for *liberalised corruption* in India. Every opportunity is there for one to get corrupt and evade the same at safe destinations. So rather than diminishing corruption, liberalisation promotes corruption in great numbers.

Economic liberalisation has made governments soft which are committed to the interest of the business houses than its citizens. The soft governments usually show reluctance in taking action against the corrupt. Even when the foreign nations are ready to provide the list of persons having bank accounts in their land, they don't want the same. This attitude gives confidence for the corrupt to invest their unaccountable money in the safe tax heavens. Once out of the land, it is hard to bring this money back. This is because in most of the tax havens, tax evasion is not a criminal offence (Dhiraj and Sandheep 2011: 19). So even for getting information about the listed money, it needs to be presented a case of money laundering, corruption or drug running which is much harder than straight forward tax evasion case. The investigation becomes complicated and expensive in nature. So without political support all efforts will flop, as the big fishes usually relies on that a support.

Corruption is an anti-social activity and when it comes to the defence forces it becomes an anti-national activity. Whoever does such a crime should be considered as anti-national because in one way or other they are threatening the existence and integrity of the nation. So corruption needs to be curbed with an iron hand. Only a combined effort with the help of the academia, civil society, bureaucrats, politicians and the judiciary can produce the results. An apolitical approach to corruption is not advisable and the political leadership needs to take a bold stand. It is the duty of the higher bureaucrats and the common man to pressurise the political ministers to have such a stand. The corrupt should be severely punished and their properties should be attached. Imprisonment should not end with Sukram or Bengaru Lakshman and attachment of property should not end with Jaganmohan Reddy or the Joshis, it should go on to all the corrupt. Suitable penalty measures should be taken against companies, including cancellation of deal together with blacklisting of them, when charges of corruption are clear. Only such stringent steps can deter companies and persons from engaging in corrupt practices. Above all the vigilance of the public is an important factor in curbing corruption.

End Notes

1. Statistics provided by the Director General of Commercial Intelligence and Statistics (DGCI & S) indicate that the number of drug companies have come down from 252 in 1996-97 to 205 in 2002-03. The Organisation of Pharmaceutical Producers of India (OPPI) is currently having a membership of 72 companies. The Herfindahl Index of Concentration doubled from 0.008 in 1996-97 to 0.016 in 2002-03 (CMIE 2004) implying that the competition is slowing down. This represents the formation of a cartel in pharmaceutical industry.

References

Anupama, Katakam (2012): "Towards Trial," *India Today*, 29(14), July 27, 24-26.

—— (2010): "House of Scandal," *India Today*, 27(24), July 14-27, December 3, 28-32.

Baksi, Soham; Pinaki, Bose and Manish, Pandey (2009): "The Impact of Liberalisation on Bureaucratic Corruption," *Journal of Economic Behaviour and Organisation*, 72, 214-24.

CMIE (2004): *Corporate Finance*, Centre for Monitoring Indian Economy, Mumbai.

Deccan Herald (2011): "Tainted IAS Couple Worth Rs 360 crore," *Deccan Herald*, January 19, http://www.deccanherald.com/content/130426/tainted-ias-officer-couple-worth .html accessed on 30-01-2013.

Dhiraj, Nayyar and Sandheep, Unnithan (2011): "The Great Indian Robbery," *India Today*, XXXVI(5), January 31, 18-24.

DNA (2010): "CBI Books 2 Senior Home Ministry Officials for Corruption," *Daily News Analysis*, April 28, http://www.dnaindia.com/india/report_cbi-books-2-senior-home-ministry-officials-for-corruption_1376737 accessed on 30-01-2013.

Express News (2012a): "Opposition Demands JPC Probe into Walmart Lobbying," *The New Indian Express*, Kochi, December.

—— (2012b): "Congress the Richest Party, Others Catching Up," *The New Indian Express*, Kochi, September.

—— (2012c): "Rs 2,490-cr Tax-free Income!," *The New Indian Express*, Kochi, December.

—— (2012d): "Probe into Donations for Cong, BJP: EC," *The New Indian Express*, Kochi, October.

—— (2012e): "Corruption Eats Away the Steel Frame," *The New Indian Express*, Kochi, April.

Financial Express (2012): "CBI Probes a Record Number of Babus," *The Financial Express*, August.

Gangadhar, Patil (2012): "Of 89 Sanctions to Prosecute IAS Officers, 55 Just Against 2," *Daily News and Analysis*, November 12, http://www.dnaindia.com/india/report_of-89-sanctions-to-prosecute-ias-officers-55-just-against-2_1763466 accessed on 14-12-2012.

Gurumurthy, S. (2009): *Business Standard*, New Delhi, April 22. (0:41 IST).

India Today (2010): "MHA Official Leaked Secrets for Sex, Money; Aide Arrested," *IndiaToday.in*, November 23, http://indiatoday.intoday.in/story/mha-official-leaked-secrets-for-sex-money-aide-arrested/1/120922.html accessed on 30-01-2013.

Indian Express (2011): "MHA Joint Secy Under CBI Scanner for Graft," *The Indian Express*, http://www.indianexpress.com/news/mha-joint-secy-under-cbi-scanner-for-graft/795103 accessed on 30-01-2013.

Jitha, S.R. (2010): "Bureaucratic Corruption in a Liberalised Society," *Pragati*, 4(111), Jan-March, 45-53.

Kerala Kaumudi (2012a): "2G Adhikarathinte Maravile Kodiya Azhimathi," *Kerala Kaumudi*, Kochi, February.

—— (2012b): "2G: 122 Licensukal Supremekodahi Radhakki," *Kerala Kaumudi*, Kochi, February.

—— (2012c): "India-kkarude Kallapana Nikshepam 24,50,000-kodi," *Kerala Kaumudi*, Kochi, February.

Mathrubhumi (2013): "1100 Sarkar Jeevanakarkku Ethire Anveshanam: Vigilance Director," *Mathrubhumi*, Thiruvananthapuram, February.

MIB (2011): "Interaction with Newspaper Editors," *Ministry of Information and Broadcasting*, Government of New Delhi.

Outlook (2011): "CWG Deal: Shunglu Panel Indicts Lalli, Aruna Sharma," *OutlookIndia.com*, February 1, http://news.outlookindia.com/items.aspx?artid=710466 accessed on 30-01-2013.

Priya, Ranjan Das (2008): "Slow Down My Foot, Economy is in the Black," December 18, http://www.mydigitalfc. com/economy/slowdown-my-foot-economy-black-483.

PTI (2012a): "IAS Officer Pradeep Shukla Arrested by CBI in NRHM Scam," *Business Standard*, May 10, http://www.business-standard.com/article/pti-stories/ias-officer-pradeep-shukla-arrested-by-cbi-in-nrhm-scam-112051000348_1.html accessed on 30-01-2013.

PTI (2012b): "Maharashtra: Deputy Collector's Assets Worth Rs 118 crore Unearthed," *Daily Bhaskar*, March 15, http://daily.bhaskar.com/article/MAH-OTC-maharashtra-deputy-collectors-assets-worth-rs-118-crore-unearthed-2975931.html accessed on 30-01-2013.

Rahul, Tripathi (2012): "CBI Probes a Record Number of Babus," *Screen India*, August 27, http://screen. indianexpress.com/news/cbi-probes-a-record-number-of-babus/993485/0 accessed on 30-01-2013.

Sanakan, V.S. (2012): "Kalkarippadangal Kittiya Kambanikal Rashtriya Partikalkku Kodikal Ozhuki," (M) *Kerala Kaumudi*, Kochi, September.

Srinivasa, Rao (2011): "Andhra Pradesh Mining Scam: CBI Arrests IAS Officer But Spares Minister," *Mail Today*, November 29, http://indiatoday.intoday.in/story/andhra-mining-scam-cbi-arrests-ias-officer-spares-minister/1/161944.html accessed on 30-01-2013.

Sujay, Mehdudia (2012): "Now, Coal Burns Rs 186,000-crore Hole in Exchequer," *The Hindu*, Thiruvanant-hapuram, August.

Sunday Express (2012): "Mother of all Scams: Rs 3.78 lakh crore," *The New Sunday Express*, Kochi, August.

The Hindu (2012a): "Supreme Court Scraps UPA's 'Illegal' 2G Sale," *The Hindu*, New Delhi, February 2, http://www.thehindu.com/news/national/article2853159.ece accesses on 10-02-2012.

TOI (2012a): "CBI Books IAS Officer in CWG Case," *The Times of India*, August 28, http://articles. timesofindia. indiatimes.com/2012-08-28/india/33449073_1_ias-officer-eks-contract-sports-ministry accessed on 30-01-2013.

——(2012b): "Senior IAS Officer Held in Rs 125-cr Scam," *The Times of India*, February 2, http://articles.timesofindia. indiatimes.com/2012-02-02/kolkata/31016809_1_ias-officer-pratap-biswal-bharat-inmate accessed on 30-01-2013.

Vishwas, Kumar (2012): "Judgment Vindicate CAG Report," *The New Indian Express*, Kochi, February.

—— (2011): "Spectre of Trial," *The New Indian Express*, Kochi, October.

Yatish, Yadav (2012): "Action Against 70 IAS Officers for not Filing Asset Info," *The New Indian Express*, Kochi, November.

10

Bureaucracy and Human Rights

Human Rights are the basic rights. These rights are inherent to all human beings, whatever be the nationality, place of residence, sex, national or ethnic origin, colour, religion, language, or any other status. All are equally entitled to human rights without any discrimination. So, Human Rights are those rights which are inherent in our nature and without which one cannot live as a human being (Daren 2005: 399). Equality and Justice are at the heart of all human rights. It includes adequate and decent food, water, health, freedom from slavery, fair treatment under law, shelter etc. All these rights are interrelated, interdependent and indivisible. These rights enable a person to develop his personality and lead a decent life on earth. Under the shadow of human rights all people are entitled not to starve, not to suffer from preventive disease, to have opportunity to better their economic condition, to have access to knowledge and information and to decide on anything that affect their life (Anita and Sriprapha 2003: 4).

These basic human needs and values are at the foundation of universal ideas of human rights and which is described in Article (2) of the Universal Declaration of Human Rights (UDHR), which states:

> "Everyone is entitled to all the rights and freedoms set forth in the Declaration, without distinction of any kind such as race, colour, sex, language, religion, political or other opinion, national or social origins, property, birth or other status. Furthermore, no distinction shall be made on the basis of the political, jurisdictional or international status of the country or territory to which a person belongs, whether it be independent, trust, non self-governing or under any other limitation of sovereignty."

Bureaucracy is an important instrument of the state to administer its people and to manage the affairs. It consists of officials at all levels, who are expected to carry out the day-to-day administration without any fear or favour. The duty of the bureaucracy is to understand the problems of the people and to create a balanced socio-economic and political environment, so that citizens could lead a meaningful life. Human Rights means all human beings have the right to live with dignity at all times regardless of these legal or political statue. The state is supposed to be the most important protector of human rights as they are the solemn reminder that a state owes to its citizens. Bureaucracy being the instrument of state therefore is the forerunner in the protection of human rights (Jitha 2011: 143), which is stated in the Universal Declaration of Human Rights, in various articles like:

> *Government officials must be accountable for their actions through clearly formulated and transparent process, and more particularly the legitimacy of a government must be regularly established through a well-defined open process of public choice* (Article 21).
>
> *The safety and security of citizens must be assured* (Article 3 and 5); *The rule of law must prevail and citizens must be protected from arbitrary or capricious actions by public authorities* (Articles 7, 8, 9, 10 and 11).
>
> *Everyone has the right to an adequate standard of living and necessities of life which should be provided for the benefits of all citizens in inequitable manner* (Articles 22, 23, 24 and 25).
>
> *Freedom of association and expression of opinion must be permitted and information must be readily amiable to ensure accountability* (Articles 19 and 20).

Basically, bureaucrats are human rights protectors. They do this in their capacity as administrators in various departments. Whichever be the department they works in, their actions have a direct or indirect impact on human rights. So the role of bureaucrats in the protection of human rights is manifold and multi-dimensional. Laws, Declarations, Conventions, and Protocols, etc., do not solve the problems, unless they are implemented promptly. The agency to implement this is the bureaucracy. This makes them the important protectors of human rights.

Development is a means of protecting or ensuring human rights. Development and human rights are interdependent. It is the UN General Assembly Declaration on the Right to Development, 1986, that links human rights and development. The declaration defines *development as a comprehensive economic, social, cultural and political process, which aims at the constant improvement of the well-being of the entire population and of all individuals on the basis of their active, free and meaningful participation in development and in the fair distribution of benefits resulting from it.* The declaration reaffirms development as a universal and inalienable right and an integral part of fundamental human rights. Anitha Cheria (2003: 25) observes, the definition of development by the UN General Assembly Declaration on the Right to Development makes several significant points and reflects several aspects as to the content of the right to development. First of all, all human rights and fundamental freedoms are indivisible and interdependent; second, the participation of all individuals in development must be active, free and meaningful; third, development should be seen in the context of basic needs and social justice; fourth, it emphasises both national policies and programmes and international cooperation.

By interpreting the definition of development by the UN General Assembly, and the observations of Anitha Cheria we can substantiate that:

1. As all human rights and fundamental freedoms are indivisible and interdependent, equal attention and consideration should be given to the promotion, protection and implementation of all human rights. This is because absence of one right can scuttle the other. In this sense civil, political, economic, social and cultural rights have equal importance.
2. Development demands participation of all sections of the society especially with regard to the formulation of developmental goals and activities. This is for ensuring inclusion in the process of development. Women must have an active role in the development process. Education will enable all persons to participate freely so prime importance should be given to education in the process of development.
3. Development and social justice are inseparable. The benefits of development should trickle down to all and there should be no concentration of benefits in few hands. Social justice speaks of a society that offers individuals and groups fair treatment and an impartial share in the benefits of societal development by rejecting monopolies, special privileges and other exclusionary social barriers to economic self-reliance (Reinhart 2009: 48).

At this points the increased responsibility of the state in the process of development for the protection of human rights. As this task is done by the bureaucrats it becomes their responsibility, which can be numbered as follows:

1. To improve the general well being of the entire population, of all individuals from all sections of the society.
2. To create equality of opportunity for all in their access to basic resources, education, health services, food, housing, employment and the fair distribution of income.

3. To ensure and encourage the free and active participation of all the individuals especially the women and weaker sections of the society.
4. To develop a human rights-based approach to development in which control over their destiny must be returned to the people themselves.
5. Developmental activities should be planned in such a way that its burden will be shared depending upon one's capacity to hold it. Proper measures to rehabilitate the victims should be taken in advance of displacement.
6. To distribute the benefits of development to all in a fair fashion, such that instead of tricking down from the top it should spring up from the bottom.
7. Special care should be given to the needs of the indigenous population, marginalised, helpless, women and children so as to ensure their inclusion in the process of development.
8. To curb concentration of wealth, monopolies, exclusionary social barriers, corruption, and all sort of such activities that are stumbling blocks in the path of equity and justice in society, and development of the nation.
9. To promote and foster self-reliance among the individuals and creation of a self-reliant economy for the nation.
10. To create an atmosphere in which citizens can enjoy their rights in a free manner commensurate with the development of the nation.

From long back development and human rights are moving in dichotomous direction instead of going together. The gap between development and human rights is widely prevalent. Quite often development is pursued at the cost of human rights. A large number of indigenous population, peasants and the like are displaced in the name of development, that too without providing adequate compensation and rehabilitation packages. Here the development of one is pursued at the expense of human rights of the other. The sufferers are not becoming the beneficiaries of development under such conditions. So what is occurring is the accumulation of wealth in the hands of a few by dispossessing many from their spaces and resources, a process that David Harvey (2003) calls as "Accumulation by Dispossession." The age of globalisation and free-market fundamentalism further increases the gap between development and human rights. When the rich and educated becomes the beneficiaries of development, the burden of it heavily falls upon the common man.

When development lacks its inclusive character it becomes a human rights violation. *Inclusion is needed when sharing the burden for development and in sharing the benefits out of development.* But the present day development totally neglects this principle. We can see that in India vast majority are deprived of the benefits of development. When an overwhelming

836 million people or 77 per cent of the total population live on a per capita consumption of less than Twenty Rupees a day (Argun Sengupta 2007) we cannot claim inclusion. Poverty has become a grave issue in Indian society. To a great extent, though not fully, the Public Distribution System (PDS) in India found a solution to that. But with the restructuring of the PDS system in 1997 in accordance with the policies of liberalisation, matters began to get upside down. The universal PDS was replaced with targeted PDS (TPDS), in which the populations were classified into above poverty line (APL) and below poverty line (BPL) and subsidised food were made eligible only to the BPL households. There occurred major mismatches between household's classification as APL and BPL and PDS became narrowly targeted. The result was that even the BPL holders were not provided adequate food grains. At the same time there occurred a steep increase in the price of food grains in the open market. Neither the politicians nor the bureaucrats did something effective to hold the market from staggering the price of food grains.

While on the one hand thousands are not getting adequate access to food grains, on the other hand million tonnes of food grains are getting damaged each year. Between 1997 and 2007, 1.83 lakh tonnes of wheat, 6.33 lakh tonnes of rice, 2.20 lakh tonnes of paddy and 111 lakh tonnes of maize were damaged in different FCI (Food Corporation of India) godowns (Hindustan Times 2010). In 2012, the amount of food grains that was damaged in the stock rooms of FCI in Kerala alone was 50,000 tonnes (Sunil kumar 2012: 1). Punjab, the food granary of India wasted over 70,000 tonnes of wheat in 2011 (Times Now 2012). In a country where food prices break the back of the common man, an estimated 231 million people go hungry every day, each minute, five Indians die of hunger - i.e., 7000 each day and 2.5 million people every year, this is criminal wastage. If the FCI officials have worked in a responsible manner this much damage could have been avoided. By providing better infrastructure to the godowns and by ensuring adequate movement of food grains from godowns to the fair shops, the damage could have been averted. This would have also ensured adequate quantity of food grains to the needy at a reasonable price from the fair shops together with a fair price for food grains in the open market.

Together with this, income inequality in India is rising at an unprecedented rate because the top 10 per cent of the population owns 52.9 per cent of the total wealth i.e. more than half of the nation's wealth (Manas 2010). Twenty years of globalisation in India has not trickled down the benefits of development to the bottom. If such was the case 77 per cent of the population wouldn't have been living with an income of less than 20 rupees a day, when India is having a GDP of 89.12 trillion rupees (Economic Survey 2012: 2). Year by year, or day by day the rich is becoming richer while the poor poorer. All this is due to the income re-concentration effect in the economy, favouring a few. The decline of agriculture, cottage and small scale industries, traditional indigenous sectors etc. affects the mean income of the poor and they are being forced to work in conditions that are not familiar to them. The large influx of migrant workers to Kerala from West Bengal, Bihar, Odisha is all due to this.

Here we can see only paradoxes of development. When the Planning Commission wants those below the poverty line to live with a per capita daily consumption of Rs. 28.65 in cities and Rs. 22.42 in rural areas (The Hindu 2012a: 14), its Deputy Chairman, Dr. Montek Singh Ahluwalia wants at least lakhs daily. *Kerala Kaumudi* (2012a: 12) quotes *Statesman News Service* reporting, Dr. Ahluvalia spending Rs 36.40 lakh for his four foreign trips in between the months of May and October in 2011. The average spending per day is Rs 2.02 lakh as he spent 18 days for his foreign trips during this period. In between 2004 and 2011 Dr. Ahluvalia has conducted 42 foreign trips, of which 23 were to America. In total he spent about 274 days in foreign countries during this period. It is to be noted that several of these trips are not connected with his duties as Deputy Chairman of the Planning Commission. Criticizing the wastage of public money, P. Sainath says, "it is hypocrisy to impose one approach on an impoverished people while practising another entirely different – for himself, with their money - public money" (The Hindu 2012b: 13). The other paradox is with regard to the construction of two toilets at the Planning Commission's Office, New Delhi, at an expense of Rs 35 lakh, with Rs five lakh on restricted access door (Aman 2012: 1; Kerala Kaumudi 2012b: 12). When this is the case with Planning Commission, what the government has given for the construction of toilets in rural areas for a household was Rs 4,600, during that time (The Hindu 2012c: 15). Now the amount has been raised to Rs 10000.

Displacement is another development induced human rights violation in India. Large tracts of lands have been acquired in many parts of the nation in the name of Special Economic Zones (SEZ), the once watchword of development in the neo-liberal era. It is very difficult to calculate the total area of land that has been acquired all over India. Cold blooded murders were occurred at Odisha, Haryana, Uttar Pradesh, Andhra Pradesh, Madhya Pradesh and West Bengal in the name of SEZ. Violence reached its zenith with the Singur and Nandigram incident where the Communist Government under Buddhadeb Bhattacharya led the massive violence. In Nandigram chemical hub of Salim Group would have required the acquisition of over 14,000 acres (57 km^2) of land and Tata in Singur needed 997 (4.03 km^2) acres of land. Both are multi-year crop lands. Because of stiff resistance from the public the government and the companies were forced to withdraw from the project, together with this it ended the 30 year long spell of communist government in West Bengal. The rest of India also witnessed strong protest against the compulsory and violent acquisition of lands, most of which are bloody in nature. In November 2006, farmers from the Jamnagar District in Gujarat moved the High Court of Gujarat and later even the Supreme Court to challenge the setting-up of a 10,000-acre (approx. 4,000-ha) SEZ by Reliance Infrastructure. They alleged that the acquisition of large tracts of agricultural land in the villages of the district not only violated the Land Acquisition Act of 1894, but was also in breach of the public interest (Jona 2008: 73, 74). This together with the Singur and Nandigram issue in West Bengal led the Government to "consider" putting a ceiling on the maximum land area that can be acquired for multi-product zones and decide to "go slow" in approving SEZs.

Protest against land acquisition took place in over 40 districts in 17 states in the past three years. Tens of thousands of acres were taken over with the farmers and the dependants on land being given meagre compensation and no rehabilitation measures. The Ganga Expressway, a 1047-km stretch which seeks to link Greater Noida in western Uttar Pradesh (UP) with Ballia in eastern UP requires more than 10,000 hectares of land and will displace 5,000 villages. Similar is the case with the Yamuna Expressway in Greater Noida (UP), where about 6000 acres of land is being acquired by infrastructure company Jaiprakash Associates (Vandana Siva 2011). The hi-tech city associated with the Yamuna expressway is expected to affect seven lakh people of 334 villages in six districts of UP (Ajoy 2011a: 10). The East-West Corridor and North-South Corridors are the other mega road projects under the National Highway Authority of India that induce massive displacement. The total land acquired for the 3000 kilometers East-West four-lane Corridor connecting Silchar in Assam with Porbander in Gujarat is 1,825.68 hectares. Schools have also been evicted for the project (Sushanta 2011: 18).

States like Odisha, Chhattisgarh and Jharkhand with rich mineral resources are becoming the horror grounds of displacement to the tribals and peasants. POSCO and Tata's Greenfield in Odisha, Vedanta in Chhattisgarh are the mega projects that induced massive displacement. When POSCO necessitates 3,693 hectares of land (Venkatesan 2012: 35, 36), the Greenfield wants 2,000 hectares (Purnima 2012: 32) and Vedanta 1,070 hectares of land. According to the estimates of government agencies itself, a total of 1.71 lakh hectares of agricultural land have been diverted for non-agricultural purpose in Chhattisgarh. In Madhya Pradesh, 150 companies have been allowed to acquire 2.44 lakh hectares of land out of which 1.94 hectares are private land acquired from farmers (Venkitesh 2011: 8). It is without adequate compensation these lands have been "encroached." For example, in the case of Ganga expressway in UP, what the government offered was Rs 880 for a square metre in Tapal which is near to Delhi and Noida where the market rate was over Rs 25,000 for a square metre. Other projects also follow the same line. In Chhattisgarh, the displaced had got only between Rs 7,000 and Rs 25,000 an acre from Vedanta (Ajoy 2011b: 10). There can be seen huge differences between the market value and the amount given as compensation. The issue is that once displaced it is hard to get placed in a better area.

A study about displacement in India shows that it is nothing but, *state sponsored terrorism* in the name of development. *State and its agencies are becoming the worst human rights violators*. The human rights principles associated with development are blatantly violated across the nation. First and foremost one is that *these projects are against the interest of those who are affected.* Not only are they given inadequate compensation but also deprived of their source of livelihood. For a common man in Assam or in any other states he cannot use the expressways because they are toll plazas, similar is the case with hi-tech cities. Alienation of the poor can be heavily seen in these projects. So long as the construction work is going on, the labour of the masses is needed, once it is over they will be deprived access when the barrier of finance comes in. So *the benefits of development are not reaching the one who suffered its burden.* The benefits exclusively go to some sections of the society, who haven't lost anything for the project. Thus *the principle of inclusion goes off the show*. Together with all these we can see *a phenomenon of washing away the classes of peasants, agricultural labourers and tribals to a single class known as have-nots or in the practical sense slum-dwellers, a bye product of accumulation by dispossession*.

Land acquisition everywhere went on a bullet speed but rehabilitation and compensation is having only tortoise speed. It is without the consent of the holders this much land has been taken away. The BSP government under Mayawati used its emergency powers to acquire land from Greater Noida to Agra for the Yamuna expressway project (Ajoy 2011a: 10). The villagers in Odisha claim that the public hearings on the Collectorate premises which declared overwhelming support from the villages for the project (POSCO) were stage-managed (Purnima 2012: 33). Here the finger points to the District Collector, the top bureaucrat of the district. District administration, revenue and police officials are behaving in a brutal manner with regard to displacement. This is not an exemption even to the cent per cent literary state Kerala. There too bureaucrats behave like agents of some vested interests. Moolampally in Kerala showcases the brutality of bureaucrats. It was in a very brutal manner that the special team under Ramadevi, Deputy Collector and Suseela Jacob, Special Tahsildar Land Acquisition, accompanied by a large police force demolished the houses of 10 families at Moolampilly. It was done not only without prior intimation but also by not giving any time for the households to remove their household articles. Brute force was something that was used to evict the families there, by destroying cooked foods, throwing away the books and study materials of students, a kind of utter barbarism by state force. In Kinallur, Kerala, the public including women and children were brutally lathicharged when they tried to stop the survey for a proposed four-lane road (Mathrubhumi 2010: 4).

Rehabilitation of victims or the affected is a big issue, either with regard to land acquisition or some other damages. The victims of Bhopal Gas Tragedy (1984) have been bitterly treated by the governments and its agencies. When all was set to help Warren Anderson go out of India nothing was done to protect the victims[1]. The Government of India and the State Government of Madhya Pradesh were aware that the Bhopal plant used hazardous substances and processes. There were also public warnings by the local media (Upendra 2012: 49) and by workers' unions in the plant about dangerous conditions at the plant, as well as several accidents, some fatal. Two years before the tragedy, i.e., on 1982 itself, Rajkumar Keswani, a local journalist wrote a series of articles in Hindi titled, "Bhopal in the edge of an volcano" predicting that a disaster was waiting to happen[2] (Gurumurthy 2010: 9). The state environmental board had recorded the presence of poisonous gases inside the plant to be in excess of permissible limits. Journalist Jyoti Punwani reports, "The plant's union had, in late 1982, written to the Union Home Minister and State Chief Minister about the spate of mishaps inside the plant" (Jyoti 2010: 10). Ignoring this warning the state government granted legal titles to thousands of people who had built homes around the plant site, just months before the accident. Nor did the government impose strict safety standards or press Union Carbide Company (UCC) to review safety mechanisms. Leave the politicians who act as the agents of the corporates, if any one officer of the environment board had done their duty, a catastrophe could have been avoided. It was their legal duty but they ignored it in front of the political and money power of US corporate Carbide.

The culpability of the Union Carbide doubles because it knew that the safety measures were not in place. When the safety loops came in picture on December 3, 1984, an estimated 10,000 or more died and around 5,00,000 suffered agonising injuries with disastrous effects (Upendra 2012: 49), because of the leakage of Methyl-Iso-Cynate from the factory. Despite this massive catastrophe, by mocking people, the government released UCC Chairman Anderson and allowed him to fly in a state aircraft to Delhi, from where he escaped to the US. The government also didn't press for a civil and criminal liability from the company. As if all was not enough, the government of India took away from the victims the right to represent them and vested itself with the exclusive right to represent victims by enacting the Bhopal Claims Act, 1985. Then in 1989 the government agreed to a settlement with Union Carbide Corporation (UCC) (Jyoti 2010: 10). In return for a modest and arbitrarily determined financial payment to victims, the settlement bestowed sweeping civil and criminal immunity on UCC, trading off its legal liability, excluding the victims of the disaster from shaping the end of the case. As all loopholes were set for the culprits to escape, despite the graveness of the tragedy the culprits got only two years imprisonment and a penalty of 1 lakh rupees. The verdict of the court on the case was disappointing as not only the punishment granted was meagre but also as there was no order for reinvestigating the case (Kerala Kaumudi 2010a: 1). Bhopal tragedy exposed beyond any doubt the incapability of country's legal system and the government itself in defending the human rights of Indian citizens against the culpability of foreign multi-nationals.

The payment of compensation to victims did not, however, begin until 1992 and involved numerous problems, including payment of inadequate sums, delayed payments, arbitrary rejection or downgrading of claims. Excessive bureaucracy in the claims process led to the entry of middlemen and rampant corruption, further reducing the amount of compensation money that victims were able to finally get. In 1994, the Indian Council for Medical Research (ICMR) stopped all further research on the medical effects of the Bhopal disaster without explanation. The full results of the research carried out and the data with the ICMR have yet to be published. The state government efforts to provide rehabilitation have proven largely ineffective. The poor quality of the health care system has meant that most survivors have had to spend most of their compensation money on private medical treatment. The hospitals set for the treatment of gas victims provide only symptomatic treatment. The social and economic rehabilitation measures have been poorly implemented and have failed to lessen the impoverishment of already economically vulnerable survivors. Those orphaned and widowed by the gas leak are in a particularly precarious condition. Government and its agencies have the primary responsibility for protecting the human rights in the community endangered by the activities of companies, such as those employing hazardous technology.

The victims of Endosulfan in Kadsaragod are also no better than that of Bhopal victims. Even after two decades of the worst crisis, the victims were not given proper care and attention by the government. The problems that started with breathing problems, irritation in eyes, cough and skin diseases escalated to genetic, epilepsy, cancer and various unnamed diseases. Three decades after the issue, the National Human Rights Commission in 2012 had recommended giving Rs five lakhs each to 24,536 victims, who were seriously ill or mentally retarded. It had also recommended giving Rs three lakhs each to other kind of victims (Express News 2012a). So, years after a very few got this paltry amount which couldn't meet even a single share of their medical expenses. Many haven't got the full amount awarded by the commission. As the government hospitals were not equipped to treat these victims, they were forced to depend upon private hospitals where out-of-pocket expenditure is very high. Even, the Government of Kerala doesn't have a proper list containing the name of all endosulfan victims. Such is the case with the Plachimada Victims too. The water supply project promised for the victims years back is not implemented till date (January 30, 2103), citing technical reasons.

Getting things done without delay itself is a way of protecting human rights (Jitha 2010: 68). We know that Justice delayed is justice denied. Common man often complains about the cold response of the bureaucrats towards their problems. In the present day the influential are always going for short cuts and are trying to infringe the basic human rights of the individual but common man are tied with red-tapism and hierarchical delay to enjoy their basic rights. Laws for the common man and shortcuts for the influential are the reality now-a-days. The administrative procedure is so complicated and cumbersome that the file of the common man needs to climb up and down the bureaucratic ladder. So to get something done from an office one has to go there a number of times. For the poor this is an additional burden. For example, repeat visits to the district headquarters to get registered or to get a card meant loss of wage or opportunity, apart from “harassment”. Additional costs are involved like the “travel cost” for visiting the point and cost of meals, especially if it is distant from the place of residence. The TII-CMS India Corruption Study 2007 conducted among the BPL households points out some examples for the serviccs for which three or more visits were reported that includes: as in-patient for getting bed (29 per cent), electricity bill related (37 per cent), land records (23 per cent), filing a complaint with police (46 per cent), bill payment of water (45 per cent), plot/house allotment (69 per cent), for getting selected or job card in NREGA (56 per cent), to open new account in Bank/Post Office (37 per cent) and for new ration card (37 per cent) (TII-CMS 2008: 8). All these cases involve violation of human rights. The number of repeat visits cannot be altogether avoided but it needs to be minimised, not only to avail the basic services but also to enjoy human rights.

Corruption is more likely where and when the number of visits a citizen has to make to get a particular service is more. Corruption is no doubt a human rights violation. The Supreme Court of India has validated this argument through its observation that “corruption is only a punishable offence but also undermines human rights, indirectly violating them, and systematic corruption, is a human rights’ violation in itself, as it leads to systematic economic crimes.” (Hindustan Times 2012). The court made this observation while setting aside an order of the Bombay high court that suspended a two-year jail term imposed on the superintendent of Central Excise department for corruption. The court in its observation clearly states the relationship between human rights and corruption and exhorts that curbing corruption is a necessity for ensuring human rights. We can see that corruption in its multi-dimensional aspects is a violation of human rights.

When payment for services becomes the rule, denial of services to those who cannot pay gets accepted in a corrupted atmosphere. This is dangerous as vast majority of the population will be denied of the services unavoidable for them. When corruption plays down merit it puts its damage on the society in the form of lack of efficient, honest and hardworking personnels. When it comes to industrial firms and so on, the number of pollutants or unaccountable ones will spring up. Its damage on the society is direct and harsh. Together with eating up the resources of the nation, corruption in its various forms as tax evasions and hawalas will reduce the capacity of the state to invest in public welfare. Lack of resources will plague the attempts of the state to initiate measures for the creation of infrastructure, spread of education and health care, improvements in the field of science and technology, welfare schemes and more than that affects enhancing the security of the nation itself. This in a big way affects the development programmes of the state and there by human rights.

The most important human right that needs to be protected now-a-days is the human right to water. This is an urgent necessity not only because water is needed for sustaining life on earth but also as lack of water and sanitation clearly has an impact on the enjoyment of other human rights, such as the rights to education, health and work, which form an essential basis for poverty elimination and human development as well. Even though such was the importance of right to water, it lacked a universally applicable legal binding document for a long time and this led to the gross abrogation of human right to clean and safe drinking water with indigenous people as the victims of water theft, contamination of water on their territories and forcible displacement from their land and watersheds (Reinhart 2012: 48). At the same time many nations have legally recognised the right to water as an essential and inalienable right. South Africa included water as a human right in its constitution (1996) and is first among various nations that recognised the human right to water. Ethiopia, Ecuador, Kenya, Bolivia and Dominican Republic followed suit.

The interference of judiciary can be seen in many nation states for ensuring the right to water. India has to its credit the largest number of jurisprudence regarding the environmental aspects of the constitutional right to life. The Supreme Court of India, in various cases interpreted Article 21, expanding its ambit to include Right to Safe Drinking Water, Right to Health and Clean Environment, there by establishing a clear and straight relationship between fundamental rights and environmental rights (protection). The Article 21 of the Indian Constitution reads that *No person shall be deprived of his life or personal liberty except according to procedure established by law.* In *Attakoya Thangal vs. Union of India*, the Court held that "right to sweet water and the right to free air are attributes of right to life" and in *Subash Kumar Case,* the Court said that right to life includes the right to enjoyment of pollution free water and air for full enjoyment of life (John *et al.* 2004: 47). The Supreme Court held in *Virendra Gour and Others vs. State of Haryana* (1995), that "environmental, ecological, air, water pollution, etc., should be regarded as amounting to violation of Article 21." The *Narmada Bachao Andolan vs. Union of India* (AIR 1991) was a landmark in the field of legal decisions, where the Supreme Court recognised the relationship between the quality of human environment and the enjoyment of basic human rights:

> Water is the basic need for the survival of human beings and is part of right to life and human rights as enshrined in Article 21 of the Constitution of India. ...it is a matter of great concern that even after half a century of freedom, water is not available to all citizens even for their basic drinking necessity violating human rights resolution of UNO and Article 21 of the Constitution of India.

Right to water got a legally binding status when the United Nations recognised it as an important human right. Earlier in 2002, the Economic and Social Council in its General Comment No. 15, interpreted Articles 11 and 12 of the International Covenant on Economic, Social and Cultural Rights so as to include right to water as pre-requisite for the realisation of other human rights, and confirmed the right to water in international law (ECOSOC 2002). But there was no obligation on state parties to implement the covenant's provision immediately. On July 28, 2010, the United Nations General Assembly adopted a Resolution 64/292[3] which acknowledges that clean drinking water and sanitation are integral to the realisation of all human rights and calls on States and International Organisations to provide financial resources, build capacity and transfer technology, particularly to developing countries, in scaling up efforts to provide safe, clean, accessible and affordable drinking water and sanitation for all (UN News Centre 2010). Two months later, in September, the UN Human Rights Council (2010) adopted a resolution affirming that water and sanitation are human rights — *the human right to safe drinking water and sanitation is derived from the right to an adequate standard of living and is inextricably related to the highest attainable standard of physical and mental health, as well as the right to life and human dignity*. The Council specified that right to safe drinking water and sanitation are part of international law and reaffirmed that states have the primary responsibility for the realisation of all human rights. This is an important step as state parties to the ICESCR can no longer deny their responsibility to provide safe water and sanitation for all individuals. The UN Declaration got universal acceptance and judiciary too accepted its sanctity.[4]

With the recognition of right to water, three obligations are imposed upon the states. The first one is the *Obligation to Respect*, where by the state must refrain from any action or policy that interferes with the enjoyment of the human right. This means that no one should be denied access to water because of the inability to pay. No government now has the right to remove existing services, as the government of Botswana did to the Kalahari Bushmen, or as authorities in Michigan of United States did to ten of thousands of residents when they cut off their water supply because they could not afford to pay the rising water bills. Under the *Obligation to Protect*, the state is obliged to prevent third parties from interfering with the enjoyment of the human right. It sounds that the state should protect the local communities from pollution and inequitable extraction of water by corporations (or governments). The third one is the *Obligation to Fulfill*, where by the state is required to adopt any additional measures directed towards the realisation of the right. This demands the extension of public water and sanitation facilities to those communities and people not covered now on account of their inability to pay (ECOSOC 2002; Barlow 2011: 15, 16, 17; Reinhart 2012: 56). All the above said obligations form the responsibility of the bureaucracy in each domestic system.

The Human Right to Water suggests that each person needs 20-50 litres of safe freshwater a day to ensure their basic needs for drinking, cooking and cleaning (UN-Water 2010). The water supplied must be clean and safe and should be of an acceptable colour, odour and taste for each personal or domestic use and must be accessible to every human being within the vicinity of less than 1000 metres. The charges associated with securing water must be affordable that they should cost no more than three per cent of the average family income (UN-Water 2011). Scarcity of water and its commodification are becoming the major stumbles in the path of realisation of right to safe drinking water. Already fresh water is a scarce resource as the total usable freshwater supply for eco-systems and humans is less than one per cent. This amount too is fast depleting due to increased pollution. The world's rivers, the single largest renewable water resource for humans and a crucible of aquatic biodiversity, are in a crisis of ominous proportions. Adding to this is the global climate change that on the one hand shrinks the fresh water resources through serious droughts and pollutes the same on the other hand through floods, storms, cyclones and the like. The circle of water crisis is completed by the commodification of water.

Commodification is a greatest enemy of human rights. Commodification encloses the commons and makes them private goods, the access to which is determined by the laws of market. Application of market principles in water supply, known as *market environmentalism* has resulted in the pricing of water, that too at a height unreachable to the common man, denying access to the poor. That happened in Tombel, Bolivia, Ghana, Uruguay, Michigan, Wisconsin etc. In Tombel as a result of privatisation of water supply, the price of water rose dramatically from 7.7 FCFA/m^3 in 1963 to 70.5 FCFA/m^3 in 1971 and to 129 FCFA/m^3 in 1982. By April 1982 there occurred a steep rise to 225 FCFA/m^3 (Ben 2005: 297, quoted from *Cameroon Tribune*, 13 January 1982; 18 August 1982). Water rates jacked up by nearly 35 per cent in Cochabamba after the entry of Bechtel Corporation. Families with monthly incomes of around $ 100 have seen their water bills jump up to $ 20 per month (Barlow and Clarke 2002: 155). After seven years of water privatisation in Manila, Philippines, under a Suez company (Maynilad Water) contract, water rates increased in some neighbourhoods by 400 to 700 per cent (Global Exchange 2010). In Argentina, Suez charged high consumer rates and cut off water access for citizens unable to pay (Robbins 2003: 1078), leaving those most in need without access to a life-sustaining natural resource. Corporate exploitation resulted in the depletion of water reserve and environmental pollution, affecting not only the present generation but also the coming ones in Plachimada, Michigan and many other areas. Water quality seriously declined in Colombia, Alberta, Grenoble, USA and in Canada. Commodification thus is against sustainable development also.

Drawing out from the three *Obligations to Respect, Protect and Fulfill* with the recognition of human right to water, the role of bureaucracy with regard to ensuring it includes *the protection of fresh water sources, extension of water supply to all and resisting commodification of water*. The first duty goes hand with environmental conservation. As water is not something that can be created in a laboratory for massive consumption all efforts should be made to preserve it. The India Infrastructure Report 2011 points out water pollution as a serious problem in India as almost 70 per cent of its surface water resources and a growing percentage of its groundwater reserves are contaminated by biological, toxic, organic, and inorganic pollutants. Remaining freshwater sources like river basins, lakes, ponds, streams, wetlands, glaciers etc. are in the risk of pollution or extinction. Pollutants and pesticides are brimming the fresh water sources. Not only the major river systems like Ganga and Yamuna are polluted but also other river systems and its tributaries. The Performance Audit of Water Pollution in India done by the CAG during 2011-12 shows that rivers like Gomti, Godavari, Musi, Cauvery, Cooum, Mahananda, Khan, Kshipra, Vaigai, Chambal, Rani Chu, Mandovi, Sabarmati, Subarnarekha, Bhadra/Tungabhadra, Pennar, Pamba, Betwa, Krishna, Sutlej, etc., continue to be plagued by high levels of organic pollution, low level of oxygen availability for aquatic organisms and bacteria, protozoa and viruses which have faecal-origin and which cause illnesses. These rivers are the lifeline of India and its States and people depend on them not just for water but also for livelihood.

Despite more than 27 years of implementation of programmes, including the Water, Prevention and Control of Pollution Act, 1974, to control pollution, water in our rivers remains critically polluted. In many cases, these sources have been rendered unsafe for human consumption as well as for other activities, such as irrigation and industrial needs. India's 14 major, 55 minor and several hundred small rivers receive millions of litres of sewage, industrial and agricultural wastes. The most polluting source for rivers is the city sewage and industrial waste discharge. Presently, only about 10 per cent of the waste water generated is treated; the rest is discharged as it is into our water bodies. Due to this, pollutants enter rivers, lakes and groundwater. Scientific report from the Centre for Water Resources Development and

Management (CWRDM) on water quality of the rivers in the state of Kerala calls for immediate actions as even the relatively virgin rivers such as the Chalakkudy river and the Anjarakkandy river that have their origins in the pristine forests of Nelliampathy and Kannoth respectively have been found to be highly polluted. For the samples taken for the study, 81 per cent from Pampa basin were found to be bacteriologically contaminated and coloured and in the case of Chalakkudy river basins Ecoli was present in 70 per cent of groundwater samples during pre-monsoon and 62 per cent in post monsoon season. In the case of Anjarakkandy river basin, 85 per cent of ground water samples were found to be contaminated during pre-monsoon and 38 per cent in the post monsoon season (Reema 2011: 4). War timed efforts should be made to protect the fresh water sources because once extinct it is hard to recharge them.

Together with fresh water scarcity is increasing the population of India. As a result the per-capita water availability is also decreasing. In a Question Hour reply to Rajya Sabha, Water Resources Minister Pawan Kumar Bansal informed that the per capita availability of water in the country has declined to one-third in the past 65 years. The per capita availability of water in the country declined to 1545 cubic meters as per the 2011 census, compared to 1816 cubic meters as per the 2001 census (PIB 2012). By 2025 India will be in the list of countries with water stress, if things go like this. Lack of access to safe drinking water is one that haunts millions in our nation. As the Census of India 2011 shows only 32 per cent of total population has access to piped drinking water from treated source – 62 per cent in urban and 17.9 per cent in rural areas. When this is the case, instead of ensuring every one equitable access to water, the state is abandoning its responsibility of providing free and safe drinking water in favour of private for-profit corporate interest, by citing lack of finance to run the water supply project, a clear violation of the obligation to *protect and fulfill.* The disappearance of the traditional sources of water or its pollution, and inability to afford the high water rates set by the newly privatised water services; have forced many to rely on sources contaminated by their own untreated human waste as well as industrial poisons for drinking.

Commodification of water entered its rail in India with the sale of River Shenoth, Ganga and Bhavani (2003). The sale of Bhavani has been made by the government even while the state (Tamil Nadu) was reeling under severe drought, ground water levels have reached depths of over 1,000 feet, and water riots and water-related murders have become an everyday occurrence (IRC 2003). World Bank and Asian Development Bank are the agents of privatisation of water in India. To them, subsidising water as a public good will lead to wastage of the resource. The World Bank schemes works on the basis of user charges, full cost recovery and benefit principle. It has openly advised governments round the world, not to give any subsidies to ameliorate the increase in water tariffs (Barlow and Clarke 2002: 155). The Draft Water Policy of India, 2002 provided ample scope for the privatisation of water supply delivery systems in the nation and the New Draft Water Policy of 2012 vigorously advocates the market environmentalist principle in water supply. Section 7 of the policy says that *over and above the pre-emptive uses for sustaining life and eco-system, water needs to be treated as an economic good and therefore, may be priced to promote efficient use and maximising value from water.* Section nine says that *there should be a mechanism in every State to establish a water tariff system and fix the criteria for water charges based on the principle that the water charges shall reflect the full recovery of the cost of administration, operation and maintenance of water resources projects.* The Draft Water Policy of India 2012 not only failed to address the question of water security but also opening the doors of water supply across the country to domestic and foreign companies, by advocating corporatisation and private sector participation. This is a clear violation of the human right to water together with violation of judicial interpretation making right to water a fundamental right under Article 21 of the Indian Constitution (AIR 1991). A situation is emerging in which instead of providing assured drinking water, the right to purchase bottled water is being pushed in (Express News 2012b: 8), and it is dangerous.

By shedding the state run water supply system many states are now running the 'ambitious' *Jalanidhi Project* which is the re-emergence of the market model in the name of Community Driven Project under the assistance of the World Bank. Kerala is not an exemption to this[5]. Jalanidhi does not aim to cover all people, only those who demand it and are willing to pay 15 per cent of capital costs (of which at least half must be cash and the rest may be labour) and 100 per cent of Operation and Maintenance costs. The Beneficiary Groups have to deposit 15 per cent of the capital cost and the Grama Panchayat's shares 10 per cent and the rest 75 per cent by the World Bank. Where STs constitute more than five per cent of the population the beneficiary contribution is limited to 10 per cent, two per cent of the capital cost need to be paid as cash, and the rest can be contributed as labour (Jalanidhi 2010). The investment of the World Bank is one term and after that the beneficiary groups themselves have to meet the recurring costs of operation and maintenance. This normally will be a burden to the "consumers" of the project. Studies by the Kerala State Planning Board found that the average cost of water supply per household in each Panchayat varies from Rs 7112 to Rs 17410 and the poorest of the poor (10 per cent) who are unable to pay the beneficiary share of 15 per cent as stipulated in the Project are kept away from the benefit of project (Planning Board 2009: 129, 130). Like other World Bank projects, in Jalanidhi too non-state actors play a key role in the implementation and maintenance of the project. NGOs and private sector consultants have an important role in the project, from preparation of the project to getting administrative and technical sanction, supervision of work and preparation of bills. Once the project is over, the supporting NGOs will withdraw and beneficiary groups have to carry on the activities. Experiences round the world shows that similar projects in the long run, due to economic reasons, incapability of beneficiary groups, combined with the role of non-state actors, got privatised fully, denying common man access to free drinking water.

The World Bank project, which calls for demand driven investments, user charges, benefit principle and full cost recovery denies the common man human right to water. We are going to implement the same market principles that have been rejected by many nations of the world because of its grave havoc to humanity and the environment. When water becomes a commodity under law, denial of water because of economic reasons gets legitimised. In accordance with the policies of the World Bank and that of the Asian Development Bank, a vigorous attempt to lock up the public taps is going on around the nation. Advice has been given to all Local Self Government Institutions in Kerala to lock up the existing public taps and prefer individual household connections (Jayaprakash 2012). This has a hampering effect on the access to water and the worst affected are the tribals, slum-dwellers, and those who lives in colonies. When finance acts as a stumble in their path to access private connections they are forced to collect water from sources that are polluted, resulting in serious health hazards. So *a circular trap or padhmavyuha is going to be there for the common man i.e. on the one side, the government withdraws from its primary responsibility and in that gap private for-profit institutions emerge in the scene; on the other side with the shift from social equity to economic equity, only the financially sound can have access to water; at the same time the remaining public taps are going to be locked up; fresh water has become a scarce resource added up by severe droughts and pollution*. The burden of this will be high on women and children who fetch up water from long distances to meet household needs.

Water shortage affects agricultural production, industry and the whole economy too. The water foot print of agriculture is so high and increases with increase in the production of food grains both for consumption and for exports. It requires about 160 litres of water to produce 1 kg of potato, 900 litres to produce 1 kg of maize, 1300 litres to produce 1 kg of coconut, 1300 litres to produce 1 kg of barley and 4500 litres of water to produce 1 kg of rice. Water intensive crops, increased demand for cash crops and the number of agro-based industries changes the water consumption patterns. The shortage is to such an extent that even water is purchased for agricultural activities. Time demands a change in the cropping and irrigation pattern that is being followed from the very past. Drip irrigation can reduce the quantity of water needed to a large sum. Shortage of water affects the economy too because water plays an important role in world economy as a solvent for a wide variety of chemical substances and facilitates industrial cooling and transportation.

The role of water in world economy can be understood from the statistics that it takes 100 litres of water to produce 1 kg of paper, 1500 litres to produce 1 kg of sugar, 4500 litres to produce 1 tonne of cement, 20,000 litres of water to produce 1 tonne of steel and 40,000 litres to make a car.

Right to water has a security aspect also, as it is something affecting the life of individuals. This not only includes the physical security of one while accessing water but also the security of nation-states themselves. Scholars of international relations have expressed growing concerns about the possibility of militarised intrastate and interstate conflicts over environmental resources, particularly over shared water resources (Homer-Dixon 1999; Kahl 2006). If this comes true, as prophesied by Ismail Serageldin, former vice-president of the World Bank, the wars of the twenty-first century would be no doubt over water. Trans boundary river systems usually brings in problems with regard to its sharing, like the disputes between India and Pakistan with regard to the sharing of the waters of Indus, and that with Bangladesh regarding the Farakka. This conflicts or concerns can be seen within nation states themselves, like the sharing of the Cauvery water between Karnataka and Tamil Nadu. The dispute has brought the people of both states to the streets in many-a-times. The Mullaperiar also has a security aspect in India. While a dam collapse can wash away the life of thousands in Kerala, scarcity in supply can threaten the life of many in Tamil Nadu as a result of crop failure. Even though, nation states have not engaged in an armed conflict for water till now, direct conflicts can be seen within the systems. The Mullaperiar issue brought the Kerala-Tamil Nadu border similar to Wagah for many days. Human security in the future no doubt depends upon access to clean and safe water. All these shows that water issue is a hot bed that needs to be handled cautiously.

The track record of bureaucracy with regard to right to water is not good. Exemptions are there. Through the commoditisation of the commons, especially water, criminal negligence was made by the bureaucracy, not only in India but also in other parts of the world. Instead of cautioning the government about the ill-effects of water privatisation, what the bureaucracy has done was preparation of detailed plans for privatisation. The possibility of getting money makes bureaucracy chalk out plans for water privatisation. The best example of criminal negligence was the actions of Department of Water Resources at Plachimada (Coco-Cola bottling plant). They have not dared to conduct inspection at the factory site, even though the fact was known that Coco-Cola was violating the Kerala Ground Water Act. The decision of the Panchayat Director (IAS Officer), cancelling the order of Panchayat barring licence to the company is another example (Mathrubhumi 2005: 27, 28). Bureaucrats have not uttered a single word, when the Government sold River Ganga and River Bhavani to satisfy the corporate greed on 2003. Bureaucratic apathy failed to ensure safe drinking water to all. For example, the people of

Vagaman has complained about the illegal check dam constructed by a resort that enclosed the local river named *Narakakuzhi*, which has been the water source for 400 families. Even after one year of complaint to the District Collector and at the Secretariat to demolish the check dam that has been constructed illegally by the resort that too in the encroached government land, no action has been taken till date (January 25, 2013). Nearby there is another enclosure by a private resort that created an artificial lake for boating, by closing a tunnel that carries water to the Idukki Dam (Mangalam 2013: 17).

Instead of all these bureaucrats especially higher bureaucracy has a major role in the enforcement of right to water. If action starts from the top the bottom will be forced to act. They can do a lot to prevent pollution and for conserving the water sources. Mega water projects are unsustainable and not capable of ensuring water to all. Take the case of Japan Water Project in Kerala. The feasibility of this 2000 crore project is now in question because most of the identified water sources in the initial stage of the project have got dried up. What needed is water management at the local and its allocation. By maintaining ponds, streams and wetlands water crisis can be to a great extend prevented. Through rain water harvesting the ground water can be recharged and this will keep the water level up. The water resources department and the land use department can do yoemen service in this regard. Taking into consideration the seriousness of the problem, the civil servants have to initiate a *water literacy* programme, just like the literacy programme that has been initiated to remove illiteracy. The citizens should be made aware of the prudent management of water resources and its sustainable use. They should also be brought together in the efforts to overcome the fresh water crisis. Success stories are there, K.J. Alphonse IAS in his capacity as the Land Use Commissioner of Kerala, initiated such an attempt, which to a great extend succeeded in creating awareness among the people about the need for rain water harvesting. It brought in ideas of constructing concrete tanks for storing rain water, rain pits for ground water recharge, and rejuvenation of the traditional sources of water and water shed management.

Human Rights today occupy top-level priority internationally as well as nationally. The general idea of human rights has today widespread acceptance. The situation of human rights in developing societies has been complex and it intensified with the advent of globalisation. History shows that bureaucracy is the only group that hasn't been much affected by the onslaught of globalisation. So the responsibility before bureaucracy in developing societies is much higher than that in developed societies. In these societies what is need from bureaucracy is protection from petty corruption and getting things without delay. They have to root out corruption and use their knowledge, experience and political neutrality to identify the good things. In strengthening the social sectors the bureaucrats have to play a constructive role. Public Distribution System and the health care system should be strengthened to reduce the social crisis of liberalisation. They should resist the onslaught of multinationals and for that the challenge before the bureaucracy is to initiate decentralisation, people's empowerment through devolution of power and encourage local self-governing institutions to administer and meet collective over social needs while encouraging the market to meet the individual needs. Above all, the civil servants should keep in mind that they are the servants of society, not masters.

End Notes

1. Prominent newspapers and channels with video clippings reported the role of government machinery in helping Warren Anderson to escape from India. Media reports have cited the de-classified records of CIA, which disclosed that the then Prime Minister Rajiv Gandhi had instructed the then Madhya Pradesh Chief Minister Arjun Singh to free Anderson after he was arrested on December 7, 1984. Anderson was treated as a state guest and sent back to Delhi in the state plane (Gurumurthy 2010: 9). The revelations of P.C. Alexander who was Principal Secretary to Prime Minister Rajiv Gandhi, supports the media reports. He stated that it was the order of the Rajiv Gandhi to the Madhya Pradesh Government that let Anderson who has to be kept under arrest, free. Even the higher officials were unaware of all that has happened to help Anderson. (Kerala Kaumudi 2010: 10).
2. Rajkumar Keswani later got the prestigious B.D Goenka Award for Excellence in Journalism for his investigative work on Union Carbide India Limited.
3. The Resolution was adopted with a vote of 122 in favour to none against and 41 abstentions. The countries that strongly opposed the UN Resolution are Canada, the United States, Australia, New Zealand and the United Kingdom and they abstained from voting. The Resolution was pressed in the Assembly by Bolivia.
4. Citing the UN resolution the Botswana Court of Appeal quashed the decision of the High Court (made one week before the General Assembly voted to recognise the right to water and sanitation) that denied the Bushmen access to their broken borehole and upheld the right of the Bushmen to use their borehole as well as the right to sink new boreholes. The court called the treatment of the Botswana Government towards the Bushmen as degrading (Barlow 2011: 18).
5. Jalanidhi entered its second phase and Jalanidhi II intends to cover 80 more Gram Panchayats (GP). Jalanidhi I was started in 1999, with an estimated cost of Rs 381.5 crore, to cover 92 GPs spread over the four districts of Thrissur, Palakkad, Malappuram and Kozhikode. Later it was extended to 110 GPs by adding 18 GPs spread over the remaining nine districts, excluding Alappuzha (Jalanidhi 2012). Alappuzha was not covered under this project because of the disinterest of the people (Planning Board 2009: 7). The nodal oversight agency of Government of Kerala (GoK) to implement the project is the Kerala Rural Water Supply and Sanitation Agency (KRWSA), registered as an autonomous society. The flow of funds in Jalanidhi is from the World Bank to the GOI, thence to the GOK/KRWSA, thence to the District Project Management Units (DPMUs) of the KWRSA, thence to the GPs, and thence to beneficiary groups (BGs) that actually execute and maintain subprojects.

References

AIR (1991): *Narmada Bachao Andolan vs. Union of India*, 2 SCC 718.

Ajoy, Ashirwad Mahaprashata (2011a): "Uttar Pradesh," in "Standing Up to the State," *Frontline*, 28(12), June 17, 9-11.

——(2011b): "Chhattisgarh," in "Standing Up to the State," *Frontline*, 28(12), June 17, 13-16.

Amen, Sethi (2012): "Hard at Work, the Very Special Correspondent," *The Hindu*, Thiruvananthapuram, June 8.

Anitha, Cheria Edwin and Sriprapha, Petcharamesree (2003): *A Human Rights Approach to Development: A Source Book*, Books for Change, Bangalore.

Argun Sengupta (2007): *Report on the Conditions of Work and Promotion of Livelihood in Unorganised Sector*, National Commission for Enterprises in the Unorganised Sector, Government of India, New Delhi.

Barlow, Maude (2011): *Our Right to Water*, The Council of Canadians, Ottawa.

Barlow, Maude and Clarke, Tony (2002): *Blue Gold, The Fight to Stop the Corporate Theft of the World's Water*, Left World, New Delhi.

Ben, Page (2005): "Paying for Water and the Geography of Commodities," *Trans Inst Br Geogr*, 30, 293-306.

C and AG (2012): *Performance Audit of Water Pollution in India*, Comptroller and Auditor General of India, Report No. 21, 2011-12.

Census (2011): *Census of India's Houselisting and House Census Data Highlights – 2011*, Office of the Registrar General and Census Commissioner, Government of India, Ministry of Home Affairs.

Economic Survey (2012): *Economic Survey 2011-12*, Ministry of Finance and Economics, Government of India, New Delhi.

ECOSOC (2002): *The Right to Water (Articles 11 and 12 of the International Covenant on Economic, Social and Cultural Rights), General Comment No. 15 (2002)*, Committee on Economic, Social and Cultural Rights, United Nations Economic and Social Council.

Express News (2012a): "Only 101 Endosulfan Victims Given Compensation," *The New Indian Express*, November 25, http://newindianexpress.com/cities/thiruvannthapuram /article1353749.ece accessed on 12-01-2013.

—— (2012b): *Editorial*, *The New Indian Express*, Kochi, July19, 8.

Global Exchange (2010): *SUEZ-LYONNAISE DES EAUX*, "Some of the *Most Wanted* Corporate Human Rights Violators," http://www.globalexchange.org.

GoI (2012): *Draft National Water Policy 2012*, Ministry of Water Resources, Government of India.

Gurumurthy, S. (2010): "Dishonesty, Fraud, Breach of Trust," *The New Indian Express*, Kochi, June 14, 9.

Harvey, D. (2003): *The New Imperialism*, Oxford University Press, New York.

Hindustan Times (2012): "Corruption is a Violation of Human Rights, Says SC," *Hindustan Times*, October 17, http://www.hindustantimes.com/India-news/NewDelhi/Corruption -is-violation-of-human-rights-says-SC/Article1-945805.aspx accessed on 18-10-2012.

——(2010): "Food Grains Rot in FCI Godowns Across India," *Hindustan Times*, July 27, http://www.hindustantimes.com/India-news/NewDelhi/Food-grains-rot-in-FCI-godowns -across-India/Article1-578444.aspx accessed on 12-01-2013.

Homer-Dixon, Thomas (1999): *Environment, Scarcity and Violence*, Princeton University Press, Princeton, N.J.

IRC (2003): *Sale of River Bhavani, India Resource Centre*, http://www.indiaresource.org /issues/water/2003/bhavaniriver.html accessed on 10-11-2009.

Jayaprakash, S.N. (2012): "Stopping Public Taps (M)", *Mathrubhumi*, March 5.

Jalanidhi (2010): *Kerala Rural Water Supply and Sanitation Agency*, jalanidhi.ac.in.

Jitha, S.R. (2011): "Bureaucracy and Human Rights Under Liberalisation," in P. Sukumarannair (ed.), *Human Rights in a Changing World*, Kalpaz Publications, New Delhi, 141-49.

—— (2010): "Bureaucracy and its Role in the Protection of Human Rights," *UCJPS*, 5(1 and 2), March, 67-73.

John, Scanlon; Angela, Cassar and Noemi, Nemes (2004): *Water as a Human Right?* IUCN Environmental Policy and Law Paper No. 51, UNDP.

Jona, Aravind Dohrmann (2008): "Special Economic Zones in India – An Introduction," *ASIEN*, 106, January, 60-80.

Jyoti, Punwani (2010): "Who didn't help Carbide?" *The New Indian Express*, Kochi, June 17.

Kahl, C.H. (2006): *States, Scarcity and Civil Strife in the Developing World*, Princeton University Press, Princeton, N.J.

Kerala Kaumudi (2012a): "Parakkan Divasam 2 Laksham," (M) *Kerala Kaumudi*, Kochi, June 7, 12.

—— (2012b): "Asoothrana Commission-nte Chilavuchurukkal Engana," *Kerala Kaumudi*, Kochi, June 7, 12.

—— (2010a): "Veendum Dhurantham," *Kerala Kaumudi*, Kochi, June 8, 1.

—— (2010b): "P.C. Alexander-ude Velipeduthal: Anderson-ne Vidan Uttaravittathu Rajiv Gandhi,"(M) *Kerala Kaumudi*, Kochi, June 12, 10.

Manas, Chakravarty (2010): "Distribution of Wealth of Nations," *livemint.com and The Wall Street Journal*, http://www.livemint.com/2010/10/13203814/ Distribution-of-wealth-of-nati.html accessed on 20-09-2011.

Mangalam (2013): "Vagamannil Kayyettam" *Mangalam Daily*, Thiruvananthapuram, January 25, 17.

Mathrubhumi (2012): "Kinallur Sambhavam Daurbhagiam," (Editorial) *Mathrubhumi*, Kottayam, May 8, 4.

—— (2005): *Plachimadayile Jalachushanavum Janakeeya Prathirothavum*, Mathrubhumi Books, Kozhikode.

PIB (2012): "Per Capita Water Availability," *Press Information Bureau*, Government of India, New Delhi, Release ID: 82676.

Planning Board (2009): *An Evaluation Study of Jalanidhi Projects in Kerala*, Kerala State Planning Board, Thiruvananthapuram, October.

Purnima, S. Tripathi (2012): "Battle of Bastar," *Frontline*, 29(8), May 3, 32-4.

Reinhart Philip (2012): "The Human Right to Water," *Pragathi*, Quarterly Research Journal, 6(121), July-Sept., 47-59.

—— (2009): "Economic Development and Social Justice," *Competition Success Review*, XLV(11), May, 48-50.

Reema, Narendran (2011): "River Basins Brimming with Pollutants, Pesticides," *The New Indian Express*, September 30, 4.

Robbins, Peter T. (2003): "Trans-national Corporations and the Discourse of Water Privatisation," *Journal of International Development*, 8(15), 1073-82.

Sunilkumar, C.G. (2012): "FCI Godownukalil Nashichathu 50,000 Tonne," *Kerala Kaumudi*, Thiruvananthapuram, December 10, 1.

Sushanta, Talukdar (2011): "North-Eastern States," in "Standing Up to the State," *Frontline*, 28(12), June 17, 17-18.

The Hindu (2012a): "Inequality has gone up, notwithstanding dip in Poverty," *The Hindu*, March 21.

——(2012b): "Foreign Travel is Expensive But Necessary for the Discharge of Official Duties," *The Hindu*, Thiruvananthapuram, May 24, 13.

—— (2012c): "Now More Spending for Toilets in Rural Areas," *The Hindu*, Thiruvananthapuram, June 8, 15.

TII-CMS (2008): *India Corruption Study 2007, With Focus on BPL Households*, Transparency International India and Centre for Media Studies, New Delhi, June.

Times Now (2012): "*Criminal Wastage of Food Grain in Punjab*," *Times Now*, May 4, http://www.timesnow.tv/Criminal-waste-of-food-grain-in-Punjab/articleshow/4401 414.cms accessed on 12-01-2013.

UN-Water (2011): "Water Scarcity," International Decade for Action, Water for Life 2005-2015, *UN Water*, UNEP.

—— (2010): *The Human Right to Water and Sanitation*, Resolution A/RES/64/292, United Nations General Assembly, July 28.

UN Human Rights Council (2010): *Human Rights and Access to Safe Drinking Water and Sanitation*, A/HRC/15/L.14, September 24.

UN News Centre (2010): "General Assembly Declares Access to Clean Water and Sanitation is a Human Right," *News Centre*, United Nations.

Upendra Nath, Sharma (2012): "No Lessons Learnt From Bhopal Gas Tragedy," *The New Indian Express*, Kochi, 80 Years Special Edition, 49.

Vandana Siva (2011): "The Great Land Grab: India's War on Farmers," *Al Jazeera*, http://english.aljazeera.net/indepth/opinion/2011/06/201167117566679 87.html accessed on 07-06-2011.

Venkatesan, V. (2012): "Posco in Limbo," *Frontline*, 29(8), May 04, 35-7.

Venkitesh, Ramakrishnan (2011): "The Great Land Grab," *Frontline*, 28(12), June 17, 4-8.

11

Bureaucracy and Health Sector

Health and health care are key factors determining the development of a nation. No nation can become a developed one when majority are teaming in poverty and crippling with bad health. Infant mortality rate, child mortality rate, maternal mortality rate, longevity, literacy, etc., are key factors determining the status of a nation as developed or not. The Human Development Index takes into account the three dimensions of Health (longevity), Education (literacy) and Living Standards (Gross National Income Per-capita) to rank countries in the tires of development. All are complementary and mutually contributing and in the absence of one, others cannot be satisfied. All the developed nations have world class health care facilities and gives prime importance to health care as it provides competitive human resource to the nation. Even though machines have replaced man in many fields, man behind the machines can be seen everywhere. Why Japan could have technological progress, US could have military progress and Eurone could have industrial progress is all due to their better human power or brain. Most third world nations cannot make such a progress because their human resources are daunting with poverty and diseases. Those nations that could overcome these problems can make progress and are doing so.

Simply put health is the absence of illness or diseases. The Alma-Ata Declaration (1978: 1) declares health as a state of complete physical, mental and social well-being, and not merely the absence of disease or infirmity. Health care implies the provision of assistance to persons in need of care, cure, education, prevention, or help related to trauma, illness, disease, disability or dysfunction by other persons knowledgeable and skilful in providing such assistance (Pellegrino 1999: 247). Health-care is a complex set of practices integrating a variety of goods. Together with the personal relationship between a health professional and a person seeking help there are other facilities, medications, instruments, dressings and other disposable items used in health care. These things as Pellegrino (1999: 247) points are in one sense commodities, since they can be owned, consumed, bought, traded and donated. To a large extent these things are subjected to market forces. But in the interest of common good, they become the subject of ethical and public concern when their scarcity threatens human well-being.

Health care provision depends on efficiently combining financial resources, human resources, and supplies, and delivering services in a timely fashion distributed spatially throughout a country. This requires a "system" that mobilises and distributes resources, processes information and acts upon it, and motivates providers, appropriate behaviour by individuals, health care workers, and administrators. In a well-functioning health system, the relationship between all actors should be balanced. A harmonious relation between the state, providers and citizens is inevitable for the smooth running of the system. The state due to its sovereign status and importance in society enjoys an upper hand and becomes the controlling actor. It should direct and control the health care providers for the common good. The state should be responsive to the interests of the citizens, *i.e.,* quality care should be made available at affordable rates. The voices of the clients/citizens should be taken into consideration while making policies and regulations. When the citizens provide client power to the providers they should provide services in return. However, recent years saw the decline in role of the state and usurping of powers by the providers to such an extent that they dictates the terms and conditions in the health care "business". The providers as controlling actors are not conducive to the interest of the citizens and to the system as a whole and have totally disharmonised the system, giving least or no attention to the voices of the needy (Patients).

The concept of health as a fundamental human right has been reaffirmed by the Alma-Ata Declaration of 1978, which was adopted at the International Conference on Primary Health Care, Almaty (formerly Alma-Ata, USSR), currently in Kazakhstan, 6-12 September 1978, attended by virtually all the members of the WHO and the UNICEF. As per the declaration, attainment of the highest possible health is the most important worldwide social goal because the promotion and protection of the health of the people is essential to sustained economic and social development and contributes to a better quality of life and to world peace. The declaration affirmed health as a fundamental human right and called for a transformation of conventional health care systems and for broad inter-sectoral collaboration and community organising with people having the right and duty to participate individually and collectively in the planning and implementation of their health care. The Alma Ata declaration has also outlined the eight essential components of primary health care which includes: *education concerning prevailing health problems and the methods of preventing and controlling them; promotion of food supply and proper nutrition; an adequate supply of safe water and basic sanitation; maternal and child health care, including family planning; immunisation against the major infectious diseases; prevention and control of locally endemic diseases; appropriate treatment of common diseases and injuries; and provision of essential drugs*. The responsibility for the health of their people is on the Governments which have to be fulfilled by the provision of adequate health and social measures. The declaration also underlines that primary health care should be universally accessible to all individuals and families in the community at a cost that can be affordable.

In the neo-liberal movement health care also became a commodity and the commodification of health care raises many questions. The fundamental dictum of managed care is that the cost, price, availability, and distribution of health care should be left to the free workings of a free marketplace constrained by a minimum of governmental regulation (Pellegrino 1999: 244; Hong 2000: 30). Through the usual mechanisms of competition a "quality product" should emerge since providers will compete with each other in quality, price, and satisfaction of consumers to keep their market-share and/or profits. The "consumers" and "purchasers" will be free to choose among providers selecting the best "buy" suited to their individual needs. Costs will decline, and quality will be maintained or will improve. More care will be accessible to more people on their terms, not the doctor's (Pellegrino 1999: 244). The laws of competition will reduce waste, overuse, and error to everyone's advantage. Medicine will be demystified, physicians will become employees, and physicians' decisions will be shaped to conserve society's resources. To Stefen and Rene, (2009: 24) commodification in the health care sector benefits patients by bringing new products to market, legitimising diseases, and raising awareness of treatment options.

Under the free market model, health is no longer an inalienable right or an absolute human need but a private good. As health care is a commodity, it is something we possess and can sell, trade, or give away at our free will. This implies that, like any commodity, ownership of medical knowledge upon which health care depends resides with health professionals or those who employ or invest in them (Nozick 1974: 160). In this view, there would be no duty of stewardship over medical knowledge which would require its use on behalf of those who need it but cannot pay for it. Nor can there be any valid moral claim by the sick on society for its allocation or distribution (Pellegrino 1999: 247). In a free market there is no room for the non-player, the person who can't "buy in" - the poor, the uninsured, the uninsurable. The special needs of the chronically ill, the disabled, infirm, aged, and the emotionally distressed are no longer valid claims to special attention. Under the free-market system there is no economic justification for the extra-time required to explain, counsel, comfort, and educate these patients and their families since these cost more than they return in revenue. Under such circumstances the poor will be marginalised from acquiring the needy health care services.

Globalisation and Health Care in India

The policies of privatisation and liberalisation implemented from 1991 onwards by the central government had its impact all over India. An important recommendation of the World Bank was that public funding to the service sectors like education and health shall be reduced. Accordingly, the central government is reducing investment in the health sector. Though health is a subject under the state list, the central government has cut short the share of the several centrally sponsored health care and preventive programmes. The impact of globalisation on health sector manifested in various forms like stagnating government health expenditures; increasing unregulated privatisation of the health care sector; the sky rocketing price of drugs and rising cost of health services; and the change in doctor-patient relations.

One of the most obvious indicators of the inadequacy of public health spending in India is the very small amount of such spending relative to Gross Domestic Product (GDP). In developed countries, especially those with ageing populations, government health spending accounts for around five per cent of GDP or more. Even in Asian developing countries excluding India, the average is around three per cent of GDP (ERF 2006: 12). India's government health expenditure amounts to less than one per cent of GDP, whereas France spends 10.4 per cent and Japan spends eight per cent (Monali 2010: 3). Further, this ratio is not only low internationally, but is even low compared to past experience. In the mid-1980s, health expenditure of central and state government taken together was more than 1 per cent of GDP, but now it is only around 0.9 per cent. Further, it has fallen as low as around 0.8 per cent in 2001-02. The government's allocation for healthcare remains a paltry 0.36 per cent of GDP in the 2010-11 budget, 0.25 per cent in 2011-12 and 0.34 per cent in 2012-13. The allocation for health care in the 2012-13 budget was Rs 20,882 crore (Urmi 2012: 40). For a country with more than 1000 million populations where a high level of people can be adjudged as poor, this amount is not only paltry but also a matter of serious concern.

The shortage of funds has severely affected the government health care mechanisms. It resulted in shortage of medicine, less availability and utilisation of technology, and poor infrastructural facilities. The inadequacy in facilities alienated people from government health care services. A survey in Kerala where the public health care system is far better compared to other states in India, points out that only 23 per cent of households regularly utilises the public sector (Nabae 2003: 143). Even in the poorest stratum the share was as low as 33 per cent. The reasons stated for not using government institutions included: non-availability of drugs in government hospitals, lack of proper attention and better behaviour in private institutions (Raman Kutty 2000: 105). Because of financial and managerial reasons many of the facilities in public sector remains under-utilised. The untapped potential for utilisation are estimated to be 12.3 per cent for doctors, 25.7 per cent for nurses, 25.7 per cent for beds, 53.2 per cent for building spaces and 59.3 per cent for land, in Kerala alone (Nabae 2003: 143).

Normally medicine and diet, provided free of cost to persons below a certain income level will benefit the lower income group at the expense of the non-poor tax payer. Similarly, an increase in hospital accessories and construction will be neutral across income classes but it will benefit, especially those who depend on publicly provided health services. When investment on drugs, supplementary nutrition, equipments and buildings are reduced, consumers of the publicly provided health services in general stand to lose. The worst affected will be the poor, who would have received them free of cost. So, if the purpose of government provision of health services is to ensure availability of health facilities to the poor, actions should be taken to increase the spending on medicine, accessories and infrastructure (Reinhart 2010a: 164).

Private health care system in India has grown vastly over these years and is well-established and flourishing. But the number of the private providers of health care services in India is largely unexplored due to paucity of data. At the time of Independence, the private health sector accounted for only five to 10 per cent of total patient care. Until the mid-1980s, public hospitals were the dominant providers of in-patient care, especially for the poor, even though patients increasingly resorted to the private sector for out-patient services (Gita 2003: 19). Although this varied considerably across states, public hospitals provide an important alternative to the private sector and at significantly low cost. But by mid-1990s private sector became dominant in terms of both in-patient and out-patient services. Planning Commission (2008: 68, 69) data shows that by 2004, the share of private sector in total hospitalised treatment was 58.3 per cent in rural areas and 61.8 per cent in urban areas and in the case of non-hospitalised treatment, government sources account for only 22 per cent in rural areas and 19 per cent in urban areas. The National Family Health Survey (NFHS) III data also confirms that the private medical sector remains the primary source of health care for the majority of households in urban areas with 70 per cent and in rural areas with 63 per cent. Private Doctors or clinics are the main source of care in the private sector, catering to 46 per cent of the urban and 36 per cent of the rural households (IIPS and Macro International, 2007: 436). Studies by *Northbridge Capital* shows that nearly 75 per cent of all the hospitals and 40 per cent of hospital beds in the country are in the private sector and they provides 60 per cent of all out-patient care in India and as much as 40 per cent of all in-patient care (Monali 2010: 5).

After the reforms of 1990s private health care providers got growing support. This included a variety of subsidies for corporate hospitals, in the form of subsidised sale of land, reduced import duties and tax concessions for medical research (Baru 2000), reduced utility charges, discounted or free land, and low-interest loans (Chakraborty 2003) and urban land in prime locations in exchange for their providing a proportion of their services free to the poor (Gita 2003: 19). But there is increasing evidence of non-compliance with this condition by major private hospitals in metro areas. According to the Report on Private Medical Institutions in Kerala there are about 413 medical institutions, which are registered under "Charitable Trusteeship" acts. But only two per cent of inpatients could receive 'free ward' facilities in 2004. This underlines the fact that free delivery of inpatient care services in the so-called 'charitable institutions' is negligible (Dilip 2008: 30). There is sizeable decline in proportion receiving treatment from free wards. The so-called charitable institutions are working as for-profit institutions and the ill effect of this seems to be on the poor, who are the major beneficiaries of the free ward facilities.

The policy of liberalisation has its impacts on the pharmaceutical industry too. When deregulation facilitated the entry of a number of pharmaceutical companies, price decontrol set the pricing of pharmaceutical items to the market forces of demand and supply. This resulted in the pricing of medicines many a times higher than its actual cost. Though medicines are in one sense commodities, because of their peculiar importance with regard to life saving and cure they cannot be subjected solely to the same laws and principles of the market as shoes, lampshades, mobiles or computers (Reinhart 2011: 63). The effects of industrial deregulation on drug prices began to be felt in the 1980s and these continued and accelerated in the 1990s. It resulted in spiralling costs of drugs and the continued absence of a regulatory list of essential drugs resulted in the market being flooded with irrational drugs (Gita 2003: 19). The rise in cost of prices increased the cost of both in-patient and out-patient health care in rural and urban areas. In India, expenditure on drugs accounts to 74 per cent of the total out-of-pocket (OOP) spending, 76 per cent in rural areas and 70 per cent in urban areas (William and Mishra 2009: 14). So normally when the price of drugs increases the cost of medical care also increases.

Till 1970 all drugs were under price control. Profitability allowed on price-controlled drugs ranged from 40 to 75 per cent (Godwin and Varatharajan 2007: 43). By 1979 the number of drugs under price-control has come down to 347, 163 in 1987 and again brought down to 76 by 1995 (Gita et al. 2002: 1346). Allowed profitability too went up to 150 per cent. By 2002, the share of drugs under price control went further down to 25 per cent or just 32 drugs. As shown in the website of the National Pharmaceutical Pricing Authority (NPPA), the list of drugs under price control in India currently is 74. It needed the intervention of the Honourable Supreme Court to revise the list of essential drugs in India. The revision of National List of Essential Medicines (NLEM) will result in a price contrcl of about 40 per cent of the medicines sold in the market, i.e., for 354 medicines, broadly categorised within 27 therapeutic categories such as ophthalmological preparations, cardiovascular medicines, immunologicals, anti-allergic and others. The move, if successful could bring more than half of the country's Rs 65,000-crore (Rs. 650 billion) medicine market under price control. The NPPA is the medicine price regulator but ironically it functions within the administrative control of the Ministry of Chemicals and Fertilizers. Prior to 1995 when the number of drugs under price control was revised downward, the annual price rise of drugs was estimated at 10-50 per cent (Godwin and Varatharajan 2007: 43). Under price decontrol the annual price rise of drugs is much higher.

The impact of the liberalisation of the drug industry is evident in the sky rocketing costs of drugs since the 1980s. An analysis of drug prices between 1980 and 1995 revealed a 197 per cent increase overall for 778 drugs. The sharpest increases were evident for imported drugs (Gita *et al.* 2002: 1346). The last five years saw a doubling in the price of medicines. In case of patent medicines there is a rise of 10-20 per cent within a single year (Aneesh 2011). It is a fact that the people are not aware of the rise in price of many medicines that are coming to market in new names and designs. Reports from Kerala shows that medicines, including life saving medicines are being sold at a price that is ten-fold than the cost price. About 250 drugs including the commonly used Pantoprazole, Azithromycin, Amoxicillin, Cefuroxime, etc., are sold at these higher prices. These medicines are brought to Kerala from other states, mainly from the tax free zones of Himachal Pradesh (Jayan 2010: 1). Pantoprazole – 40 whose cost price is just 60 paise is being sold at Rs six, i.e., at a price higher than 1000 per cent. Azithromycin – 500 that is available at Rs 12.60 is sold at Rs 42. Similar is the case for Cefuroxime Sodium Injection - 750 and Cefuroxime - 500. The selling price of Cefuroxime is Rs 199, which is five times higher than the original price of Rs 38.50. Cefuroxime - 500 whose cost price is Rs 23 becomes Rs 118 when it comes to market. All these are occurring when there is order of the Drugs Controller that the Maximum Retail Price (MRP) of medicines should not exceed 100 per cent of the manufacturing cost.

The differences in price can be noticed even in case of same drugs. Different companies are producing the same medicines in various brand names. For example, Clopidogrel, a regular drug for heart patients is sold under various brand names by different companies. The MRP of each strip of 10 tablets varies with its brand name. When Bluecross produces Clopidogrel with the brand name Antiban its MRP is Rs 32. But when it comes to Thinrin of Biocon the strip costs Rs 69 and further increases to Rs 192 when it comes to Clopigrel of U.S.V. Similar is the case with Pantoprazole, a drug that blocks the production of acid by the stomach. Mankind Pharma produces Pantoprazole under the brand name PANTAKIND and the MRP of a strip is Rs. 27.15 and this is the lowest price for the branded one. The highest price is quoted by Sun Pharmaceuticals for its PANTOCID, i.e., Rs 70. The price of branded Pantoprazole varies between Rs 27.15 and Rs 70. We can also see that one company sells the same drug with different costs under various brand names. Azithromycin is manufactured by Cipla under the various brand names Azipro, Azimax and Azee. A strip of 3 500 mg tabs of Azipro has an MRP of Rs 42, of Azimax it is Rs 62.40 and when it comes to Azee it is Rs 71 (Primary Study).

The first-ever study conducted by the National Pharmaceutical Pricing Authority on cancer medicines has found huge price variations among different brands of same medicines sold in the country. The price difference is the highest - 3,210 per cent, among different brands of breast cancer medicine Letrozole. While a 10-tablet strip of Letrozole 2.5 mg from Swiss drug maker Novartis costs Rs 1,986, the same strip by Hyderabad-based Hetero carries a price tag of Rs 60. When Novartis price a 10-tablet strip of Imatinab 400 mg at Rs 41,152, the same is priced by Glenmark at Rs 3,000. For other drugs the corresponding highest and lowest figures are Nozolamide 250 mg (5 capsule) - Dr. Reddys (Rs 22,282) and Sun Pharma (Rs 4,485); Pemetrexed 500 mg (vial)– Eli Lilly (Rs 73,660) and Glenmark (Rs 11,990); Exemestane 25mg (30 tablet) – Pfizer (Rs 4,315) and Natco (Rs 1,290). Of the 75 medicines that were subjected to analysis, the price difference of over 100 per cent was seen in 30 cases (Joe 2010). Cancer drugs are typically taken for months and high drug prices result in huge cost for patients.

The vast difference in the prices of drugs procured by the government agencies and maximum retail prices of the same drugs when sold through retail pharmacies exposes the huge profiteering indulged in by pharmaceutical companies. Kerala Medical Services Corporation Ltd. (KMSCL), a Kerala government undertaking which is functioning under the State Ministry of Health, is procuring drugs from a large number of drug companies at a price which is much lesser than the MRP. During the year 2011-12, KMSCL procured the cancer drug Amifostine injection (500 mg) at Rs 430 while the same injection is available at the private medical stores at Rs 4,225, an increase of almost 1000 per cent. Similarly, heart disease drug Dobutamine HCL Inj. – 50 (5 ml) is procured by the KMSCL for Rs 19.35 against the MRP of Rs 320. In the case of drugs for kidney diseases, Sprionolactone (25 mg, unit 10 × 10) is procured by the KMSCL for Rs 48.40 but the same is being sold at the retail shops at Rs 200. For a large number of life-saving medicines, especially for treating cancer, heart ailments, kidney diseases, etc, some of the companies are charging more than 1000 per cent of the procurement prices. This is not the case for medicines alone, surgical items, stents, acetabular caps, femoral components too are charged at higher prices. Stents that are used for angioplasty are priced Rs 60,000 to Rs 1,50,000 despite its actual cost of Rs 10,000 to Rs 20,000 (Reinhart 2011: 67).

The proliferation of for-profit medical care institutions, together with the rising cost of drugs is increasing the cost of health care. Private hospitals are for-profit institutions that charge the "consumers" heavily. The out-of-pocket health expenditure in private hospitals is much higher than that in government hospitals. According to the 60th round of NSSO 2004, the average medical expenditure on account of hospitalisation in rural areas was Rs 3,238 in government hospitals and Rs 7,408 in private hospitals, in urban areas the corresponding figures were Rs 3,877 and Rs 11,553, respectively (Planning Commission, 2008: 69). Together with this we have to read that the major share in health care spending comes from the households. Parvati and Dinesh (2008) notes, "in terms of the sources and determinants of health care financing, the burden of health care expenditure in India largely falls on individual households, indicating relatively less involvement and inadequate support structures generated by the government in this regard." National Health Accounts 2007 shows that household spending on health care accounts to 68 per cent of the total health care spending in India and government spending comes second with 25 per cent, one-fourth of the total spending (Reinhart 2010a: 174). By 2012 the share of spending from private sources increased to 70 per cent which made the Union Rural Development Minister Jairam Ramesh, say "India is a unique country in the world where 70 per cent of the health expenditure is private expenditure" (Express News 2012: 1). So, an increase in health care expenditure directly affects the individuals.

Rising cost of care is a critical concern for the poor people, because the household spending on medical treatment by the poorest income groups was higher than the average for all income groups (Gita 2003: 19). The rising cost of health care has a range of possible impacts on the poor, including: cuts back on other consumption such as food, which has a direct impact on health; increased indebtedness; growing untreated illness; and growing gender biases in health seeking behaviour. The high cost of inpatient treatment in the private sector makes health care unaffordable to the poor and disadvantages, raising the issue of affordability and equity. The World Bank (2001: 156), study shows that more than 40 per cent of all the patients admitted to a hospital in India have to borrow money or sell assets, including inherited property and farmland, to cover their medical expenses; and 25 per cent of farmers are driven below the poverty line by the costs of their medical care. A study on Indian poverty by Anirudh Krishna of Duke University also found that expenditure on health is the primary reason for families to decline into poverty (Urmi 2012: 40). The statement of the Union Minister, Jairam Ramesh that the expenditure on health care is the single most important reason for rural area indebtness in India (Express News 2012: 1), validates this argument.

Primary data collected from the patients of a Neuro ICU of a private hospital in Kerala shows that the total expenditure incurred for a period of 10 days is five times higher than that in a government hospital. In government hospital too out-of-pocket (OOP) is there as one has to take medicines, lab facilities, scanning etc. from outside. In many cases even the poor prefer private hospitals. The doctor concerned is the main factor in selecting the service, travel and accommodation convenience forms a part of selection also. Data collected from a Critical Care Unit (CCU) of a private hospital shows that the average expenditure per day is around Rs 10,000, while using ventilator and oxygen. From CCU they will be shifted to the ward before discharge and this usually takes a week. So the total expenditure will be at an average of Rs 30,000 – Rs 50,000. Majority of those who seek care in these hospitals are from the middle class. For them the high cost of medical care is a burden. When it comes to cancer and heart patients, a major share of their income will be washed out for treatment (Primary Study).

It is also noted that the private sector has outgrown the public sector through the direct and indirect patronage of the state governments. Narayana (2003) argues of that in Andhra Pradesh where private corporate hospitals received huge amounts of public funds in the form of reimbursements from public sector undertakings and the state and central governments (e.g., the Central Government Health Scheme CGHS) for treating their employees. Under the Rajiv Gandhi Arogyasri scheme implemented by the Andhra Pradesh government, about Rs 800 crore (89 per cent of the premium) went to private hospitals (CII and HOSMAC 2011: 36-39; Rao 2012: 15). Similar is the case with the Health Insurance Cards in Kerala, by which the patients can avail services from the listed private hospitals too. Case study conducted among the patients who availed such services in private hospital shows that the private hospitals are making huge profit from this. A card holder can avail the services amounting to Rs 30,000 in a year and at least three days admit in a single turn is needed for availing the benefit. A vast majority prefer private hospitals and as there is no specific criterion regarding the treatment mode, most private hospitals prefer the most expensive so as to make the total expenditure include their profit also. The benefit of the insurance card goes to the private hospitals. So by weaning away resources from the government private hospitals are replacing public hospitals rather than complementing them.

With the rise of neo-liberalism health care became a market rather than a service and this market is one of the thriving markets not only in India but also round the world. The rise in population in India is making it a hub of hospitals. India that shares 16 per cent of the world population contributes 20 per cent of the global disease burden, it is also known as the cardiac and diabetes capital of the world. Each year around 43,000 peoples are being diagnosed for various kinds of cancer in Kerala alone (Primary Study). Both these diseases warrant constant medical care and are expensive in nature. Eyeing this various hospitality brands liked Anil Ambani's Reliance Health, Hindujas, Sahara Group, Apollo Tyres and Panacea Group has started aggressive expansion in the country. Share of private expenditure as a per centage of total expenditure on healthcare has grown to nearly 80 per cent over the last decade and it is further expected to increase. It is estimated that the Indian hospital industry would be worth US$ 280 billion by 2020 as against US$ 44 billion in 2010. Foreign companies are waiting for their turn to invest in the health care sector of India only because of the high turnout from such an investment. But such a market is highly deleterious to the interest of the common man and the society because in such a market the denial of care for the poor gets legitimised.

Commodification of health care is not something that can be welcomed in any society because it makes health care a commodity purchasable by the "ability to pay." The application of the principles of cost recovery, profit-maximisation, cost-benefit analysis, deregulation, etc., increased the cost of medical care while the entry of private hospitals made health care a profit making business (Reinhart 2010b: 165). Globalisation hasn't demystified medicine; instead it made medicines a means for profit-making, legitimising profit-making as the sole aim of pharma industry. The rise in price of drugs ultimately increases the out-of-pocket expenditure in health care. The high cost of medical care deters many from availing timely health care, slipping to dangerous conditions including death. Most of the diseases warrant constant medical attention and treatment and sustained medical treatment is beyond the wherewithal of the average households. What is needed is quality care at affordable conditions. The private health care system cannot be an answer because of the high average cost of treatment. This warrants greater and sustained efforts by the state.

Studies on the health care system in Kerala show that *the active role of the state government has been a key factor in the expansion of health care facilities*. The initial period of rapid growth in health care facilities in Kerala was dominated by the public sector that was up to the 1980s. This period has witnessed considerable spending of the state on health sector. Investment in education and health infrastructure has been a consistent policy of all elected governments in Kerala, whatever their political leaning. It was the tradition of government support for health development that has been a catalyst for advancement of health care in the state. The number of institutions and beds increased sharply. There are more than 300 hospital beds per 1,00,000 population in Kerala, which is probably one of the highest ratios in the developing world (Raman Kutty 2000: 106). This corresponds to that found in the US and many other developed regions. Only countries like Japan, Germany and UK had a bed-population ratio higher than that prevailing in Kerala (Dilip 2008: 13). But by mid-1980s because of the fiscal crisis and other problems, there occurred a slowdown in government expenditure. All these resulted in slowing down the growth of public health institution, both in quantity and quality. The private sector took lead from the decline of government health care facilities. It is the public sector that sensitised the population to the need for sophisticated care. Even today government continues to play a leadership role in the training of all strata of health professionals, who are then largely absorbed by the private sector.

Kerala's remarkable achievement in health care was to a large extent based on its vast network of public health institutions. The hall mark of the Kerala model of health care was the low cost of health care, universal accessibility and availability to the poor sections of the society. Many of its health indicators surpass those of other Indian states; some are even par with developed countries. Life expectancy at birth in Kerala is higher than the levels achieved by the developing countries. The average life expectancy of a man in Kerala is 71.3 and this means that a man in Kerala can expect to live nine years longer than the average Indian man. Similarly, a woman in Kerala can expect to live to the age of 73.8, 12.4 years longer than the average Indian women. The birth rate in Kerala is much lower than the birth rate for all of India. Improved child health and higher levels of education, particularly female education, are among the most important reasons for Kerala's low and declining birth rate and the general acceptance of a small family norm (Kannan *et al.* 1991). The proportion of infants and children who are getting vaccinated are much higher in Kerala than rest of India. Immunisation coverage improved substantially and studies point that incomes were not the major determinant of immunisation of children in Kerala. Kerala has almost attained universalisation of immunisation (Planning Commission 2010: 308). Female empowerment in Kerala is vital to its achievements in respect of child health and health conditions in general. Female literacy and girls' schooling rates are high in Kerala, and is critical to this high performance.

The death rate in Kerala has declined steadily, more rapidly than the Indian average. So has the infant mortality rate. The infant mortality rate in Kerala is 12 per 1000 compared to the national average 55 per 1000. The decline in infant mortality rate in Kerala has been associated with improvements in pre-natal and post-natal care and higher levels of institutional child birth (Parayil 2000: 91). 99 per cent of deliveries in Kerala are institutional. The low infant mortality rate of 12 per 1000 live births and under-five mortality rate of 14 per 1000 live births (Census 2011: 12, 16) places Kerala higher than the average for developing countries with high human development. The decline in maternal mortality rate (MMR) is associated with the quality care they are getting during pregnancy and child birth. NFHS (2005-06: 203) reports, 99 per cent of pregnant women gets antenatal care in Kerala. The MMR in Kerala is as low as 85 per 1,00,000 live births, while the all-India average is 212 (Census 2011: 5). The average age of women at the time of birth of her first child is also higher in Kerala than in any other state (NFHS 1998-99; Kannan *et al.* 1991: 87). The health care system is considered to be the principal factor for attaining the high level of health status in Kerala. These achievements have occurred despite its low economic status. Key factors contributed to these outcomes are effective health care system and non-health care sector contributions including widespread education, land reforms, public distribution of food and housing, in other words the active involvement of the state.

For any system to have a better health care facility the active role of the state apparatus is thus needed. The current crisis in the health sector of Kerala owes to the withdrawal of the state. So in order to improve the health care scenario, the Government of India should invest more on health care and it should be an active controlling actor of the system. Already there is a shortage of health care facilities in India and its rank 171 in a list of 175 countries on public health spending. The goals of the National Rural Health Mission cannot be achieved without augmenting the budgetary share, as it necessitates development of rural health care infrastructure; fill in vacancies of doctors, auxiliary nurse, midwives and paramedics. Of the total 23,391 primary health care centres only 27 per cent, i.e., 6,329 are fully functional. There exists shortage of doctors and accredited health care activists (ASHA). Quoting the words of the Rural Development Minister, "public health care system does not exist in many parts of the country" (Express News 2010: 1). There is shortage of health care activists with only 15 per cent of the primary health centres having an auxiliary nurse midwife; female assistants are available only in 38 per cent of the centres. When the accepted norm for ASHA workers is one per 1000 persons the average is currently 0.74 per 1000 persons. The health care system of the country is totally plagued with lack of resources and persons.

The challenge now-a-days before us is to expand the health care machinery to the rural areas. As reduced health care spending has become a rule, what can be done is preventing the under-utilisation of the sanctioned amounts. The track record of health administration's utilisation of allocated funds is not stellar. Out of the sanctioned Rs 348 crore in the Budget 2011-12 for human resources for health, only Rs 248 crore was utilised (Urmi 2012: 41). The shortage of personnels is one affecting the health care system and it is one that forces to seek care in private hospitals. To prevent the mushrooming growth of private hospitals and clinics is another major challenge because they are literally exploiting the public. It is the absence of regulatory mechanisms that resulted in the proliferation of private for-profit health care institutions, private scanning centres, labs that exploit the common man. The Drugs Control Department in many states are not having adequate personnels. This usually affects the quality checking of medicines and their price fixation. The drugs control department in Kerala is having a strength of only 62 personnel but it has to control 152 pharma companies and 16,950 medical shops in the state (Santhosh 2011: 6).

We can see that the drugs that are selling at higher prices are those not included in the price-control list of the central government. To prevent the increasing cost of health care, the sky rocketing rise in the price of medicines have to be halted. Only price control can facilitate the same. The NPPA has to be strengthened and should be brought under the control of the Ministry of Health from its current position under the Ministry of Fertilizers and Chemicals. This needs a political decision-making. The urgent revision of the National List of Essential Medicines and its continued monitoring is essential to prevent the irrational increase in the price of medicines. Usually what happens is that when a medicine comes under price control, the pharma companies will change the combinations to avoid those ingredients that are under price control and they escape from price cap. This demands the continued vigilance of the drugs control department. They can also play a big role in determining the price of the medicines as it is their duty to ensure that the MRP of drugs includes only the cost price and allotted profit. There also exist vast difference between the actual cost of medicines and its MRP. Absence of a better regulatory mechanism and the unholy nexus between manufacturers-distributors and doctors are creating this climate for exploitation. This can be understood by comparing the selling price of drugs in cooperative, *neethi*-medicals with other medical shops. From *neethi*-medicals we get medicines below the MRP and both MRP and selling price will be marked in the bill. By going through the difference between MRP and selling price we can say that selling at MRP is exploitative. With ample evidence we can say that "life saving medicines are priced (MRP) 25 times higher than the actual price" (Reinhart 2011: 68). Like the *neethi*-medicals in Kerala *Jan Aushadhi* shops are now opening in the Northern States of India. In Jan Aushadhi shops in Delhi, antibiotics that are available at Rs 55 in medical shops are given at Rs 11.10, a price reduction of five-fold or 496 per cent. The official website of Jan Aushadhi (http://janaushadhi.gov.in/) exhibits the comparative prices of generic medicines sold at *Jan Aushadhi Stores vs. Branded Products*. By increasing the number of such subsidised medical shops the price of medicines can be reduced.

When government agency determines the price of medicines that are to be distributed exploitation can be taken away. But in many cases the druggists associations determines the price of medicines. The price of medicines distributed in Kerala are determined not by any government agency but by the All Kerala Chemists and Druggists Association (AKCDA). The association issued a circular that warns about taking actions including fines and stoppage of supply of medicines to those medical shops that are selling medicines at a low price as against the one determined by the association (Manorama News 2011). Doctors are getting fixed commissions from the distributors and this adduces them to prescribe costly medicines even if they were not needed (Reinhart 2011: 66). A number of duplicate drugs and there combinations together with banned ones are still available in the market. Even though laws relating to drug production and maintenance are violated in a large scale, little or no action is being taken. No attempt is there to ensure the quality of the drugs available in the market. If the quality of the generic drugs can be ensured there can be a shift from the branded ones which can drastically reduce the expenditure on health care as a whole. Strengthening the drugs control department can only do the same.

If the higher bureaucrats are determined it is possible to make some changes in the health care system. The Office of the Controller General of Patents under the leadership of P.H. Kurien did a giant leap in ensuring medicines at affordable rates. It was under him the Country granted its first compulsory licence (CL) to a firm to produce a patented drug. The CL was given to Nacto Pharma, to produce and market the generic versions of an anti-cancer drug Sorafenib used in the treatment of patients diagnosed as being in the advanced stages of affliction with liver or kidney cancer. The patent for Sorafenib is held by the German Pharmaceutical giant Bayer which was supplying it under the brand name Nexavar that was being priced at Rs 2.8 lakh for a month's dosage of 120 tablets. The CL will enable the Nacto to produce generic versions of Sorafenib, which will reduce the cost of a month's dosage (120 200 mg tabs) to Rs 8,800 (The Hindu 2012: 17). It is to be noted that Rs 8,800 includes the six per cent royalty on the net sales to Bayer. So even after paying the royalty Nacto could produce the drug at a price that is less than 97 per cent of Bayer's Rs 2.8 lakh (Ramachandran 2012: 18). The CL came in the wake of the conclusion of the Controller General that the high price of Nexavar makes its unaffordable and only a small fraction of less than two per cent of those who required the drug have been treated with it (Chandrasekar 2012: 9, 10). Though the provision of CL was there right from the beginning of TRIPS, ideology or international pressure had held back the system from issuing it. The CL will force the phrama companies to sell their medicines at an affordable rate.

The role of bureaucracy with regard to health didn't stop here. They have to ensure a better condition conducive to the health of each and every individual. For that the stumbles in the path for good health like pollutions, hazardous chemicals etc. have to be met with. So, for the protection of health, waste management is necessary. The working of health care system itself produces waste and with the increase in health care units, labs, dispensaries etc. the amount of these wastes are increasing. Bio-medical wastes are highly dangerous and can cause potential damage to human beings and for the environment as a whole. This includes both infectious and non-infectious and hazardous and non-hazardous. Some hospitals or pathological laboratory wastes may contain toxic chemicals, like mercury, xylene and formalin which are hazardous. Hospital waste normally poses a risk for patients and personnel who handle these wastes and the improper disposal practices of hospital waste affects the people who come in direct contact with it. Waste piles also attract a variety of disease vectors, including mosquitoes and flies and can cause environmental pollution, unpleasant odours, and growth of insects, rodents and worms; it may lead to transmission of diseases like typhoid, cholera, HIV, Tuberculosis, Hepatitis B and C through injuries from sharps contaminated with human blood. Also antibiotics poured down the drain can kill beneficial microbes and bacteria in septic systems and dumping of healthcare waste in uncontrolled areas can have a direct environmental effect by contaminating soils and underground water (Kamalakanta and Akhilesh 2012: 63). There is no clear cut data regarding the amount of bio-medical waste that are generated in India but it is estimated that about 0.33 million tonnes of hospital waste is being generated per year. Except a few hospitals most of the hospitals and dispensaries including the government ones doesn't have adequate waste disposal mechanism. The dangerous precedence is that the used bandages, syringes, human tissues, used culture media containing microorganisms are dumped in the open bins or into the water bodies or allowing it to mix with other wastes. So it is not shocking that India is in the verge of an HIV epidemic and the WHO has already cautioned about that. Bio-medical waste management should be given top priority by the government.

In India, cities and towns generate 50 million tonnes of solid waste and 38 million litres of sewage every year. Local bodies entrusted with the task of disposing it have neither resources nor capability to do that resulting most of these wastes get dumped up and untreated. This not only has a hampering effect on the environment but also on the human right to health. Environmental degradation due to accumulation of waste materials results in the outbreak of diseases like plague, chikungunya, dengue and jaundice. Fall in waste management normally affects the dual cardinal rights to pollution free environment and right to health. These interrelated rights can be protected only through better waste management. e-Wastes now have become a major polluter and its redundancy a major health and environmental challenge to developing countries including India. India is having an increased consumption of electronic goods and is becoming a major destination for manufacturing these goods, especially after the opening up of its market or economy in 1991. Unfortunately, India has also been shortlisted by the United States and European Countries to dump their e-wastes such that over 50 thousand tonnes of e-wastes come to India every year (Gopalji and Priyamvada 2009: 9) blatantly violating the BASEL convention norms, a negative aspect of globalisation.

No definite official data exist on how much e-waste is generated in India or how much is disposed of but there are estimations based on independent studies conducted by the NGOs or government agencies. According to the

Comptroller and Auditor General's (CAG) report, over 7.2 MT (million tonnes) of industrial hazardous waste, four lakh tonnes of electronic waste, 1.5 MT of plastic waste, 1.7 MT of medical waste, 48 MT of municipal waste are generated in the country annually (Rajya Sabha Secretariat 2011: 4). To the Delhi based non-governmental organisation (NGO) Toxics Link, India annually generates $1.5 billion worth of e-waste domestically, with the booming IT sector being the largest contributor, as 30 per cent of its machines reach obsolescence annually. Bangalore, the IT hub of India, alone generates 8,000 tonnes a year (Gopalji and Priyamvada 2009: 6). The main sources of electronic waste in India are the government, public and private (industrial) sectors, which account for almost 70 per cent of total waste generation. The contribution of individual households is relatively small at about 15 per cent; the rest being contributed by manufacturers. The top ten states that generate 70 per cent of the total e-waste generated in India are Maharashtra followed by Tamil Nadu, Andhra Pradesh, Uttar Pradesh, West Bengal, Delhi, Karnataka, Gujarat, Madhya Pradesh and Punjab in the list of e-waste generating states in India. Among top ten cities generating e-waste, Mumbai ranks first followed by Delhi, Bangalore, Chennai, Kolkata, Ahmadabad, Hyderabad, Pune, Surat and Nagpur (ENVIS 2007: 3).

All our metros are in the risk of e-wastes that can corrode India's vast human resource, due to the increased presence of lead. Mumbai faces grave health and environmental risks posed by a whopping 19,000 tonnes of electronic waste produced there. Bangalore generates 10,000 to 15,000 tonnes of e-waste and Chennai ranks third, according to the Central Pollution Control Board (Gopalji and Priyamvada 2009: 6). e-Waste comprises extremely diverse substances which vary from products across different categories. More than a thousand substances fall under hazardous e-waste categories. Broadly, they consist of ferrous and non-ferrous substances. e-Waste is classified as hazardous when elements like lead, mercury, arsenic, cadmium, selenium, hexavalent chromium and brominated flame retardant are present. The most common thing found is that most places have no proper facilities to recycle the waste. So it is resorted to uncontrolled burning, disassembly, disposal, land filling and poor processing. Land filling e-waste, one of the most widely used methods of disposal and is the most dangerous as this waste contains substances such as mercury, cadmium and lead, which are among the most toxic agents which can cause a wide variety of human ailments if they leach into the soil and water. In addition, landfills are also prone to uncontrolled fires, which can release toxic fumes. The recycling of e-waste is a major concern in India. The workers in the recycling sector are dominated by the urban poor with very low literacy levels and hence they have very little awareness regarding the potential hazards of e-waste. Among the urban poor, there are a substantial number of women and children engaged in various recycling activities which further exaggerate the problem of e-waste as they are more vulnerable to the hazards from this kind of waste.

Air pollution is another problem that affects human health. Mainly the cities and the people living there are being exposed to high levels of air pollution. The graveness of the issue is that, as per the World Bank estimates, Indians are spending Rs 4550 crores every year on treatment of diseases caused by ambient air pollution (Current Science 1999: 334). Increased pollution causes decline of the lung function or increase in respiratory symptoms such as cough, shortness of breath, wheezing and asthma attacks. The rate of respiratory diseases in metros like Delhi has been medically assessed to be eight to nine times higher than the national average (Gopalji and Priyamvada 2009: 6). This is partly because of automobile emissions, and other 'normal' pollutants, but also partly because of the substances found in e-waste. Inhaling and coming into contact with them on a regular basis can damage the brain, nervous system, lungs, kidneys and the reproductive system. Innocent people become victims of what can only be described as environmental crimes. Working in poorly ventilated or enclosed areas without masks and technical expertise, results in exposure to death by slow poisoning. All these will increase morbidity.

Air pollution is also induced by the careless handling of pesticides. Though this is a routine issue, the use of Endosulfan in Kasaragod created grave health hazards in human beings. Endosulfan is a chlorinated hydrocarbon insecticide of the cyclodiene subgroup which acts as a contact poison in a wide variety of insects and mites. Endosulfan can enter the body through inhalation by breathing air contaminated with endosulfan, from eating and drinking contaminated products, or through skin. It is lethal and increased exposure to it can cause death. Though its aerial spraying was strictly prohibited, the Kerala Government owned Plantation Corporation sprayed it in the cashew plantations in Kasaragod to contain the menace of the tea mosquito, since 1978, till 2001 regularly three times every year (GoK 2011: 9). It was the district collector who gave permission for the aerial spraying of endosulfan, but it was without taking into account the harmful effects of it. At the same time the plantation corporation followed the conditions for name sake only. The terrain was unsuitable for aerial spraying considering the relatively high rainfall and geographical structure. The result was that endosulfan totally polluted the air and water bodies in that area and unusual diseases began to spring up. Today children are living with congenital anomalies, mental retardation, physical deformities, cerebral palsy, epilepsy and hydrocephalus. Psychiatric problems are also on the increase and suicidal tendencies are high. Doctors have reported many cases of cancer, especially of the liver and blood (GoK 2011: 9, 11; NIOH 2003: 5; Thanal 2002: 3).

Since 1979, farmers and the local media have raised the concern that endosulfan and its aerial spray is the cause for the ailments seen in cattle and later in human beings (Thanal 2002: 7). But the health department and the plantation corporation did not pay much heed to the concerns of the people. The approach of the District Collector was apathetic as he didn't issue orders to stop aerial spraying. The Kerala State Pollution Control Board came with a report that there is no trace of endosulfan on the waters of Kasaragod (Thanal 2002: 8). When the members of the *Down to Earth* met P.C. John, the District Collector, his comment was that "when ministers and elected representatives were discussing the matter it wasn't proper for him to say anything." The same person was reported as saying in an interview with Star News – *How to stop it (aerial spraying)? Why should I stop it? I am giving consent as per rule?* (NIT 2006: 22). No government machinery came for the support of the local population and at last in October 2001 the Hosdurg Munsif court ordered the permanent prohibition of use of any insecticide by air. Later, the Munsif Court of Kasaragod suspended all pesticide applications in Kasaragod taluk in February 2001. By the time the use of endosulfan was banned the worst damage had occurred in the surrounding areas where it was sprayed. Today villages in Kasaragod District are complaining from peculiar and complex variety of diseases unprecedented in this part of the country. The peculiar set of diseases has affected at least 15 panchayaths in the District.

Water borne diseases are on the rise as a result of water pollution. Growing population, lack of sanitary condition, poverty, poor planning, industrial pollution, over exploitation of natural water and natural disasters are the main reasons of pollution of water. Only a small fraction of the sewage gets treated and the rest flows into water bodies as a result water gets polluted with pathogenic microorganisms, parasites, and toxic chemicals, all mostly due to human intervention. Those who are exposed to polluted water are in the risk of diseases like cholera, diarrhoea, hepatitis A, E and typhoid. Unclean water and poor sanitation has been identified as the second biggest killer of children worldwide. Every year, 3.5 million people die of waterborne diseases and half the hospital beds on Earth are occupied by people suffering from waterborne disease (General Assembly 2010). Every 20 seconds, a child dies as a result of poor sanitation i.e. 1.5 million preventable deaths each year (UN 2011). Diarrhoeal diseases are major public health problems among the children under the age of five years and mortality and morbidity levels due to water borne diseases are high in India. Of the 37 diseases identified as major causes of death in developing countries, 21 are related to water and sanitation.

Health care management is a complex task that demands multifaceted actions. On the one hand, the public health care machineries have to be strengthened and expanded to even remote areas. Quality care needs to be ensured that too at free of cost to the poor, if not possible, at least at an affordable rate to all sections. This is essential as majority in the country lags behind economically. The high cost of medical care will jeopardise the interests of the poor, marginalised, destitute and the women. Private sector because of its for-profit nature is no longer an alternative to the public health care institutions. As the morbidity pattern is increasing which in many cases demand prolonger care, the private sector due to its high cost involved cannot be depended upon. Together with this the spiralling cost of medicines and other pharma and surgical items should be kept under control. Medicines are an integral part of health care and the modern health care is unthinkable without the availability of necessary medicines. Medicines not only saves life and promote health but also prevent epidemics and diseases. Medicines being the weapon of mankind to fight diseases and illness, accessibility to medicines form the fundamental right of every human being. Medicines being a Hobson's choice, an exorbitant increase in the price of medicines will adversely affect the poor who are in need of medical care.

Together with cure prevention has a major role in health care. Better externalities have to be created so that illness can be prevented. This includes a pollution free surrounding, safe drinking water, adequate food and sanitation. The generalist bureaucrats have a major role in these areas, when the specialists can take care of the cure part. They should facilitate the timely devolution of the allotted fund for the various activities so that the policies and programmes can be completed in the stipulated period. As food supplements health, the public distribution system should be strengthened to ensure adequate food grains to all. Similar is the necessity of safe drinking water. Ensuring basic things of sustenance for all will to a great extend help in protecting health. Waste management needs to be taken as a priority as it corrodes human health and the environment alike. Vector borne diseases are on the rise due to lack of sanitation and piling up of wastes in and around cities and its outskirts. Until and unless proper measures to prevent diseases are put into action, health cannot be an assured one for all. Determination from the bureaucracy and active role with the citizens can make all these accessible and real. People won't hesitate to help the bureaucrats if they work in a responsible manner. What is needed is bureaucracy should take the lead role.

References

Aneesh, Nair (2011): "Marunninupolum Mariyadhaellathe....," (M) *Malayala Manorama*, June 6.

Baru, R.V. (2000): "Privatisation and Corporatisation," *Seminar*, 489, May, http://www.india-seminar.com/2000/489/489percent20baru.htm.

Census (2011): *Maternal and Child Mortality and Total Fertility Rates*, Office of the Registrar General and Census Commissioner, Ministry of Home Affairs, Government of India, July 7.

Chakraborty, S. (2003) "Private Health Provision in Uttar Pradesh, India." in Yazbeck, A.S. and Peters, D.H. (eds.), *Health Policy Research in South Asia: Building Capacity for Reform*, World Bank, Washington DC, 257–77.

Chandrasekhar, C.P. (2012): "A Big Step Forward," *Frontline*, 29(8), May 4.

CII and HOSMAC (2011): *Partnership in Health Care: A Public-Private Perspective*, White Paper, Confederation of Indian Industry and HOSMAC, March.

Current Science (2007): "Urban Air Pollution," *Current Science*, 77(3), August 10, 334-6.

Dilip, T.R. (2008): *Role of Private Hospitals in Kerala: An Exploration*, Working Paper 400, Centre for Development Studies, Thiruvananthapuram.

ENVIS (2007): "E-Waste Indian Perspective," *ENVIS*, Urban Municipal Waste Management Newsletter, November.

ERF (2006): *Government Health Expenditure in India: A Benchmark Study*, Economic Research Foundation, New Delhi.

Express News (2012): "Public Health System has Collapsed, Says Jairam," *The New Indian Express*, Kochi, November 17, 1.

General Assembly (2010): *Resolution Recognizing Right to Water* and *Sanitation*, Resolution A/RES/64/292, United Nations General Assembly, July 28.

Gita, Sen (2003): "Inequalities and Health in India," *Development*, Sage, New Delhi, 18-20.

Gita, Sen., Aditi, Iyer and Asha, George (2002): "Structural Reforms and Health Equity: A Comparison of NSS Surveys, 1986-87 and 1995-96," *Economic and Political Weekly*, XXXVII(14), April 6-12, 1342-50.

Godwin, S.K. and Varatharajan, K. (2007): "Drug Price Differentials across Different Retail Market Settings," *Health Administrator*, XIX(1), 41-7.

GoK (2011): *Report on Health Effects of Endosulfan And Progress of Rehabilitation Activities in Kerala*, Department of Health and Family Welfare, Government of Kerala, April 20.

Gopalji, Malviya and Priyamvada, M. (2009): "India is yet to Realise e-Waste Hazards," *The New Indian Express*, Kochi, July 16, 9.

Hong, Evelyne (2000): *Globalisation and the Impact on Health, A Third World View*, Third World Network, Penang.

IIPS and Macro International (2007): "Morbidity and Health Care," *National Family Health Survey (NFHS-3), 2005–06, Volume I*, International Institute for Population Sciences and Macro International, Mumbai.

IIPS and ORC Macro (2000): *National Family Health Survey (NFHS-2) 1998-99*, IIPS, Mumbai.

Jayan, Mohan (2010): "Ten-fold Price for Medicines in Kerala," (M) *Malayala Manorama*, June 21, 1.

Joe, Mathew C. (2010): "NPPA Study Finds Huge Gap in Cancer Drug Prices," *Business Standard*, October 13.

Kamalakanta, Muduli and Akhilesh, Barve (2012): "Challenges to Waste Management Practices in Indian Health Care Sector," *IPCBEE*, 32, 62-67.

Kannan, K.P., Thankappan, K.R., Kutty, V.R. (1991): *Health and Development in Rural Kerala*, Kerala Sastra Sahitya Parishad, Thiruvananthapuram.

KMSCL (2012): Kerala Medical Services Corporation Ltd., Thiruvananthapuram.

Manorama News (2011): 17 June 2011, 01:10 pm IST.

Monali, Doshi (2010): *Hospital Sector Research*, Northbridge Capital, November.

Nabae, Koji (2003): "The Health Care System in Kerala – Its Past Accomplishments and New Challenges," *Journal, National Institute of Public Health*, Department of Public Health, Toho, 140-5.

NIOH (2002): *The Investigation of Unusual Illnesses Allegedly Produced by Endosulfan Exposure in Padre Village of Kasargod District (N.kerala)*, National Institute of Occupational Health, Ahmedabad.

Nozick, R. (1974): *Anarchy, State and Utopia*, Basic Books, New York.

Parayil, G. (2000): *Kerala: The Development Experience*, London: Zed Books.

Parvati, Iyer and Dinesh, Abrol (2008): "Financing of Health," *India, Science and Technology*, www.nistads.res.in accessed on 08-07-2010.

Pellegrino, E.D. (1999): "The Commodification of Medical and Health Care: The Moral Consequences of a Paradigm Shift from a Professional to a Market Ethic," *Journal of Medicine and Philosophy*, 24(3), 243-66.

Planning Board (2010): *Economic Review 2009*, State Planning Board, Government of Kerala, Thiruvananthapuram.

Planning Commission (2008): "Health and Family Welfare," *Eleventh Five-Year Plan, 2002–2007*, Vol. II, Chapter 3, Planning Commission, Government of India, New Delhi.

Rajya Sabha Secretariat (2011): *E-waste in India*, Research Unit, Rajya Sabha Secretariat, New Delhi, June.

Ramachandran, R. (2012): "Western Warning," *Frontline*, 29(8), May 4, 18-21.

Raman Kutty, V. (2000): "Historical Analysis of the Development of Health Care Facilities in Kerala State, India," *Health Policy and Planning*, Oxford University Press, 15(1), 103-9.

Rao, P.H. (2012): "The Private Health Sector in India: A Framework for Improving the Quality of Care," *ASCI Journal of Management*, 41 (2), 14–39.

Reinhart, Philip (2011): "De-regulation, Drug Prices and the Human Right to Health," *Pragati*, 5(117), July-September, 62-9.

—— (2010a): *Commodification and Commercialisation of Health Care: The Impact of Globalisation with Special Reference to Kerala*, M.Phil Thesis, Department of Politics and International Studies, Pondicherry Central University, Puducherry.

—— (2010b): "Commodification of Health Care: The Expansion of Market to an Under Marketised Sphere," *Holistic Thought*, IX(2), July-December, 158-67.

Santhosh, M.B. (2011): "Maruninum Venam Milma Model," (M) *Kerala Kaumudi*, Kochi, October 12, 6.

Stefan, Timmermans and Rene, Almeling (2009): "Objectification, Standardisation and Commodification in Health Care: A Conceptual Readjustment" *Social Science and Medicine*, 69, 21-7.

Thanal (2002): *Preliminary Findings of the Survey on the Impact of Aerial Spraying of Endosulfan on the People and Ecosystem in Kasaragod, Keralam, India*, Thanal, Thiruvananthapuram.

The Hindu (2012): "MNCs Fear Side Effects of Nexavar Ruling," *The Hindu*, Thiruvananthapuram, March 14, 17.

Urmi, Goswami (2012): "Investing in Social Sector," *Yojana*, April, 38-42.

Wiliam, Joe and Mishra, U.S. (2009): *Household Out-of-Pocket Healthcare Expenditure in India: Levels, Patterns and Policy Concerns*, Working Paper 418, Centre for Development Studies, Thiruvananthapuram.

World Bank (2001): *Raising the Sights: Better Health Systems for India's Poor*, Health, Nutrition, Population Sector Unit India, South Asia Region, World Bank, Washington DC.

UN (2011): "Drinking Water and Sanitation," United Nations Water Statistics, *UN Water*, http://www.unwater.org/statistics_san.html accessed on 08-11-2011.

12

Bureaucracy and Environmental Conservation

Conservation of the Nature has got added attention these days, most specifically in the age of Global Warming. It was too late for the human beings to understand that the progress he achieved during the last ten or twelve decades had created imbalances in the nature and it gripped to such an extent that if not taken into consideration, one day or other the earth will perish. In the surge for profit, man ignored the importance of the environment — the forests, rivers, lakes, streams, wetlands, glaciers, seas and oceans and the innumerable animal and plant species living in that. By the time when human beings became aware of the need of protecting the environment, irreparable damage had occurred to the eco-system, round the world. Almost all major river systems have got polluted. Studies conducted by the Stockholm International Water Institute points out that in the global south, more than 90 per cent of sewage and 70 per cent of industrial waste are dumped untreated into the surface water. Every day two million tons of sewage and industrial waste are discharged into the world's water (UN 2011), the equivalent of the weight of the entire human population of 6.8 billion people. Across the Globe, the water systems have become the dumping grounds of industrial, bio-medical and domestic wastes.

The damage to the nature didn't stop with the pollution of water system. Day in and day out the green caps of the world is declining at a startling rate. According to the World Resources Institute, the world has lost about half of its forest cover. Data from the UN Food and Agriculture Organisation shows that deforestation was at its highest rate in the 1990s, when each year the world lost on average 16 million hectares of forest. From 4,168 million hectares in 1990, the total forest cover declined to 4,033 million hectares in 2010 (Emily 2012). In India too forest cover showed a decline. India State of Forest Report 2011 shows that there is a decrease of 367 square kilometer in forest cover, in comparison to 2009. Forests account to 78.29 million hectares or 23.81 per cent of the geographical area of the country; of this the very dense forest accounts only 2.54 per cent. Forests are primarily threatened by land clearing for agriculture and pasture and by harvesting wood for fuel or industrial uses. Brazil, home to the Amazon forests that has 13 per cent of the world's forested area has lost 55 million hectares since 1990, an area three fourths the size of Texas. Between 2000 and 2010, Brazil lost 2.6 million hectares of forest each year, more than any other country. South America lost 40 million hectares of forest during the same period (Emily 2012).

Global rates of deforestation are not capturing up the full damage done to the world's forests. At the same time forest degradation from selective logging, road construction, pollutions, climate change, and other means compromises the health of remaining forests. Replacing natural old-growth forests with a monoculture of an exotic species is greatly reducing biodiversity in our forests. Deforestation and forest degradation directly threaten as many as 400 million people including 50 million forest indigenous people who depend on forests for subsistence. Moreover, the process of deforestation generates large amounts of carbon dioxide, equivalent to 20 per cent of global emissions from fossil fuels, making deforestation the second most important contributor to global warming and results in annual degradation of some 12 million hectares of fertile land and loss of thousands of species (Arnoldo 2000: 1).

Global Warming

Global warming is nothing but the retaliation or after effects of the damage that human beings have done to the environment. It escalated to as the only most danger to the planet earth while exempting the probability of one more world war, a huge asteroid, or a fatal plague. Global Warming is a global problem affecting the world round; damaging the aquatic eco-system in the Murray Darling basin; drying up of Yangtze due to precipitation decrease; warming up of the largest fresh water lake, Baikal; melting up of the glaciers of Himalayas; decline in the area of Lake Chad and extended dry seasons in Africa; damage to the riparian eco-systems in the Elbe region; creation of multi-year droughts in USA and Southern Canada; impairing the non-consumptive water uses in the Mississippi; shrinking of the glaciers of Andes and so on (Reinhart 2012a: 288). Warming of the isolated but enormous Lake Baikal (Russia) is a clear signal that climate change has affected even the most remote corners of our planet (Science Daily 2008).

The phenomenon of global warming has its myriad and numerous adverse effects on both the environment and human beings. That effect is extensive and covers every sphere of one's life. The effect of global warming is increasing the average temperature of the earth and the Inter-governmental Panel on Climate Change (IPCC) projects that the global mean temperature may increase between 1.4 and 5.8 degrees Celsius (C) by 2100 (Jayant *et al.* 2006: 314). This unprecedented increase is expected to have severe impacts on the global hydrological system, ecosystems, sea level, crop production and related processes. The impact would be particularly severe in the tropical areas, which mainly consist of developing countries, including India. The rise in temperature and precipitation patterns increases the frequency, duration, and intensity of other extreme weather events, such as floods, droughts, heat waves, and tornadoes (Camille and John 2005: 339-44). The total annual power of hurricanes has already increased markedly since 1975, because their average intensity and average duration have increased. While there is increased precipitation in the upper latitudes, there is a decrease in the lower latitudes, including parts of South Asia, an aspect of concern for India. When some areas of Earth will become wet due to global warming, other areas will suffer serious droughts and heat waves. Africa will receive the worst of it, and more severe droughts are also expected in Europe. All these will seriously affect the availability of fresh water all over the world, especially in Africa, where it is already a dangerously rare commodity.

Another important effect of global warming is rise in ocean level caused by expansion of water and melting of ice. Observations since 1961 show that ocean has warmed to a depth of at least 3,000 meters and has been absorbing more than 80 per cent of the heat added to the climate system. Smaller glaciers have been de-glaciated by almost 38 per cent in this period. In the Northern Hemisphere, spring and summer sea-ice cover decreased by 10 to 15 per cent from the 1950s to the year 2000; sea-ice extent in the Nordic seas has shrunk by 30 per cent over the last 130 years (UNEP 2003: 4). IPCC study reveals that melting of polar ice caps has contributed between 0.2 and 0.4 mm annually to sea level rise over the twentieth century and the sea level is predicted to accelerate from 20-30 cm over the twentieth century and to 35-90 cm over the twenty-first century (IPCC 2001). The melting of ice caps will throw the global eco-system out of balance. Ice caps are fresh water, and when they melt they will desalinate the ocean, i.e., making it less salty. The desalinisation of the gulf current will "screw up" ocean currents, which regulate temperatures. Temperature rises and changing landscapes in the Arctic Circle will endanger several species of animals. Besides all these salt water intrusion into inland water bodies like ponds, lakes, etc., will result in fresh water getting polluted (salty), increasing the grave of fresh water scarcity. As the effects of global warming are vast and cover every sphere of life, if we do not take note of the alarming rate of its growth, one day the life on earth will come to an end.

The warming of the climate system is unequivocal and as it is evident there can be no room for skepticism on global warming. The nature and its resources need to be protected, not only for catering the needs of the present generation but also for the coming ones. This demands a meticulous plan for the most efficient and rational allocation of the existing resources and preservation of the same. Being a global problem, global warming demands a global action. But the International Community failed to reach at a consensus regarding an effective action. So it is up to the domestic state systems and its inhabitants to take necessary actions. The state is expected to protect its citizens and make necessary conditions for the enjoyment of their rights. Governments must take measures to protect the forest cover including the water systems, conserve the various species and their eco systems, adopt measures to reduce various kinds of pollutions and build infrastructure to protect coastal areas and to improve management of water basins. Moreover, government intervention is necessary as there involves a question of the allocation of scarce resources (for e.g., water) to the varying and diverse needs that are increasing day by day. Bureaucracy due to its dual role in policy making and its implementation can play a lead role in this regard, rather than any other organisations.

The need for protecting the environment is clear beyond doubt, because existence itself becomes a big question without nature. So the resources of the nature are to be distributed without affecting the ecological balance. Environmental protection and human rights protection have many commonalities. It is quite natural that environmental degradation or pollution has its repercussions on environment as well as human rights. The Right to Life becomes meaningless in the absence of a clean and safe environment. The nature of environment and human rights problems are similar in all countries. Such common concerns include water pollution, i.e., lack of access to drinking water, pollution of water resources, pollution due to toxins; air pollution that includes industrial air pollution, emission of sulphur and nitrous oxides, carbon dioxide and CFC emissions; land pollution; pollution due to dumping of waste, deforestation; destruction of eco-systems and biodiversity etc. In all these cases the destruction of natural resources invariably affects the very basic fabric of human rights. Preserving the environment on the one hand thus, no doubt protects human rights.

The Constitution of India provides ample provisions for the protection of human rights and environment. A separate part (Part III) has been provided for the protection of basic rights, not only of the citizens but also of other population (it depends). As per the Directive Principles, the state is obliged to protect the environment, forest and wild life (Article 48A). It is the fundamental duty of the Indian citizen to "protect and improve the natural environment including forests, lakes, rivers and wild life" (Article 51A). Besides this, many environmental laws were enacted with the purpose of controlling pollution and promoting environmental conservation, which includes: Wildlife Protection Act, 1972; Water, Prevention and Control of Pollution Act, 1974; Forest Conservation Act, 1980; Environment Protection Act, 1986; Factories Act, 1987; and the Green Tribunal Act 2011.

During 1980's there underwent a sea change not only in administrative and legislative activities but also in judicial decisions. The Supreme Court of India widened the ambit of Article 21 (No person shall be deprived of his life or personal liberty except according to procedure established by law) to include Right to Safe Drinking Water, Right to Health, Clean Environment and so on. Maneka Gandhi case was a starting point in this regard. The Supreme Court accepted the principle of due process of law with regard to judicial review in Maneka Gandhi case (AIR 1978) and held that the right to life and personal liberty will not stand in isolation. The principle of natural justice has been brought in while analysing the reasons for the violation of the rights mentioned in Article 21 of the Constitution. In Francis Coralie case (AIR 1981), the Supreme Court ruled that right to life is not confined to mere animal existence, but extends to the right to live with basic human dignity. In Rural Litigation and Entitlement Kendra vs. State of Uttar Pradesh, the Supreme Court of India extended the scope of Article 21 to include the right to live in a healthy environment. The court upheld the right of people to live in a healthy environment with minimal disturbance to ecological balance (AIR 1985). This got concretised in Chhetriya Padushan and Subash Kumar cases, where the court declared (latter case) that "right to life enshrined in Article 21 includes the right to enjoyment of pollution free water and air for full enjoyment of life" (AIR 1991). By adopting international principles such as polluter pays principle, precautionary principle, sustainable development principle, public trust doctrine and the principle of absolute liability, the Supreme Court consolidated its position in strengthening "Right to Healthy Environment" concept under Article 21.

Here comes the importance of environment friendly development, popularly known as sustainable development. Sustainable development encompasses a number of principles: Basic needs of life should be available to all human beings; consumption of natural resources should be utility based; Economic growth should safeguarded for the interest of the future generation to come; ecological process should continue unabated; the development and maintenance of environment should run simultaneously; regional imbalance in conservation of nature should be minimised or removed; international fraternity should be united to fight the menace of pollution; a long-term view should be adopted for a better relation between human and species generation. Sustainable development thus is a moderate position between extreme of no growth verses unlimited growth and is based on the use of renewable resources in harmony with ecological system. It is moderate in the sense that there is no restriction on using the resources for development. However, there is restriction in using the resources exhaustively. Therefore sustainable development should address effectively the question of environmental degradation.

Globalisation and the Enclosure of the Greens

Globalisation, the dominant development model of our times is not one that takes into consideration the question of environmental conservation. In the unfolding of capital natural resources have been appropriated and in the stage of globalisation too the looting of the earth's natural resources forms the main objective of the dominant capital (Samir Amin 2001). Key to globalisation is commodification. New commodities are created with the expansion of markets to new geographical areas and new sectors that may not yet have been marketised. Commodification is accomplished through the deregulation of exchange mechanisms, allowing penetration of market mechanism into under-marketised spheres. Water is one such commodity and commodification of water is considered as a direct assault on the commons.

Commons are the resources that are held in common or shared among the communities. Traditionally, commons were defined as the elements of the environment — forests, atmosphere, rivers, fisheries or grazing land — that are shared, used and enjoyed by all. Today, commons comprises a wide range of shared assets and forms of community governance; some are tangible, while others are more abstract, political, and cultural. The tangible assets of the commons include the vast quantities of oil, minerals, timber, grasslands, and other natural resources on public lands... (Bollier 2002). To Richard Bocking (2003), the noted Canadian environmentalist, "Commons are those things to which we have rights just by being a member of the human family - the air we breathe, the freshwater we drink, the seas, forests, mountains, the genetic heritage through which all life is transmitted, the diversity of life itself." So commons can be defined as the free gift of nature and all are entitled to enjoy its benefits, without paying for it. The real owners of the commons are thc people and the government is the trustee and steward of these resources.

The rise of economic globalisation has resulted in what is known as Green Captivism or Captivism of the Greens. By green captivism is meant the economic captivism of the greens or the products of nature for continued profit. This captivism has been through enclosing the commons and dispossessing many (especially the indigenous population) from their access to these resources; through conquest, robbery, force, market economics and economic instruments like foreign aids and loans by the Triad Governments and Multinational Corporations, with the direct and indirect support of the international and regional financial institutions, especially the World Bank

(Reinhart 2012b). The result is a hypertrophic market that colonises untouched natural resources and public life while eroding the democratic commonwealth (Bollier 2002). The enclosure of the commons has been through the process of privatisation, commercialisation and commodification. From a neo-liberal perspective, neither privatisation nor commercialisation will ensure the conversion of resources into commodities, but commodification will. Commodification entails the creation of an economic good through the application of mechanisms intended to appropriate and standardise a class of goods or services and enabling these goods or services to be sold at a price determined through market exchange (Bakker 2005: 544). "Enclosures" disproportionately benefit the corporate class and effectively deprive ordinary citizens, of access to resources that they legally or morally own.

Economic globalisation and free market fundamentalism crashed the health and integrity of the commons. Multinational corporations gained access to the genetic, mineral, timber and water resources of even the most remote parts of the earth. Profit driven exploitation of natural resources has resulted in large scale deforestation by cutting down hectares of timber in the name of land for development. This is the case with minerals; oil and natural gas reserves. The water reserves of the world, including the ground water got severely exploited and polluted. This happened in Wisconsin (United States), Newfoundland (Canada), Plachimada (India) and many other areas. As a result of the extraction by the Cola Company the ground water level in Plachimada drowned to that extend that for drinking water the local population had to go for miles. Water shortages have occurred in Varanasi, Thane, and Tamil Nadu as well. Market exploitation, besides depleting the natural resources, degrades the environment making it harmful to the development of land, water, air, forests and other natural features of planet earth.

Fresh air is one that is going to be commodified in the near future, with the further expansion of market to the under-marketised spheres. This may appear to be utopian for many who may smile like the ones who did so when it was said that water is going to be a commodity. The air we breathe in is getting the similar circumstances that have led to the commodification of other commons, i.e., scarcity and increased demand. When the demand for fresh air (pollution free atmosphere) is on the rise, with the increase in population it is becoming a scarce resource due to the mounting pollutions. Clean atmosphere is essential for all forms of living things, not only for human beings. As per the neo-liberal school, in a situation in which the demand is on the rise and supply shorter, rational allocation of the resource can be made only through attaching a price that reflects the true value of the commodity. The true value includes what John Briscoe compounds "use cost"[1] and "opportunity cost"[2] with regard to pricing of water. Pricing based on this balance will send the appropriate signals on how the scarce resource (air) will be best allocated, distributed and consumed. An environment of free market is where this balance can be best and most easily achieved (John 1996).

The private sector will be the key player in such a market which operates on the principles of cost recovery, profit maximisation, cost-benefit analysis, demand-driven investments, etc., where access to resources is determined by the willingness-to-pay for it. Such a market not only excludes the poor who couldn't pay for the services but also legitimises such a practice. Commodification of air will work in a manner different from that of other 'commodities' as it is not possible easy to measure the amount of fresh air (oxygen) one may breath in, like that it is done in hospital (to patients who are given oxygen supply). So individual pricing is not possible in the initial stages. At the same time, from an emergency supply, the use of oxygen bottles will be fashioned as a culture, just as the use of bottled water was made a part of the middle class culture. It will manifest in the form of oxygen bottles hanging in front of the shops, first in the polluted urban spaces and later in the villages. The use of oxygen bottles will become inevitable in the industrial areas, metros and other polluted cities and near the dumping (waste) yards of corporations, in the near future. While entering the Chennai central it is the foul smell that welcomes everyone and this is the case with other metros or its outskirts and the waste dumping yards. Smoke supplements this in the industrial areas. So it is quite natural that when one passes through any of these areas that person will feel the desire of fresh air, which will be fulfilled by oxygen bottles in the near future. With the circulation of air in the atmosphere, pollution spreads to other areas and this causes the demand for oxygen bottles in the affected areas.

Like the refreshment centres and parks there will be "oxygen zones or parlours" where access is determined by the willingness-to-pay for it. Oxygen connections to individual households will only be near the so-called needy areas in the initial stages. The needy areas mean those polluted areas where the people are willing to pay for the supply. The larger market will replace the present carbon credit system with a corporate controlled market system where it is not the polluter who is going to give the price but the "needy." Like commodification in other areas it is the Third World that is going to be the worst affected. Pointing the inefficiency and financial crunch of the state, private sector will come for the 'purification of the air' on what we can call the BOT basis. But as it is not possible to have a toll plaza in this case tax or cess like instruments will be used to recover the cost involved together with profit. New instruments of market may come in picture in the latter stages. Commodification of air will result in grave consequences, much higher than that of commodification of water. The non-availability of clean atmosphere and inability to pay for it will force a large section of the population including the slum dwellers to depend on the polluted atmosphere to breathe in, creating serious health hazards leading to either a sudden or a slow death, the denial of human right to life and the associated rights for a dignified life.

Bureaucracy and Environmental Conservation

Bureaucracy has a positive role in ensuring environmental conservation. Being the one who are steering the wheel of administration they can do a lot of things that can promote development and at the same time can protect environment, natural resources and ensure equity in the distribution of the resources. The things include adequate measures for waste management; protection of all forms of eco systems including wet lands and paddy fields; conservation of rivers, lakes, watersheds and ponds; preventing the bulldozing of mountains. In all these tasks the lower bureaucracy has a prominent role. It is not possible for the District Collector to conduct raids round the clock for checking the sand mafia, a village officer or the block level officer can do this task more easily and frequently than the collector. But the illegal nexus between the sand mafias-police-politicians and local bureaucrats thwarts many efforts to stop illegal sand mining in our rivers. Experiences from Kollam and Calicut districts of the Kerala State shows that when the higher echelons in service were determined to stop the illegal mining, the lower echelons were forced to act. Under pressure from the Kollam City Police Commissioner, the local police was forced to act upon the sand mafias and when it came to a stage that emptied their pockets, they began requesting the sand mafias to get the Commissioner transferred (Malayala Manorama 2012: 3). In Calicut, the District Collector K.V. Mohankumar IAS personally led the operation against the sand mafias. Though the illegal nexus chalked out plans to assassin the City Police Commissioner of Kollam City (The Pioneer 2012); or dared to attempt twice at the life of the Calicut District Collector, the same day while on an operation to stop illegal sand mining (The Hindu 2012: 1; Kerala Kaumudi 2012: 7), both were not ready to retreat from their mission and the result was a sharp decrease in the number of illegal mining.

The most specific example for an MNC attack over the local environment is in Plachimada of the Palakkad District in the State of Kerala. Plachimada is the living example of the ill effects of the enclosure of the commons; inglorious exploitation of the local resource by a corporate giant named Coco-Cola; apathy of the bureaucracy and politicians towards the problems of the common man and when it comes to our subject matter how the bureaucracy shouldn't be towards environmental issues. An ideal bureaucracy should be one that does the opposite of what bureaucrats concerned with the issues in Plachimada has done. In making the situation worse, both to the humans and to the environment, the role of the District Collector, RDO, other officers of the Revenue Department, officers of the Ground Water Department, State Pollution Control Board etc. cannot be overlooked.

Coco-Cola, which was banned in India in 1977 returned to India in 1993 when the decision was made in 1991 by then ruling government to initiate an economic reform that opened the doors of the country to globalisation and privatisation. On October 8th 1999 Hindustan Coca-Cola Beverages Pvt. Ltd. applied to Perumatty Panchayat for permission to set up a bottling plant in Plachimada. Early the following year, on January 27th, the panchayat granted a license to Coca-Cola for setting up and running the factory. The Coca-Cola plant was built on a 15-hectare plot of what used to be multi-cropped paddy land. It has a working capacity of 15,00,000 litres (Anna 2008: 4) water-based product; that around 85 truckloads of soft drinks and mineral water leave the compound every day carrying approximately 600 cases each containing 24 bottles sized 300 ml. (Eva 2004: 30; Jananeethi Report 2003: 4).

Plachimada is located in a rain shadow region in Chittur taluk of the Palakkad district in the south Indian state of Kerala. Plachimada gets very little rainfall. So the entire region has to rely upon dam irrigation canals and ground water resources for domestic and agricultural water requirements. The Coca-Cola bottling plant at Plachimada in the Perumatty Panchayat started its production on a 42 acre plot, of what used to be multi cropped paddy land. It is argued that the plant was started in violation of Clause (6) of the Kerala Land Utilisation Act, 1967, intended to prevent the use of agricultural land for non-agricultural purposes. Clause (6) specifically prohibits any land cultivated with any food crops not to be cultivated with any other food crop except on a written permission of the Collector including Revenue Divisional Officer (RDO). Sub-Clause (1) says that no holder of any land which has been under cultivation with any food crop for a continuous period of three years immediately before the commencement of this Order, shall convert or attempt to convert or utilise or attempt to utilise such land for the cultivation of any other food crop or for any other purpose except under and in accordance with the terms of a written permission given by the Collector. Sub-Clause (2) similarly prohibits any holder of any land with any food crop for a continuous period of three years at any time after the commencement of this order, shall after the said period of three years do the above said acts except under and in accordance with a written permission given by the Collector/RDO. The Cola company was not having the requisite permission from the District Collector/ RDO to convert or fill up the multi-cropped paddy land for constructing the factory (Mathrubhumi 2005: 27). So the company made its construction by filling up the paddy lands without the required permission. Neither the Collector, nor the RDO, took note of this issue and bended the provisions of the Kerala Land Utilisation Act for the 'good will' of the company.

The action of Department of Water Resources at Plachimada showcases the best example of criminal negligence. They have not dared to conduct inspection at the factory site, even though the fact was known that Coco-Cola was violating the Kerala Ground Water Act. The company had the permission to have only two wells. From the note of the factory dated 16-06-2002 it has only two open wells and six functioning bore wells which extracts only 0.4 to 0.6 million litres of water. Even when that is right, the six functioning bore wells are without permission. Regarding the water extraction at Plachimada, Dr. A. Acuthan, noted hydrologist and environmentalist, estimates that the quantity of water extracted per day is about 1.1 million litres. He observes that the plant has four 7.5 horse power (h.p.) pumps and two 5 h.p. pumps. The total pumping capacity is around 40 h.p. (Surendranath 2003). In Plachimada, Kerala, Coca-Cola extracted 1.5 million litres of deep well water, which they bottled and sold under the names Dasani and BonAqua. The company extracted 7-15 lakh litres of water for production daily (Shaji 2007), leaving back 12 lakh litres of it as waste water, daily (Mathrubhumi 2005: 53). There was uncontrolled extraction and at the same time pollution. Studies conducted by BBC, India Resource Centre, People's Union for Civil Liberties, All India People's Resistance Forum etc. supports this claim.

The Plachimada Cola factory clearly violated the Water (Prevention and Control of Pollution) Act, 1974 and Environment (Protection) Act, 1986. "Under Section 24 of the Water Act, 1974, no person shall knowingly cause or permit any poisonous or polluting matter in excess of the standards to enter into any well or land." Well water studies of the place in question reveal excessive calcium carbonate, magnesium, chloride, salinity and alkalinity, sulphide etc. The groundwater was severely depleted, affecting thousands of communities with water shortages and destroying agricultural activity. The remaining water became contaminated with high chloride and bacteria levels, leading to scabs, eye problems, and stomach aches in the local population. What is worse, there was a visible and steep increase in groundwater pollution after this plant started working. Not only well water made totally unfit for drinking, it was found to be so highly acidic and full of toxins that it was unusable for agriculture or even for washing clothes. In short, a few years of the operation of the Coca-Cola plant had turned the local groundwater into poison (EPW 2010: 8). The State Pollution Control Board is not powerless to deal with the situation. It can issue orders in consonance with Section 24 to stop the pollution. Similarly Section 7 of the Environment Protection Act restrains any person carrying on any industry discharging any environmental pollutant in excess of any standard prescribed. The studies on the sludge collected from the factory reveal excessive cadmium, lead and chromium (Hazards Centre 2006; Mathrubhumi 2005: 28, 81). When this was the case, the Secretary of the State Pollution Control Board gave clean chit to this Multinational Company by suppressing the real data.

The Panchayat Director, an IAS officer played his role for the company by cancelling the order of Panchayat banning licence to the company (Mathrubhumi 2005: 27). The license issued to Hindustan Coca Cola Beverages Ltd. by the Perumatty Panchayat was valid until 31-2-2003. For extending the license for another year from 01-04-2003 onwards, the company applied to the Panchayat on 26-02-2003, paying a licence fee of Rs 30,000. The Panchayat Board decided NOT to renew the licence issued to the Coca-Cola factory on the ground of "protecting public interest," as the company was "causing shortage of drinking water in the area through over-exploitation of ground water sources." The copy of the decision was communicated to the Chief Minister, the Minister for Industries, the Opposition Leader, the District Collector, and the Deputy Director, Local Self Government Department, Government of Kerala. Subsequently, the Panchayat also issued a show-cause notice to the company (as to why the licence should not be cancelled) on 09-04-2003, granting the company 15 days (i.e., upto 24-04-2003) to reply to the notice. The Company moved to the High Court and got an order to move to the appellate authority, viz., the Deputy Director of Panchayats, Government of Kerala, to give his decision on the matter within one month.

The Deputy Director of Panchayats referred the case to his higher-up official, the Director of Local Self Government Department (LSGD). The Director, LSGD has ordered a status quo on the matter, granting the company permission to operate the plant till a final decision is made after hearing the claims of the Panchayat. A first round of hearing was held on 27-06-2003. Further discussion was held on 18 July 2003. The Secretary to Government LSGD, P. Kamalkutty submitted the report on 13th October 2003, in which he said that the Government had examined the whole issue in detail and arrived at the following conclusions: "It is a fact that the Panchayat has not conducted any scientific enquiry or obtained any report from competent agencies before taking the drastic step of canceling the licence already issued by it. It is an admitted fact that the water level in the nearby wells have gone down, but it is not conclusively proved that this is due to the over extraction of ground water by the Company. It is also admitted that the quality of water in at least some of the wells in the area got deteriorated, but there is no clinching evidence to prove that this is due to the activities of the Company... In short, though there is no conclusive evidence to prove the adverse effects of the activities of the Company on the environment and health of the people in the locality, an investigation is ordered into the allegations levelled against the Company and its products. The Panchayat is bound to take a decision only after the investigation team puts its findings on the table. Till then the stay granted by the Government on 12-06-2003 against the order of cancellation of licence by the Panchayat will continue in operation." This lukewarm stand taken by the Secretary LSGD clearly was intended to buy more time for the Government and to let the Company to function without any legal hazards (Hazards Centre 2006).

Criminal negligence of the bureaucracy and apathy of the government and that of political parties in the initial stages added to the crisis of the common man living there. Despite clear violations of the provisions of Kerala

Land Utilisation Act, Water Act (1974), Environmental Protection Act (1986), Coco-Cola was able to continue their operation due to the criminal negligence of the officials of Land Revenue, Water Resources, Pollution Control and Panchayat Raj. Commodification of water in Plachimada too is mixed up with corruption like that of in other cases. When the officials of the Water Resources Department haven't dared to conduct an inspection at the factory site to prevent the excessive exploitation of water, the Pollution Control Board gave a clean chit for the company by providing a white washed report. By the time Cola has to wind up its operation due to popular resistance, the worst human rights and environmental rights violation has occurred. The crime of the company manifests in different layers with varying effect and long term consequences, which includes: denial of right to water; denial of right to livelihood; pollution due to over extraction of ground water and dumping of toxic sludge; cheating the farmers by distributing the sludge by impressing them that it is a good manure; violation of Kerala Land Utilisation Act (1967), Ground Water Act, Environmental Protection Act (1986); violation of human rights and that of women and children; and causing serious health hazards. If any one of the officers of any of the above mentioned departments has acted as per their entrusted duty, an environmental damage could have been averted in Plachimada.

The callous the bureaucracy didn't stop with this. Even after years bureaucracy had its sympathy to the cola company, not to the common man. It was T. Balakrishnan IAS, Principal Secretary, Industries Department of the Government of Kerala who came openly supporting the Cola (Express News 2010: 1). Addressing a seminar organised by the Industrial Development Corporation, Balakrishnan commented that "it was sad that Coco-Cola factory at Plachimada can't be saved." His argument is that as a result of the closure of the cola factory numerous job opportunities have been lost, together with a revenue loss of Rs 500 crore to the state exchequer in the form of taxes. To him, it was because of the "will power" of the Industries Department that Pepsi factory hasn't been closed (The Hindu 2010; Kerala Kaumudi 15 May 2010: 1). The comment of the bureaucrat was so open, the Industries Minister of the Government of Kerala, was also sharing the dais. The argument of the Principal Secretary is baseless and far away from the reality. What the panchayat got as tax is only Rs 7 lakh per year (Mathrubhumi 2005: 15) that too for only two years. The cola company employed only 70 permanent workers and approximately 150-250 casual labourers (Jananeethi Report 2003:4). But, the damage that the company has done to Plachimada, as estimated by the high-level committee appointed by the Government of Kerala, headed by the Additional Chief Secretary, K. Jayakumar IAS is that of Rs 216.26 crore. The report also points that the company had done severe ground water exploitation and it needs years to retain the normal ground water level (Kerala Kaumudi 2010: 1).

When Plachimada showcases the negative role of the bureaucracy the positive role of bureaucracy can be seen in Dindigal and in Silent Valley. Dindigual District Collector, K. Nagarajan ordered the closure of five companies manufacturing packaged water in different parts of the district, on the charges of pumping ground water massively without obtaining prior permission (The Hindu 2011). Nagarajan personally visited the sites when there arouse allegations that the companies were exploiting ground water excessively. This action of the District Collector is an ideal model for all bureaucrats. Such type of actions can preserve the natural resources of the nation together with protecting the rights of the common man, which is a challenge before every leaders and administrators (Jitha 2011: 30).

In Silent Valley, the timely intervention of the Palakkad Collector and the Wild Life Warden averted another "plachimada". Silent Valley is a National Park and is considered as an ecologically sensitive area, home for many endangered species including the Lion Tailed Macaque. The bottling company of the J and J Minerals was proposed to set up on the banks of Karuvarathodu, a tributary of River Kunthi. The company started its construction on 2010 itself but due to the 'unfavourable' report of the Forest Department, District Collector K.V. Mohankumar issued stop memo to the company. The Forest Range Officer of Anavai, N. Anilkumar charged a case against the company. The promoters approached the court and the High Court of Kerala directed the District Collector to hear arguments from both sides and take a "logical" decision based on the hearing. The Collector heard arguments from both sides and in the examination of evidence, S. Sivadas, the Wild Life Warden of Silent Valley, took a stiff stand against the bottling plant. He argued that the excessive pumping of water from the Karuvarathodu will make it dry and this will affect the Adivasi population living nearby. Together with this he pointed out the encroachment of a local stream named Thanichottil Thodu by the company for construction. Taking seriously the report of the wild life warden and pointing out the "possibility" of environmental and water exploitation in such a sensitive area, P.M. Ali Askar Pasha, the District Collector of Palakkad, denied permission to the J and J Minerals to set up the bottling plant at Silent Valley (Madhyamam 2012: 14). The stand of the wild life warden and the acumen of the collector saved not only the environment but also the human rights, especially right to water of the adivasi population in Silent Valley.

Illegal human encroachment is ravaging the country's forests. According to a government document, prepared based on the information provided by the state governments in 2010 and 2011 and 2012, nearly 1.25 million hectares of ecologically fragile areas have been illegally occupied by humans. This is mainly in the states of Andhra Pradesh, Assam and Chhattisgarh. In Assam, 2,59,700 hectares of forest areas are under encroachment and in Andhra Pradesh around 2,56,000 hectares of forestland have been illegally occupied by humans. Forest areas under encroachment in Chhattisgarh is estimated to be 1,18,494 hectares. Chhattisgarh is also an area where Maoist insurgents and legal and illegal mining in biodiversity hotspots are very active. The encroachment in various states include: Karnataka (96,014 hectares), Maharashtra (85,388 hectares), Odisha (78,505 hectares), Arunachal Pradesh (58,553 hectares), Tripura (47,758 hectares), Kerala (44,420 hectares), Gujarat (34,791 hectares), Uttar Pradesh (26,795 hectares), Tamil Nadu (14,352 hectares), and Jammu and Kashmir (13,360 hectares). The report also points the vulnerability of the ecologically fragile Western Ghats region to encroachment. Interestingly, not a single case of violation has been reported from Bihar (Express News 2012: 1).

Large tracts of dense forestlands in India are getting cleared in the name of development. Be it Niyamgiri and Nuagaon in Odisha, Jharsuguda in Jharkhand, Bastar in Chhattisgarh or any other mineral-rich densely forested area this phenomenon is occurring, with the support of the state and central governments. So these regions are witnessing tribal people up in arms against the policies of the government that deprives them of their homely land and livelihood. Taking the case of POSCO Project, India's single largest foreign investment ever, it requires about 1,621 hectares of land, of which about 1,253 hectares is forestland. An additional 2,440 hectares of thickly forested land in Kandadhar hills, a part of the Eastern Ghats, has been identified for captive iron ore mine for the project (Venkatesan 2012: 35, 36). Thus a total of 3,693 hectares of forestland has been identified for the project. The project is for a 12 million tone integrated steel plant and port at Paradip in the Jagatsinghpur District of Odisha by the South Korean Corporation POSCO and the MoU between the Company and Odisha Government was signed on 2005 (Manshi 2009: 8). The project got Environmental Clearance (EC) and Coastal Regulation Zone (CRZ) clearance from the Environment Ministry and on May 2, 2011, Jairam Ramesh, the Minister for Environment and Forests gave final approval to the state government for the diversion of 1,253 hectares of forestland in favour of POSCO (Venkatesan 2012: 36, 37), deeply negating the interest of the environment and tribal population there. However, the newly, formed National Green Tribunal (NGT) suspended the environmental clearance given to the POSCO project citing environmental issues.

The case with Bastar in Chhattisgarh is no different from Paradip in Odisha. The Tata's Greenfield Project in Lohandigude, with a capacity to produce 5.5 million tonnes of steel a year, on an investment of Rs19,500 crore, envisages the acquisition of over 2,000 hectares of land. The project also got the Central Government's approval to divert huge tracts of forestland in the region (Purnima 2012: 32). Besides conversion of large areas of forestland, there are other associated environmental problems. The CAG in its appraisal of 48 power projects in Uttarakhand, allotted in between 1993 and 2006, found total neglect of environmental concerns. In four out of five operational projects, riverbeds downstream had almost completely dried up and water flow has been reduced to a trickle which is inadequate for the sustenance of the ecology. The muck generated from evacuation and construction is being dumped into the rivers, resulting in increased turbidity and deterioration of water quality. This has a negative impact on aquatic biota. Together with this, the diversion of river water had depleted the natural water resources used for drinking and irrigation purposes. The report also warns of about the environmental damage that can turn out, if the state government pursues with its policy of indiscriminate hydropower projects (Purnima 2010: 49). The report of the CAG was one substantiating the arguments and allegations raised by the project affected people and many non-governmental and environmental activist groups and organisations.

Express highways and mega dam projects also contribute to large scale diversion of forestlands in India. Though dams have proved to be a boon for irrigation and generating hydro-electric power, they have also severely disrupted ecosystems by interrupting the flow of major rivers, destroying freshwater habitats and leading to the disappearance of unique species; dams have also uprooted the livelihood of millions of people who rely on the unaltered flow of river water, and they have also disrupted the structure of floodplain agriculture (Srini 2008: 8). The Ganges and Brahmaputra in India is in the list of twenty-one river basins identified by the World Wildlife Federation's (WWF) Dam Initiative report at severe risk of ecological degradation (WWF 2004). The Narmada Valley Project has subdued hectares of forestland in the states of Gujarat, Madhya Pradesh and Maharashtra. The project became controversial in its early days itself on account of the need for displacing more than a million people and submergence of 350,000 hectares of forest and 200,000 hectares of cultivated land (Veena 1991: 1). It was in 1979, the Narmada Water Disputes Tribunal Award (NWDT Award) set out the plan for the construction of 30 major dams, 125 medium dams, and 3000 small dams at various locations on the Narmada River that cuts across these three states, mainly for the purpose of irrigation and electricity generation. Geneva based International Environment Law Research Centre (IELRC 1986: 1) has pointed out that on completion, the Narmada Sagar Project (NSP) and Sardar Sarovar Project (SSP) would result in the submergence of 40,332 hectares and 13,744 hectares of forestland respectively. Massive submergence of forestland is not the case only with Sardar Sarovar and Narmada Sagar projects but with all the mega dam projects.

Together with forestlands the wetland eco-systems are also encroached upon in the name of development. Wetland eco-systems which are rich in biodiversity provides home for birds, aquatic species, mangrove forests, medicinal plants and migratory birds and are of greater significance and productive in nature. The decline of Ramsar sites[3] results in the loss of fish wealth and other resources, and causes climate change and drought like situation. "A study conducted by a NASA scientist, on the land use pattern in Kerala revealed that rampant destruction of wetlands and paddy fields are the chief causes behind the drought like situation in the state."The situation is likely to worsen unless remedial measures are taken. Environmentalists say that about 80 per cent of the total mangrove forest area in Kerala has been destroyed. Of the 1,358 sq. kms of mangroves that existed in Kannur District of Kerala, in 1975 what remains is only 9 sq. kms. Mangroves are helpful in preventing high salinity and its destruction leads to saltwater intrusion. The case of backwaters is also the same. Pollution, reclamation, encroachment and tourism development activities have reduced the depth and water holding capacity of the backwaters. Shrinking wetlands reduces water availability and forces the conversion of paddy lands to residential or shopping plots which in turn affects the food security of the nation.

India has some of the most impressive legislative acts on environmental issues in the world. But lack of resources, training, corruption of officials and "lack of will," often conspire to delay in its implementation. Development for immediate and narrow economic benefits, without considering its impact on the environment has proved to be havoc in many areas and generations are now getting affected by this. Mega dams and other projects have evacuated a number of villagers and tribals from their home land and deprived them right to property, livelihood and culture. Pollution and other environmental harm have affected the agricultural lands and brought drought and climate change. It was when human being tried to become masters of the nature, all sorts of exploitations and the consequent sorrows followed. It has become very clear that only when environment is respected and when human life is in harmony with the nature, people can get everything from nature for their happiness. All efforts should be made to conserve the environment and its resources. Instead of mega energy projects, government should take initiative to tap renewable sources of energy, in areas applicable, as far as possible. This can save large tracts of forestland and there by livelihood of thousands of whom depends on the forests across the nation. Big projects are not the way for development but many often means of displacement and environmental disasters.

Green Bureaucracy

The challenges to environment and its consequences, now-a-days demand the bureaucracy to be green in nature. Green Bureaucracy refers to those "bureaucracy that takes into account the question of environmental conservation in the process of decision-making and its implementation, such that the process of development in its varied forms is in tune with the health and integrity of planet earth and its resources, for the survival of generations one after the other." In simple sense, green bureaucracy is one that addresses the central question of environment and its inclusion while making decisions and implementing it. Green bureaucracy is environmental friendly in nature and working and is the friend of the nature. A green bureaucrat knows the importance of environment and gives importance to its protection in the process of governance. They will give prime attention for the conservation of forests, lands, mountains, hills, rivers, lakes, ponds, streams, wetlands and all other resources of the nature. Steps will be taken not only to protect the gifts of nature but also to cherish the same. In the era of neo-liberalism they will use their administrative experience, skills and vigilance to prevent the captivism of the commons or the free gifts of nature, including air, water and seed. A green bureaucrat is a champion of indigenous development and won't be a fortune seeker in the pastoral yards of domestic or foreign corporates. He/she will try to strike a balance between the process of development and the question of environmental protection, in a way that the interests of the environment and sustainability of its resources gets added importance. Such a bureaucrat is patriotic and is determined to protect the land and its people from getting polluted, degraded and destroyed by any forms or means.

In one day or the other, all bureaucrats will be forced to be green in nature and working as environmental damage is one that questions the existence of life on earth. The effects of global warming are alarming and are capable of altering, damaging and destroying all the known forms of life on earth. Land, water and air pollution has its negative consequences and leaves no one in the area spreading across by it. Water is needed for all and no one can live without water. Bureaucrats by their access to power or their position cannot remain aloof from all these. When the avalanche of destruction comes in, it doesn't matter what is their position or how much money they have secured, all will be washed out in the flow. Similarly no flue or diseases will spare any one only by the reason that he/she is a bureaucrat. Basically being a human being the bureaucrats have to endure all that the fellow beings have to suffer. Without nature there can be no life on earth and without human beings no society or government. Bureaucracy that quite often leads a parasitic life in the society by clinging to the body of corporate interests and sucking out the maximum by exploiting the masses loses its habitat without society or government. When such is the case there will be no bureaucracy, be it higher or lower. So the need for survival or existence will compel them to take decisions that are environmental friendly or ecologically sustainable.

Time demands a change from the side of the bureaucrats, in the interest of society and environment on the one hand and their existence itself on the other hand. The only persons who can do something seriously to protect the environment are the bureaucrats. By their role in policy making and its implementation they can do a lot to protect the nature and its resources. Being the permanent executive and appointed by the President of the nation after a rigorous process of recruitment, the IAS and other top echelon officers are expected to play a lead role in this regard. Moreover the higher bureaucrats are the only group that has not been much affected on the onslaught of globalisation. They should use their neutrality and wisdom in analysing the policies of the multilateral lenders and corporates that has the hidden agenda of exploiting the natural resources of the domestic nation. In matters related to development, they should prioritise a balance between the needs of human beings and environment, in a way that development won't compromise the health of the environment and the resources in it. The theory at the same time keeps in mind the limitations in front of bureaucracy in the form of corporate nexuses and political interference. Whatever be the limitations, existence comes first, because it is for that all are doing whatever they can, be it good or bad.

End Notes

1. "Use cost" is defined as the amount needed for constructing and operating the infrastructure necessary for collecting, storing, treating and distributing a commodity.
2. "Opportunity cost" is a less obvious cost - that which is incurred when one user uses a commodity and affects the use of the same by another user.
3. According to the Ramsar Convention of 1971, wetlands includes lakes and rivers, swamps and marshes, estuaries, near-shore marine areas, mangroves, wet grasslands, coral reefs and manmade sites like fish ponds, paddy fields, reservoirs and salt pans.

References

AIR (1978): *Maneka Gandhi* vs. *Union of India*, SC 597.

----- (1981): Francis Coralie Mullin vs. The Administrator, Union Territory of Delhi, SC 746.

----- (1985): Rural Litigation and Entitlement Kendra vs. State of Uttar Pradesh, SC 652.

----- (1991): Subash Kumar vs. State of Bihar, SC 420.

Allam, Ahmed; Stein, Josephine (2004): *"Science, Technology and Sustainable Development: A World Review,"* Inderscience, 1(1).

Anitha, Cheria Edwin and Sripapha, Petcharamesree (2003): A Human Rights Approach to Development: A Source Book, Books for Change.

Anna, Karthika (2008): *"Bottling Up a Corporate Giant: Victory of a Mass Movement,"* Covalence Analyst Papers, Geneva, 22-06-2008.

Arnoldo, Contreras (2000): *"The Underlying Causes of Forest Declines,"* CIFOR, Indonesia, June.

Bakker, Karen (2005): *"Neoliberalising Nature? Market Environmentalism in Water Supply in England and Wales,"* Annals of the Association of American Geographers, 95(3), 542-65.

Bollier, David (2002): *"Reclaiming the Commons,"* Boston Review, Summer Issue.

Camille, Parmesen and John, Mathews (2005): *"Biological Impacts of Climate Change,"* Sinauer Associates, USA, 333-74.

Emily, Adams E. (2012): *"Forest Cover,"* Eco Economy Indicators, Earth Policy Institute, August 31, http://www.earth-policy.org//forestcover accessed on 01-01-2013.

EPW (2010): *"Plachimada Again,"* Editorial, Economic and Political Weekly, XLV (12), March.

Express News (2012): *"Encroachments Ravaging Forests,"* The New Indian Express, Kochi, December 3, 1.

----- (2010): *"Additional Chief Secretary's Comments on Plachimada Kick Up,"* The New Indian Express, May 25, 1.

Eva, Wramner (2004): *Fighting Cocacolanisation in Plachimada, Human Ecology Division,* Lund University.

Forest Report (2011): *India State of Forest Report 2011, Ministry of Forests and Environment,* Government of India.

Hazards Centre (2006): *Ground Water Resources in Plachimada Coca Cola Stores Toxics for Future Generations,* New Delhi, June.

IELRC (1986): *Environmental Aspects of Narmada Sagar and Sardar Sarovar Multi-Purpose Projects, Department of Environment and Forests,* International Environmental Law Research Centre, Geneva.

IPCC (2001): *Climate Change 2001: Impacts, Adaptation and Vulnerability,* UNEP.

Jananeethi (2003): Jananeethi Report - *On the Amplitude of Environmental and Human Rights Ramification,* Jananeethi, Thrissur.

Jayanth, Sthaye; Shukla, P.R. and Ravindranath, N.H. (2006): *"Climate Change, Sustainable Development and India: Global and National Concerns,"* Current Science, 90(3), February.

Jitha S.R. (2011): *"Bureaucracy and Sustainable Development,"* Pragati, 5(118) October-December, 23-31.

Johan, Rockstrom (2003): *Rethinking Water Management: Innovative Approaches to Contemporary Issues,* Earthscan, London.

John Briscoe (1996): *"Water as an Economic Good: The Idea and What it Means in Practice,"* Paper Presented at the World Congress of the International Commission on Irrigation and Drainage, Cairo, Egypt, September.

Kerala Kaumudi (2012): *"Attack against Collector: Case Registered against Sand Mafia,"* Kerala Kaumudi, Kochi, December 10.

----- (2010): "Plachimada: The Damage Caused by the Cola Company is 216.26 Crore," Kerala Kaumudi, Kochi, March 23.

KLU (1967): *Kerala Land Utilisation Act,* Government of Kerala, 1967.

Madhyamam (2012): *"Collector Denied Permission for Silent Valley Bottling Plant,"* (M) Madhyamam Daily, Thiruvananthapuram, September 12.

Malayala Manorama (2012): *"Please Transfer the Commissioner,"* Malayala Manorama, Kollam, December 18, 3.

Manshi, Asher (2009): *Striking While the Iron is Hot, A Case Study of the Pohang Steel Company's (POSCO) Proposed Project in Orissa,* National Study for Advocacy Studies, Pune.

Mathrubhumi (2005): *"Plachimadayile Jalachushanavum Janakeeya Prathirothavum"* (M) Mathrubhumi Books, Kochikode.

Purnima, S. Tripathi (2012): *"Battle of Bastar,"* Frontline, 29(8), May 03, 32-4.

----- (2010): "*Damning Audit*," Frontline, 27(24), December 03, 49-52.

Reinhart Philip (2012a): *"Global Warming and Water Resources,"* in Shaji Anirudhan (ed.), Understanding the Environmental History of India, PG and Research Dept. of History, S.N College, Chempazhanty, 287-97.

----- (2012b): Green Captivism and Market Governance in Water Supply: The Challenges Ahead, Paper presented at the three Day National Seminar on "*Water Management: Mounting Challenges and Responses,*" C. Achutha Menon Study Centre and Library, Thriuvananthapuram, December 22.

Richard, Bocking (2003): *"Reclaiming the Commons,"* Canadian Unitarian Council, Toronto, April 27.

Samir, Amin (2001): *"Imperialism and Globalisation,"* Monthly Review 53(2), July.

Science Daily (2008): "Global Warming Affects World's Largest Freshwater Lake," National Science Foundation, May 1.

Shaji, K.A. (2007): *"New Kerala Line: Coke Bad, Pepsi Good,"* Tehelka, April 7.

Srini, Sitaraman (2008): *"Privatisation, Efficiency, Gender, Development, and Inequality-Transnational Conflicts over Access to Water and Sanitation,"* Human Rights and Human Welfare, 8, 91-113.

Surendranath, C. (2003): *"Coca-Cola: Continuing Battle in Kerala,"* India Resource Centre, July 10.

The Hindu (2012): *"Kozhicode Collector Escapes Attack,"* The Hindu, Thiruvananthapuram, December 9.

----- (2011): *"Water Packaging Units Ordered to be Closed,"* The Hindu, Chennai, September 1.

----- (2010): *"Protest against Secretary's Stand,"* The Hindu, Thiruvananthapuram, May 25.

The Pioneer (2012): *"Police-mafia Nexus Strong in Kerala,"* The Pioneer, November 10, http://www.dailypioneer.com/state-editions/kochi/108086-police-mafia-nexus-strong-in-kerala.html accessed on 15-11-2012.

UN (2011): *"Water Pollution, Environmental Degradation and Disasters,"* United Nations Water Statistics, UN Water, http://www.unwater.org/statistics_pollu.html accessed on 08-11-2011.

UNESCO (2010): *"Teaching and Learning for a Sustainable Future,"* UNESCO-UNEP.

UDHR (2012): Universal Declaration of Human Rights, United Nations.

UNEP (2003): *"How Will Global Warming Affect My World?"* A Simplified Guide to the IPCC's "Climate Change 2001: Impacts, Adaptation and Vulnerability," France.

UNPI (2005): *"The United Nations and Human Rights,"* The UN Department of Public Information, New York.

Veena, Gokhale (1991): *"India's Narmada Valley Hydro Project,"* Environment and Policy Magazine, 1, 1-4.

Venkatesan, V. (2012): *"POSCO in Limbo,"* Frontline, 29(8), May 4, 35-7.

WECD (1987): Our Common Future, Report of the World Commission on Environment and Development, Official Records of the General Assembly, forty-second Session, supplement No. 25 (A/42/25).

WWF (2004): *Rivers at Risk: Dams and the Future of Freshwater Ecosystems,* World Wildlife Federation, June 22.

13

Summary and Conclusion

Bureaucracy is a dominant form of organisation that has occupied a significant place in the modern nation-state. It not only fulfills a number of needs of the society but also affects the social, political and economic aspects of human life. No society can carry on the process of administration without bureaucracy. Whatever be the system of government, bureaucracy is inevitable for the design and implementation of policies, programmes and governmental decisions. Though the term bureaucracy is of eighteenth century origin only, bureaucracy as a system dates back to the origin of societal administration. It prevailed under various names from the ancient primitive to the modern democracies. The characteristics and working nature of bureaucracy differed according to the various systems that it served. Under monarchy the civil servants known as the king's men, showed loyalty to the Kings and under feudalism the loyalty was to the feudal lords. Anywhere they formed a specific class who has their own class interest, intimately related to the interests of the ruling class. The attitude of the bureaucrats to consider themselves as a specific class continues in modern democracies also.

Along with the changes in political system, bureaucratic system also got changes especially in the pattern of recruitment. From being the patronage of those in ruling position, with the rise of modern democracies, bureaucratic position began to be on the basis of merit. The merit system of recruitment gave bureaucracy added importance as they are men of talents. Moreover, under democracy, bureaucracy got a legal-rational base making its authority rests upon laws, statues and regulations. Weber's ideal model of bureaucracy with its features of hierarchy, division of labour, merit based selection, impersonality, rationality and neutrality became a fashion for the modern-nation states to apply. Being selected on the basis of merit and because of impersonality and neutrality, bureaucracy was capable of achieving the highest degree of rationality in decision making. The change from patronage or spoils to merit, strengthened bureaucracy, and made them a key player in the administration of modern states. Its role has considerably increased with the state taking upon itself the task of welfarism.

Bureaucracy forms the permanent executive in every society and serves in office for a fixed period of time. One King may be replaced by the other or the Ministers may come and go, but bureaucrats remain the same. In modern democracies they are expected to serve any political masters irrespective of their party considerations. The higher bureaucrats are expected to give rational advice to the political ministers in matters related to policy making. They also have to use their administrative skills, efficiency and acumen to understand the day to day problems of administration and to sort out the same. The supervision of administration forms the other important functions of them. The bureaucracy modeled on Weberian lines is expected to act like the Guardian bureaucracy, where the bureaucrats acted as the guardian of the population as that of the ancient Chinese bureaucracy in the 960 AD and the Prussian bureaucracy in between 1640 and 1740. Whether bureaucracy fulfilled the expected functions entrusted upon them is a big question for every society.

Development was the top priority of every nation-state that got independence after the wake of the war days. The nations of Latin America, Asia and Africa that got political independence have been facing immense problems of poverty, illiteracy, unemployment, low agricultural productivity and industrial backwardness. So to overcome all these they adopted various development packages provided by the West, especially the UN and US sponsored economic and technical aid programmes. The primary task of implementing these developmental programmes was entrusted on the bureaucracy who forms the basic skeleton of administration. But the western models of development could not provide the desired results. This generated interest among scholars especially of the Comparative Administrative Group to study the administrative system of the developing countries and their research and findings revealed that Western development models and structures are not suited to the developing nations. The basic administrative structure was elitist in character and orientation and the officials do not show much interest in the actual administrative details necessary to accomplish development plans and programmes. Not only was there absence of technically qualified and trained personnel capable of performing the developmental tasks but also institutionalisation of corruption, both stumbling blocks for development.

Weberian bureaucracy is an ideal one which cannot be copied fully even by the developed societies. When the developed world comes near to this ideal model most nations of the Third World remains far away from this ideal model. What prevails in the Third World is a sala-bureaucracy, which combines the features of modernity and tradition. Modern bureaucracies of the Third World were channeled on the pattern of their colonial masters but they work in an atmosphere characterized by traditional values, customs and practices. The sala-bureaucracy was characterised by high degree of heterogeneity, formalism and overlapping. This together with the class character of bureaucracy to resist change acted as a stumble in the path of social change. But at the same time it cannot be ignored that they are the ones who can bring such a change. Time has proved that they are the only group that can withstand the avalanche of history. The change from BC to AD, from monarchy and feudalism to democracy, from colonialism to freedom, from democracy to totalitarianism or theocracy or militarism etc. couldn't replace the institution of bureaucracy. The march of neo-liberalism too couldn't replace bureaucracy. Instead of all these changes, bureaucracy as a system got strengthened and they became a power block capable of making change.

In a developing country like India bureaucracy is considered as the backbone of developmental programmers and the civil servants who are engaged in development activities constitute the development bureaucracy. The responsibility of bringing about socio-economic change has fallen upon the higher bureaucracy, which is permanent in nature. They are the one who can understand the problems of the people more than the amateur political minister. The success of developmental programmers depends upon the ability of the civil servants to understand the problems of development. They are to help the political executive to sort out the priorities and channelise the resources of the nation for the attainment of the pre set goals. They should also evaluate the process of development and inform the authority the necessity of changes, if any in the process of development. Thus in planned development bureaucracy occupies a prominent position. But the new policies of economic liberalisation downgrade the role of state. In this context bureaucracy can be either functional or dysfunctional.

The rise of neo-liberalism redefined the role of the state. Having its roots in the philosophy of liberalism that advocates the reduced role of the state and increased role of the individual in the economy or market, neo-liberalism advocates the withdrawal of the state for allowing the market forces of demand and supply to control the economy and there by politics. Neo-liberalists advocate a miminal state to maintain the law and order functions and to act as a facilitator of the market. Normally there lies the boundary of state functions. To them it is not the duty of the state to provide services like water, health care, education etc. Social security measures are a burden to the state which has neither the resources nor the capacity to provide all services to the people. So the solution lies in privatisation of services. The free play of the market forces of demand and supply will ensure quality products, be it water, health care, or any other consumer durables, or whatever goods and services to the people. The neo-liberal school succeeded in hegemonising this argument and through the instruments of World Bank, multinational donors and Triad Governments it forced the Third World to open their doors for the neo-liberal reforms.

A deliberate call to downsize the bureaucracy of the Third World was made to ensure the necessary environment for privātisation. The argument was that the Third World nations possess a jumbo bureaucracy that is much larger than enough to carry out the day to day operation. In number, the bureaucracy of the Third World is larger but compared with the large population of these states, the ratio between bureaucrats and the population is not only inadequate but also four to seven times lesser than the developed nations. When the United States has 7,681 government servants for every 100,000 residents, India has only 1,622.8. Less number of bureaucrats means adequate number of staffs is not available for the working of various departments like health care, sanitation, education, public works, water supply etc. So the downsizing of bureaucracy makes it unable for the state to operate a number of fields. The absence or lapses in safety nets affects a wide range of population who cannot survive without state support which indirectly creates murmuring against the state. This creates a favourable atmosphere for privatisation as the common man who does not know the consequences of privatisation will argue for it by pointing the inefficiency of the state. Such an opinion or an interest is getting imbibed in the minds of the common man through the neo-liberal education that creates a hegemonic culture that portrays privatisation as a symbol of efficiency and effectiveness.

The neo-liberal reforms forced the Third World nations to make a forcible shift in their indigenous development pattern molded after the failure of those western models adopted in the wake of their independence. The withdrawal of the state from the welfare activities seriously affected these nations that were already plagued with diseases and poverty. The entry of unaccountable multinational corporations let loose a set of miseries and human rights violations. Commons like water, minerals, forest products, indigenous knowledge etc. that were considered as the heritage of humanity were commodified forcing misery upon the indigenous people, women, children and the poor. The greens have been enclosed in the process of the expansion of the market to the under-marketized spheres for ensuring profit to the private corporates. The further expansion can enclose the air we breathe in by making it a commodity. With commodification, access to those resources is determined by the purchasing power of money and not as entitlement to resources by being a member of human species. The ability-to-pay principle replaces willingness-to-pay principle with regard to access to resources.

Commodification unlashed a series of human rights violations round the world, with the state either as a participant or as a helpless spectator. The private takeover of water services has resulted in gross turmoil and misery to the common man. The water bills in Cochabamba, Grenoble, Durban, Ghana and Uruguay etc. hiked manifold making water an unaffordable item. Commodification of water and its commercialisation and privatisation has made water a commodity that is out of the reach of the common people. At the same time profit accumulated to corporates, the world round. The mounting of profit by the water lords resulted in abrogation of the people's right to safe drinking water. Similar is the case with health care. Neoliberal ascendency made health a commodity purchasable by the "ability to pay." When the application of the principles of cost recovery, profit-maximisation, cost-benefit analysis etc. increased the cost of medical care, the entry of private hospitals made health care a profit making business. The rise in the cost of health care forced many to abandon medical care. This happened in Ghana, Jamaica, Zimbabwe, South Africa, Sub-Saharan States, Bangladesh, Chile and in India too. Moreover, commodification of health care made the transaction between physicians and patients to a commercial relationship. The danger with commodification is that it makes those relations commercial and in such a relationship denial of goods and services because of the inability to pay for them gets legitimized. Be it water, health care or any other services that are essential for the survival of human life, this is the case. The worst affected of these are mainly the women.

Since 1991, under the name new economic policy India adopted the same neo-liberal policies that have created much havoc to the human community. The neo-liberals reforms completed a two decade period that is enough to evaluate its performance. India's experience with neo-liberals shows that with the new economic policy kick started an unbalanced phase in the history of India's economic and social development. Wealth began to concentrate in few hands depriving the majority of their livelihood and the gulf between the rich and poor increased manifold. Agriculture, cottage, small scale and other indigenous industries that served as the backbone of the Indian economy and source of livelihood of the majority declined heavily as they couldn't withstand the pressures of the international market without the state support. The high fluctuation in prices and environmental externalities are forcing many to not only leave the profession but also to convert the agricultural land for real estate purpose, which has ecological consequences together with affecting the food security of the nation.

The withdrawal of the state let misery in the social service sector. In consonance with the policies of globalisation, the state by pointing its financial crunch withdrew itself from a number of areas ranging from healthcare to education. As a result the quality of education and health services declined deeply affecting the poor. But there occurred a rise in the number of private schools and private hospitals which are not an alternative to the state sponsored ones because only the affluent can avail the services in the private institutions. When the number of colleges and universities at the higher tier increased, the quality of education at the elementary level declined sharply. The less spending on health care, which is less than One per cent of the GDP, is a stumbling block in bringing down the infant, child and maternal mortality rate when states like Bangladesh and Sri Lanka have far improved from India. The deregulation in pharma industry increased the price of medicines manifold making access to the life saving medicines a difficult situation to the poor. When medicines got commodified, access to health care became one determined by the purchasing power of money of the individual concerned and medical profession became a profit making business.

Privatisation became a rule and disinvestment the means for it. A number of profit making public sector enterprises were disinvested or totally sold out at throw away prices. The argument put forward for disinvestment is the lack of finance. But it is clear that disinvestment is a deliberate attempt to withdraw the role of the state in the economy for allowing the private sector a free hand in the market. The increased number of private players in a liberalised economy made corruption rampant. Globalisation hegemonised corruption as a common sense culture paving the way for liberalised corruption in the society. Corruption now is accepted as a part of the society where neither rules nor regulations come on the way and it operates in an institutional manner with specific principles of **ability-to-pay**, **willingness-to-pay** and **mutual trust**. A phenomenon of trickling down of corruption known as dropping-down of corruption can be seen in the system, in which the allure of consumerism and corruption at the higher level induces the lower level to be corrupt. The fishing of sharks in the high seas by the higher bureaucrats induces the lower ones to fish in the waters of their domain. This increased corruption and concretized it as a prerogative right of the government employees. The common man's perception about corruption increased making the public office a persona of corruption. All these are highly dangerous as it sanskritises corruption.

The neo-liberal development strategy was also not in tune with the health and integrity of the planet earth. Besides enclosing the commons it resulted in the wide spread destruction of the environment, ignoring the importance of the forests, rivers, lakes, streams, wetlands, glaciers, seas and oceans and the innumerable animal and plant species living in that. Forest covers of large tracts are being cleared in the name of development, in Odisha, Jharkhand, Chhattisgarh etc. Mega dam projects and express highways are also claiming a large part of India's forest. Together with forestlands the wetland eco-systems are also encroached upon in the name of development.

Forests and wetlands are of greater ecological significance and are the source of livelihood for many indigenous populations. Pollution has got alarming proportions and all the metros are in the risk of e-wastes. For all the damages that have been done to the planet earth it is retaliating in the form of climate change, which if unchecked will destabilise life on earth. The need for protecting the environment is now clear beyond doubt, because existence itself becomes a big question without nature.

India's experience shows that neo-liberalism is not the right model of development and it is irrational, inhuman, degrading, unethical and unsustainable. It resulted in the concentration of wealth in the hands of a few, keeping the majority out of the benefits of development. The lop-sided development pattern has created a shining India and a suffering India and this development strategy is further increasing the gulf between the liberalised India of the corporates, billionaires and the booming consumerist middle class and the *Bharat* of the common man. The basic rights of the common man including the right to life, water, health care, education are getting least attention or are getting ignored in front of the purchasing power of the affluent. So the need of the hour is replacement of the outward oriented neo-liberal development strategy with an indigenous model that can ensure basic things for sustenance, equal opportunities and equitable (minimum) distribution of wealth. Higher bureaucrats because of their strategic position in administration and because of not being much affected on the onslaught of liberalisation and globalisation are the only group who can take a lead role in this regard.

Whether bureaucracy that is considered to be the guardian of the population used their administrative skills, efficiency, experience, acumen and proverbial neutrality to resist the onslaught of globalisation are matters of serious discussion. The responsibility before bureaucracy in developing societies is much higher than that in developed societies because they have to root out corruption and use their knowledge, experience and proverbial neutrality to identify the good things. They are also the persons to organise the rescue efforts in areas like agriculture, education, health, flood control, environment protection, railway, roads, bridges, defence and power. But we can see that the higher bureaucracy hasn't given any creative criticism regarding the policies of liberalisation and globalisation. Instead of that, they were interested in reaping the new opportunities of globalisation for them in various international bodies and in Multinational Corporations. So in spite of being the champions of the underprivileged, bureaucracy likes to be a parasite that sticks on to suck the benefits from the new forces of the market economy. Such a bureaucracy cannot ensure socio-economic change, equity and social justice.

What is needed is a bureaucracy that can critically analyse and can understand the prons and cons of the various policies being advocated by the IMF, World Bank, WTO and other multi-lateral and international donors. This is because neo-liberal policies come in an implicit manner and now-a-days there won't be explicit reference to such measures in various policies and programmes. While implementing the various policies they should take care that it should in no way jeopardise the interests of the common man. Together with this they have to ensure that the resources of the nation are in no way exploited by any specific group, be it foreign or domestic and that the resources of the nation are equitably distributed among the various sections for their wholesome enhancement. Sectors like agriculture, irrigation, education, health-care, and other social services are to be given more concentration in order to reduce the gulf between various peoples in the society. Higher bureaucrats can take initiative in providing a lot of welfare services, like the Abhilasha in the West Godavari District of Andhra Pradesh.

Corruption in its various forms needs to be routed out not only for protecting the rights of the individuals but also to check black money which is capable of destabilising the financial security of the nation. Besides this it leaps the poverty reduction programmes in darkness. The benefits of the various governmental programmes can reach the desired only by bridling corruption. The market has to be brought under control otherwise the poor and the needy cannot survive. The unfair policies that are crippling the welfare measures needs to be eliminated, then only these measures can improve the lots of the people. Environmental conservation has got added importance as ecological imbalance is one threatening the existence of all forms of life on earth.

The well springs and green caps of the nature needs to be nurtured and its enclosure by any means needs to be prevented. Waste management, including that of e-waste and bio-medical should be given top priority as they corrode both human health and the environment. Development needs are to be channelised such that they won't compromise the normalcy of the environment. When the greens are getting captivated, pollution becoming uncontrolled and global climate change is getting alarming proportion; the bureaucracy needs to be green in nature and action. A green bureaucracy is a solution to the mounting environmental problems and the conflicts between the needs of the human beings and environment in the process of development.

Bureaucrats can no doubt be the agents of social change in any society. They are the ones who withstood the changes of history and remains as a major power group even in this era of neo-liberal globalisation. But what is needed is their readiness to take up the responsibility entrusted upon them by the founding fathers of our Constitution. For that, rather than remaining largely indifferent with their legacies of exclusiveness and class-consciousness, which they had inherited from the ICS, the bureaucrats needs to adjust themselves and be responsive to the changing administrative goals of the nation. It is a matter of great pleasure that India is having at all times a handful of bureaucrats who considers service to the nation and its masses more importance than personal benefits. It is because of their earnest efforts the system is moving on. They can take the lead role in social change and for that globalisation demands the higher bureaucracy to be more vigilant and have original and specialised knowledge to have insight into various social, economic and political effects of the policy measures advocated by the outside agencies; creative thinking; efficient and timely advice to the political masters; stern actions to preserve the nation's values, beliefs, prosperity, bio-diversity, environment and freedom; patriotism and a humble mind to be the servants of the society.

Appendix

Appendix I

Cadre Strength of Indian Administrative Service (as on 01.01.2012)

S.l. No.	Cadre	Authorised Cadre Strength: Senior Duty Post Under State Govt. {SDP}	Posts Under Central Govt. {CDR} [not Exceeding 40% of SDP]	State Deputation Reserve {SDR} [not exceeding 25% of SDP]	Junior Posts Reserve and Leave Reserve {JP & LR} [not exceeding 16.5% of SDP]	Training Reserve {TR} [not exceeding 3.5% of SDP]	Direct Recruitment Posts {DR} [(SDP+CDR + SDR+LR+ TR)-PQ]	Promotion Posts {PQ} 33 1/3% of SDP+CDR+ SDR+TR]	Total Authorised Strength {TAS} [DR+PQ] Col.(8)+(9)]	No. of officers in Position: Direct Recruitment (includes EC/SSC/IC	Promoted	Total [(11)+(12)]
1	2	3	4	5	6	7	8	9	10	11	12	13
1.	Andhra Pradesh	204	81	51	33	7	262	114	376	196	88	284
2.	AGMUT	183	73	45	30	6	235	102	337	176	45	221
3.	Assam-Meghalaya	135	54	33	22	4	173	75	248	156	49	205
4.	Bihar	177	70	44	29	6	227	99	326	186	12	198
5.	Chhattisgarh	97	38	24	16	3	124	54	178	86	38	124
6.	Gujarat	142	56	35	23	4	181	79	260	156	52	208
7.	Haryana	112	44	28	18	3	143	62	205	131	47	178
8.	Himachal Pradesh	71	28	17	11	2	90	39	129	74	27	101
9.	Jammu & Kashmir*	75	30	18	12	2	75	62	137	61	30	91
10.	Jharkhand	114	45	28	18	3	145	63	208	93	15	108
11.	Karnataka	163	65	40	26	5	208	91	299	166	53	219
12.	Kerala	116	46	29	19	4	149	65	214	112	46	158

(Contt...)

13.	Madhya Pradesh	227	90	56	37	7	291	126	417	222	77	299
14.	Maharashtra	190	76	47	31	6	244	106	350	208	87	295
15.	Manipur-Tripura	113	45	28	18	3	144	63	207	109	28	137
16.	Nagaland	50	20	12	8	1	64	27	91	37	15	52
17.	Odisha	123	49	30	20	4	158	68	226	134	14	148
18.	Punjab	120	48	30	19	4	154	67	221	125	36	161
19.	Rajasthan	161	64	40	26	5	206	90	296	174	10	184
20.	Sikkim	27	10	6	4	1	34	14	48	26	7	33
21.	Tamil Nadu	193	77	48	31	6	247	108	355	196	90	286
22.	Uttarakhand	66	26	16	10	2	84	36	120	67	17	84
23.	Uttar Pradesh	321	128	80	52	11	412	180	592	340	36	376
24.	West Bengal	171	68	42	28	5	219	95	314	161	66	227
	Total	**3351**	**1331**	**827**	**541**	**104**	**4269**	**1885**	**6154**	**3392**	**985**	**4377**

Source: RTI, dated 16-01-2013.

Notes: *For Jammu and Kashmir, PQ is calculated @ 50 per cent of (SDP + CDR + SDR +TR).

Appendix II

Details of Expenditure Incurred on IAS Officers in Connection with their Foreign Exposure Visit During 2010-12.

IAS Phase – II (Foreign Visit)

Updated as on 30.1.2013

Year	*Total Expenditure Incurred (Rs.)*	*No. of Trainees*	*Expenditure per Trainee (Rs.)*	*Places Visited during Foreign Exposure Visit*
2010	103,97,109	112	92,831	Singapore, Hanoi (Vietnam)
2011	98,44,446	120	82,037	Vietnam, Singapore
2012	134,75,607	135	99,819	Vietnam, Singapore

Source: RTI, dated 4-2-2013.

MCTP (IAS –Phase – III, IV and V)

Year	*Total Expenditure Incurred (Rs.)*	*No. of Trainees*	*Expenditure per Trainee (Rs.)*	*Places Visited during Foreign Exposure Visit*
2010	332,16,084	252	13,1810	Seoul (South Korea), Bostan (US)
2011	320,59,255	399	80,349	Seoul (South Korea), Canada Colombia, New York (US) Singapore
2012	155,31,530	300	51,772	Seoul (South Korea), Canada, Montreal, New York, Washington, DC

Source: RTI, dated 04-02-2013.

Appendix III

Detail Statement as on 31.1.2013 for the Mid Career Training Programmes, Phase III, IV and V, Conducted by Lbsnaa, Mussoorie Since 2010

Sl. No.	*Year*	*Name of Course*	*No. of Participants*	*Places where undergone training*	*Institutional Charges (in Rs.)*
1.	2010	Mid Career Training Programme Phase III (Round 4)	93	Korea Development Institute (KDI), South Korea	49,63,149
2.	2010	Mid Career Training Programme Phase IV (Round 4)	64	Korea Development Institute (KDI), South Korea	40,36,679
3.	2010	Mid Career Training Programme Phase V (Round 4)	95	Harvard Kennedy School, USA	2,42,16,256
4.	2011	Mid Career Training Programme Phase IV (Round 5)	101	Korea Development Institute (KDI), South Korea	52,60,560
5.	2011	Mid Career Training Programme Phase III (Rund 5)	108	Lee Kuan Yew School of Public Policy (NUS), Singapore	67,14,204
6.	2011	Mid Career Training Programme Phase IV (Round 6)	105	Institute for Public Affairs, Canada	94,91,580
7.	2011	Mid Career Training Programme Phase V (Round 5)	85	Columbia University, New York, USA	1,05,92,911
8.	2012	Mid Career Training Programme Phase IV (Round 7)	115	Institute for Public Affairs, Canada	63,94,272
9.	2012	Mid Career Training Programme Phase III (Round 6)	91	Korea Development Institute (KDI), South Korea	64,65,391
10.	2012	Mid Career Training Programme Phase V (Round 6)	94	New York and Washington DC, USA	26,71,867

Source: RTI, dated 04-02-2013.

(***Note:*** Payment of 2012 courses is still going on).

Appendix IV

Rise in Population and Decrease in the Number of Governments Servants - Kerala

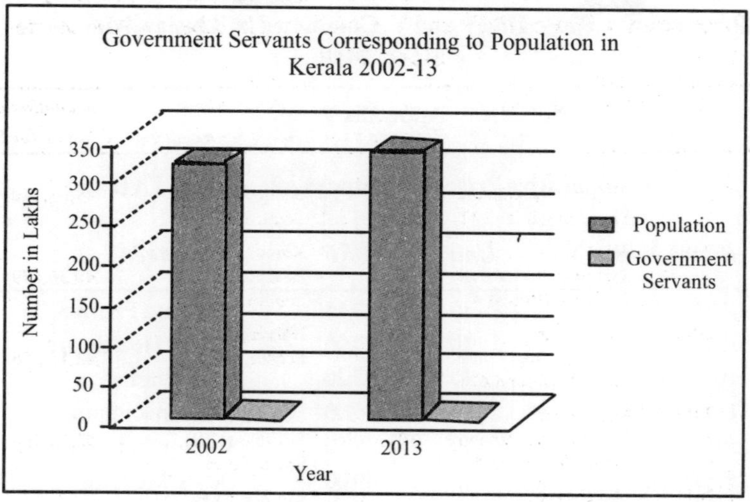

Appendix V

Comparative Prices of Pantoprazole, 40 MG TAB

Brand Name	*Unit*	*MRP*	*Marketeer*
PANTAKIND	10	27.15	Mankind Pharma
PANTONID	10	29.00	Syntro Healthcare
ACIBAN	10	33.20	IRM Pharma
PEPMARK	10	35.00	Unimarck Pharma
PENSTAL	10	38.50	Stallion Laboratories
PAZES	10	40.00	Dey's Medical
ULZAR	10	44.00	Organon India
MZOLE - P	10	47.50	Maitri Healthcare
PANTAZ	10	49.50	Medley Pharmaceuticals
TOPRAZOL	10	53.00	Karnataka Antibiotics
ZOVANTA	10	59.40	Dr. Reddy's Laboratories
PAN - 40	10	63.00	Alkem Laboratories
PANTOCID	10	70.00	Sun Pharmaceuticals

Source: Patient India.
(***Use:*** Block the production of acid by the stomach).

Appendix VI

Highest and Lowest Price of Cancer Drugs in India

Drug Name	*Highest Price (Rs.)*	*Firm*	*Lowest Price (Rs.)*	*Firm*
Letrozole 2.5 mg (10 tablet)	1,986	Novartis	60	Hetero
Imatinib 400 mg (10 tablet)	41,152	Novartis	3,000	Glenmark
Nozolamide 250 mg (5 capsule)	22,282	Dr. Reddys	4,485	Sun
Pemetrexed 500 mg (vial)	73,660	Eli Lilly	11,990	Glenmark
Exemestane 25 mg (30 tablet)	4,315	Pfizer	1,290	Natco

Source: Business Standard.

Bibliography

Official Publications

Argun Sengupta (2007): *Report on the Conditions of Work and Promotion of Livelihood in Unorganized Sector*, National Commission for Enterprises in the Unorganised Sector, Government of India, New Delhi.

C and AG (2012): *Performance Audit of Water Pollution in India*, Comptroller and Auditor General of India, Report No. 21, 2011-12.

Census (2011): *Census of India's Houselisting and House Census Data Highlights:* 2011, Office of the Registrar General and Census Commissioner, Ministry of Home Affairs, Government of India.

—— (2011): *Maternal and Child Mortality and Total Fertility Rates*, Office of the Registrar General and Census Commissioner, Ministry of Home Affairs, Government of India, 7 July.

——(2011): *Census 2011 Provisional Population Totals*, Office of the Registrar General and Census Commissioner, Ministry of Home Affairs, Government of India, 31 March, 8.

DCRB (1958): *All India Services Death-Cum-Retirement Benefits Rules, 1958*, Government of India.

Economic Survey (2012): *Economic Survey 2011-12*, Ministry of Finance and Economics, Government of India, New Delhi.

ECOSOC (2002): *The Right to Water Articles 11 and 12 of the International Covenant on Economic, Social and Cultural Rights, General Comment No. 15 (2002)*, Committee on Economic, Social and Cultural Rights, United Nations Economic and Social Council.

Forest Report (2011): *India State of Forest Report 2011*, Ministry of Forests and Environment, Government of India.

General Assembly (2010): *Resolution Recognising Right to Water and Sanitation*, Resolution A/RES/64/292, United Nations General Assembly, 28 July.

GoI (2012): *Draft National Water Policy 2012*, Ministry of Water Resources, Government of India.

——(2007): *The Constitution of India*, Ministry of Law and Justice, Government of India, New Delhi.

GoK (2011): *Report on Health Effects of Endosulfan and Progress of Rehabilitation Activities in Kerala*, Department of Health and Family Welfare, Government of Kerala, 20 April.

—(1958): *Government of Kerala, Report of Administrative Reforms Committee*, Vol. I and II, Government Press, Thiruvananthapuram.

IIPS and Macro International (2007): *National Family Health Survey NFHS-3 2005-06*, Vol. 1, IIPS, Mumbai.

India (2012): *India Year Book*, Publications Division, Government of India, New Delhi.

IMF (2007): *IMF Conditionality*, IMF Fact Sheets, Washington.

IPCC (2001): *Climate Change 2001: Impacts, Adaptation and Vulnerability*, UNEP.

MIB (2011): "Interaction with Newspaper Editors", *Ministry of Information and Broadcasting*, Government of India New Delhi.

NIOH (2002): *The Investigation of Unusual Illnesses Allegedly Produced by Endosulfan Exposure in Padre Village of Kasargod District N.Kerala*, National Institute of Occupational Health, Ahmedabad.

PIB (2012): "Per Capita Water Availability", *Press Information Bureau*, Government of India, New Delhi, Release ID: 82676.

Planning Board (2010): *Economic Review: 2009*, Kerala State Planning Board, Government of Kerala, Thiruvananthapuram.

——(2009): *An Evaluation Study of Jalanidhi Projects in Kerala*, Kerala State Planning Board, Thiruvananthapuram, October.

Planning Commission (2008): "Health and Family Welfare", *Eleventh Five Year Plan, 2002–07*, Vol. II, Chapter 3, Planning Commission, Government of India, New Delhi.

Rajya Sabha Secretariat (2011): *E-waste in India*, Research Unit, Rajya Sabha Secretariat, New Delhi, June.

UN (2011): "Water Pollution, Environmental Degradation and Disasters", United Nations Water Statistics, *UN Water*, http://www.unwater.org/statistics_pollu.html, accessed on 08-11-2011.

UN (2011): "Drinking Water and Sanitation," United Nations Water Statistics, *UN Water*, http://www.unwater.org/statistics_san.html accessed on 08-11-2011.

UN Human Rights Council (2010): *Human Rights and Access to Safe Drinking Water and Sanitation*, A/HRC/15/L.14, 24 September.

UN News Centre (2010): "General Assembly Declares Access to Clean Water and Sanitation is a Human Right", *News Centre*, United Nations.

UN Water (2011): "Water Scarcity", International Decade for Action, Water for Life 2005-2015, *UN Water*, UNEP.

—— (2010): *The Human Right to Water and Sanitation*, Resolution A/RES/64/292, United Nations General Assembly, 28 July.

UDHR (2012): *Universal Declaration of Human Rights*, United Nations.

UNDP (2009): *Human Development Report 2009*, Palgrave Macmillion, New York.

UNEP (2003): "How Will Global Warming Affect My World?" *A Simplified Guide to the IPCC's "Climate Change 2001: Impacts, Adaptation and Vulnerability"*, France.

UNESCO (2010): "Teaching and Learning for a Sustainable Future", *UNESCO-UNEP*.

UNPI (2005): "The United Nations and Human Rights", *The UN Department of Public Information*, New York.

WCED (1987): *Our Common Future*, Report of the World Commission on Environment and Development, Official Records of the General Assembly, 42nd Session, supplement No. 25 (A/42/25).

World Bank (2001): *Raising the Sights: Better Health Systems for India's Poor* Health, Nutrition, Population Sector Unit India, South Asia Region, World Bank, Washington, DC.

WWF (2004): *Rivers at Risk: Dams and the Future of Freshwater Eco-systems*, World Wildlife Federation, 22 June.

Reports

Barlow, Maude (2011): *Our Right to Water*, The Council of Canadians, Ottawa.

CII and HOSMAC (2011): *Partnership in Health Care: A Public-Private Perspective*, White Paper, Confederation of Indian Industry and HOSMAC, March.

CMIE (2004): *Corporate Finance*, Centre for Monitoring Indian Economy, Mumbai.

Dilip, T.R. (2008): *Role of Private Hospitals in Kerala: An Exploration*, Working Paper 400, Centre for Development Studies, Thiruvananthapuram.

Emily, Adams E. (2012): "Forest Cover", Eco Economy Indicators, *Earth Policy Institute*, August 31, http://www.earth-policy.org//forestcover, accessed on 01-01-2013.

ERF (2006): *Government Health Expenditure in India: A Benchmark Study*, Economic Research Foundation, New Delhi.

Hazards Centre (2006): *Ground Water Resources in Plachimada Coca-Cola Stores Toxics for Future Generations*, New Delhi, June.

Hong, Evelyne (2000): *Globalisation and the Impact on Health: A Third World View*, Third World Network, Penang.

HUNGaMA (2012): *The HUNGaMA Survey Report: 2011*, Naandi Foundation, Hyderabad.

IELRC (1986): *Environmental Aspects of Narmada Sagar and Sardar Sarovar Multi-Purpose Projects*, Department of Environment and Forests, International Environmental Law Research Centre, Geneva.

ISIS (2010): *Farmer Suicides and Bt Cotton Nightmare Unfolding in India*, Institute of Science in Society, 6 January.

Jananeethi (2003): *Jananeethi Report – On the Amplitude of Environmental and Human Rights Ramification*, Jananeethi, Thrissur.

Johan, Rockstrom (2003): *Rethinking Water Management: Innovative Approaches to Contemporary Issues*, Earthscan, London.

John, Scanlon; Angela, Cassar and Noemi, Nemes (2004): *Water as a Human Right?* IUCN Environmental Policy and Law Paper No. 51, UNDP.

Manshi, Asher (2009): *Striking While the Iron is Hot: A Case Study of the Pohang Steel Company's (POSCO) Proposed Project in Orissa*, National Study for Advocacy Studies, Pune.

Monali, Doshi (2010): *Hospital Sector Research*, Northbridge Capital, November.

Persky, Joseph; Daniyel, Felzenshtain and Virginia, Carlson (2004): *Does "Trickle Down" Work?*, Institute for Employment Research, Michigam.

Rahman, Rushidan Islam and Ali, Kamar (1996): *Structural Adjustment Policies and Health Care Services*, CIRDAP, Bangladesh.

Thanal (2002): *Preliminary Findings of the Survey on the Impact of Aerial Spraying of Endosulfan on the People and Ecosystem in Kasaragod, Keralam, India*, Thanal, Thiruvananthapuram.

TII-CMS (2008): *India Corruption Study 2007: With Focus on BPL Households*, Transparency International India and Centre for Media Studies, New Delhi, June.

—— (2005): *India Corruption Study: 2005*, Transparency International India and Centre for Media Studies, New Delhi, 30 June.

—— (2005): *India Corruption Study: 2005, Vol. II, Corruption in Income Tax*, Transparency International India and Centre for Media Studies, New Delhi.

RTI

LBSNAA (2013): *Details of Expenditure Incurred on IAS Officers in Connection with Their Foreign Exposure Visit During 2010-2012 IAS Phase-II*, Lal Bahadur Shastri National Academy of Administration, Government of India, Mussoorie, RTI Dated 04-02-2013.

DoPT (2013): *List of Members Who Retired Voluntarily From Service, 2000-2012; List of IAS Officers Who have Taken Voluntary Retirement and were Granted Permission to Join Post Commercial Employment, 2008-till date; List of Cases in Which Previous Sanction of the Central Government has been Granted, 2000-till date*, Ministry of Personnel, PG and Pensions, Department of Personnel and Training, Government of India, New Delhi, RTI Dated 08-02-2013.

—— (2013): *Cadre Strength of Indian Administrative Service (as on 01-01-2012)*, Ministry of Personnel, PG and Pensions, Department of Personnel and Training, Government of India, New Delhi, RTI dated 16-01-2013.

Unpublished Thesis/Papers

Eva, Wramner (2004): *Fighting Cocacolanisation in Plachimada*, Human Ecology Division, Lund University.

John Briscoe (1996): "Water as an Economic Good: The Idea and What it Means in Practice", paper presented at the *World Congress of the International Commission on Irrigation and Drainage*, Cairo, Egypt, September.

Reinhart, Philip (2012): *Green Captivism and Market Governance in Water Supply: The Challenges Ahead*, Paper presented at the three Day National Seminar on "Water Management: Mounting Challenges and Responses", C. Achutha Menon Study Centre and Library, Trivandrum, 22nd December.

——(2010): *Commodification and Commercialisation of Health Care: The Impact of Globalisation with Special Reference to Kerala*, M.Phil Thesis, Department of Politics and International Studies, Pondicherry Central University, Puducherry.

Books

Alfred, Saad-Filho and Deborah, Johnston (ed) (2005): *Neo-liberalism: A Critical Reader*, Pluto Press, London.

Alphons K.J. (1996): *Making a Difference*, Viking Publishers, New Delhi.

Anitha, Cheria Edwin and Sriprapha, Petcharamesree (2003): *A Human Rights Approach to Development: A Source Book*, Books for Change, Bangalore.

Aravind, S. (1992): *Indian Administration*, Himalaya Publishing House, Bombay.

Arora N.D. (2010): *Political Science*, McGraw Hill Education, New Delhi.

Avasthi, Amreshwai and Avasthi, Anand Prakash (2008): *Indian Administration*, Lakshmi Narain Agarwal, Agra.

Bakshi, P.N. (2008): *The Constitution of India*, Law Publishers, Allahabad.

Barlow, Maude and Clarke, Tony (2002): *Blue Gold: The Fight to Stop the Corporate Theft of the World's Water*, Left World, New Delhi.

Basu, D.D. (2000): An *Introduction to the Constitution of India*, Nagpur, Wadhwa.

—— (1981): *The Shorter Constitution of India*, Prentice-Hall of India, New Delhi.

Bello, Walden (1996): "Structural Adjustment Programs: Success for Whom", in Mander, J. and Goldsmith, E. (eds) *The Case Against the Global Economy,* Sierra Club, San Francisco.

Bhambhri, C.P. (1973): *Public Administration in India*, Vikas Publishing House, New Delhi.

Chakraborty, S. (2003) "Private Health Provision in Uttar Pradesh, India" in Yazbeck, A.S. and Peters, D.H. (eds), *Health Policy Research in South Asia: Building Capacity for Reform*, World Bank, Washington, DC, 257–77.

Chopra, J.K. (2009): *Unique Quintessence of Political Science*, Unique Publishers, New Delhi.

Dasgupta, Samir and Kiely, Ray (2006): *Globalisation and After,* Sage, New Delhi.

Dave, Hill and Ellen, Rosskam (2009): *The Developing World and State Education: Neo-liberal Depreciation and Egalitarian Alternatives*, Routledge, New York.

Dubashi, P.R. (1998): "Restructuring and Reforms of Indian Political, Administrative and Economic System," in T.N. Chaturvedi, *Fifty Years of Indian Administration – Retrospects and Prospects*, Indian Institute of Public Administration, New Delhi.

Dwarakadas, R. (1958): *Role of Higher Civil Service in India*, Popular Book Depot, Bombay.

Dwivedi, O.P. (1998): "Development Administration: An Overview", in Chaturvedi, T.N (ed), *Fifty Years of Indian Administration: Retrospect and Prospects*, Indian Institute of Public Administration, New Delhi.

Edward, W. Weidner (1970): "The Elements of Development Administration", in Weidner (ed) *Development Administration in Asia*, Duke University Press, Durham.

Esman, Milton J. (1966): "The Politics of Development Administration", in Montgomery and Siffin, *Approaches to Development Politics, Administration and Change*, McGraw Hills, New York.

Fred. W. Riggs (1970): "The Idea of Development Administration", in Weidner (ed) *Development Administration in Asia*, Duke University Press, Durham.

Gita, Sen (2003): "Inequalities and Health in India", *Development*, SAGE, New Delhi, 18-20.

Guham S. and Samuel Paul (2001): "Corruption in India", in S. Subrahmonian (ed) *India's Developmental Experience*, Oxford University Press, New Delhi.

Harvey, D. (2005): *A Brief History of Neo-Liberalism*, Oxford University Press, New York.

Hira, Anil (1998): *Ideas And Economic Policy In Latin America: Regional, National, and Organisational Case Studies*, Praeger Publishers, West Port, USA.

Homer-Dixon, Thomas (1999): *Environment, Scarcity and Violence*, Princeton University Press, Princeton, N.J.

Jain, R.B. (1976): *Contemporary Issues in Indian Administration*, New Vishal Publications, New Delhi.

Jitha, S.R. (2007): *Higher Bureaucracy and Development*, Kalpaz Publications, New Delhi.

——(2011): "Bureaucracy and Human Rights Under Liberalisation", in P. Sukumaran Nair (ed.), *Human Rights in a Changing World*, Kalpaz Publications, New Delhi, 141-49.

John, Montgomery (1966): "A Royal Invitation: Variation on Three Classic Themes", in Montgomery and William Siffin (eds.) *Approaches to Development: Politics, Administration and Change*, McGraw-Hill, New York.

Kahl, C.H. (2006): *States, Scarcity and Civil Strife in the Developing World*, Princeton University Press, Princeton, N.J.

Kannan, K.P., Thankappan, K.R. and Kutty, V.R. (1991): *Health and Development in Rural Kerala*, Kerala Sastra Sahitya Parishad, Thiruvananthapuram.

Laxmikanth, M. (2011): *Governance in India*, Tata McGraw-Hills, New Delhi.

Lee, Hahn-Been (1970): "The Role of Higher Civil Service Under Rapid Social and Political Change", in Edward Weidner (ed.), *Development Administration in Asia*, Duke University Press.

Mathrubhumi (2005): *Plachimadayile Jalachushanavum Janakeeya Prathirothavum* (M), Mathrubhumi Books, Kozhicode.

Max, Weber (1947): *The Theory of Social and Economic Organisation*, Oxford University Press, New York.

Michel, Crozier (1964): *The Bureaucratic Phenomenon*, The University of Chicago Press, Chicago.

Milton J. Esmon and John D. Montgomery (1969): "System Approaches to Technical Cooperation: The Role of Development Administration", *Public Administration Review*, 29(5), Sept-October.

Mishra, B.B. (1977): *The Bureaucracy in India*, Oxford University Press, New Delhi.

——(1970): *The Administrative History of India*, Oxford University Press, New Delhi.

Mittelman, James H. (2000): *The Globalisation Syndrome: Transformation and Resistance*, Princeton University Press, New Jersey.

Moreland, W.H. and Chatterjee, A.C. (1953): *A Short History of India*, Longmans, London.

Naidu, S.P. (1996): *Public Administration, Concepts and Theories*, New Age International, New Delhi.

Narayanan Nair (1973): *The Civil Service under the Law and the Constitution*, The Academy of Legal Publications, Thiruvananthapuram.

Nigro, F.A. and Nigro, L.G. (1984): *Modern Public Administration*, HorperCollins.

Nozick, R. (1974): *Anarchy, State and Utopia*, Basic Books, New York.

Parayil, G. (2000): *Kerala: The Development Experience*, London: Zed Books.

Peter, Blaue (1965): *Bureaucracy in Modern Society*, Random House, New York.

Petras, James and Veltmeyer, Henry (2001): *Globalisation Unmasked*, Madhyam Books, New Delhi.

Premlatha, Bansal (1974): *Administrative Development in India*, Sterling Publishers, New Delhi.

Pylee, M.V. (1995): *An Introduction to the Constitution of India*, Vikas, New Delhi.

Ramakanth, Rao M.G. and Mathur, Prashant, K. (1994): *Advanced Public Administration: Policy, Planning and Decision-making*, Kanishka Publishers, New Delhi.

Ramesh, Arora K. and Rajni, Goyal (2011): *Indian Public Administration: Institutions and Issues*, Wishwa Prakashan, New Delhi.

Reinhart, Philip (2012): "Global Warming and Water Resources", in Shaji Anirudhan (ed.), *Understanding the Environmental History of India*, PG and Research Dept. of History, S.N. College, Chempazhanty, 287-97.

Robert, Michel (1954): *Political Parties: A Sociological Study of the Oligarchical Tendencies of Modern Democracy*, Dover Publishers, New York.

Ruddar, Dutt (2006): *India's Economy*, S. Chand and Co. Ltd., New Delhi.

Samir, Amin (2009): *The World We Wish to See: Revolutionary Objectives in the Twenty-First Century*, Aakar Books, Delhi.

Sapru, R.K. (1994): *Development Administration*, Deep and Deep Publications, New Delhi.

Scholte, Jan Aart (2005): *Globalisation: A Critical Introduction*, Palgrave Macmillan, New York.

Sikdar, Soumyen (2007): *Contemporary Issues in Globalisation*, Oxford University Press, New Delhi.

Steger, Manfred B. and Roy, Ravi, K. (2010): *Neo-liberalism: A Very Short Introduction*, Oxford Publishers, New York.

Theodore, Harney MacDonald (2009): *Removing the Barriers to Global Health Equity*, Radcliffe Publishing Ltd., Oxon.

Tony, Schirato and Jen, Webb (2006): *Understanding Globalisation*, SAGE Publications, New Delhi.

Vishnoo, Bhagvan and Vidhya, Bhushan (2011): *Indian Administration*, S. Chand and Co., New Delhi.

Wizard (2012): *Wizard Current Affairs 2012*, Career Classics, New Delhi.

Journals

Allam, Ahmed and Stein, Josephine (2004): "Science, Technology and Sustainable Development, A World Review," *Inderscience*, 1(1).

Anna, Karthika (2008): "Bottling Up a Corporate Giant: Victory of a Mass Movement", *Covalence Analyst Papers*, Geneva, 22-06-2008.

Arnoldo, Contreras (2000): "The Underlying Causes of Forest Declines", *CIFOR*, Indonesia, June.

Bakker, Karen (2005): "Neo-liberalising Nature? Market Environmentalism in Water Supply in England and Wales", *Annals of the Association of American Geographers*, 95(3), 542-65.

Baksi, Soham; Pinaki, Bose and Manish, Pandey (2009): "The Impact of Liberalisation on Bureaucratic Corruption", *Journal of Economic Behaviour and Organisation*, 72, 214-24.

Baru, R.V. (2000): "Privatisation and Corporatisation," *Seminar*, 489, May, http://www.india-seminar.com/2000/489/489percent20baru.htm.

Ben, Page (2005): "Paying for Water and the Geography of Commodities", *Trans Inst Br Geogr*, 30, 293-306.

Bendix, R. (1959): "Bureaucracy" in *International Encyclopaedia of Social Sciences*, MacMillan, New York.

Bhaskaran, Nair M. (1989): "Evolving New Values in Civil Service and Combating Corruption", *Kerala Journal of Social Sciences*, III and IV (1 and 2), July/December.

Bollier, David (2002): "Reclaiming the Commons", *Boston Review*, Summer Issue.

Briggs, John and Ian, Yeboah E.A. (2001): "Structural Adjustment and the Contemporary Sub-Saharan African City", *Blackwell Publishing* and *The Royal Geographical Society*, 33(1), March, 18-26.

Camille, Parmesen and John, Mathews (2005): "Biological Impacts of Climate Change", *Sinauer Associates*, USA, 333-74.

Current 336 Science (2007): "Urban Air Pollution", *Current Science*, 77(3), August 10, 334-6.

EPW (2010): "Plachimada Again", Editorial, *Economic and Political Weekly,* XLV (12), March.

Gita, Sen., Aditi, Iyer and Asha, George (2002): "Structural Reforms and Health Equity: A Comparison of NSS Surveys, 1986-87 and 1995-96", *Economic and Political Weekly*, XXXVII(14), April 6-12, 1342-50.

Godwin, S.K. and Varatharajan, K. (2007): "Drug Price Differentials across Different Retail Market Settings", *Health Administrator*, XIX(1), 41-47.

Jayanth, Sthaye; Shukla, P.R. and Ravindranath, N.H. (2006): "Climate Change, Sustainable Development and India: Global and National Concerns", *Current Science*, 90(3), February.

Jitha, S.R. (2011): "Bureaucracy and Sustainable Development", *Pragati,* 5(118) Oct-Dec, 23-31.

—— (2010): "Bureaucracy and its Role in the Protection of Human Rights", *UCJPS*, 5(1 and 2), March, 67-73.

—— (2010): "Bureaucratic Corruption in a Liberalised Society", *Pragati*, 4(111), Jan-March, 45-53.

Jitha, S.R. and Reinhart, Philip (2012): "Higher Bureaucracy, Liberalisation and Social Change", *South Asian Journal of Socio Political Studies*, XII(2), Jan-June, 53-56.

Johan, Rockstrom (2003): "Rethinking Water Management: Innovative Approaches to Contemporary Issues", *Earthscan*, London.

Jona, Aravind Dohrmann (2008): "Special Economic Zones in India: An Introduction", *ASIEN*, 106, January, 60-80.

Kamalakanta, Muduli and Akhilesh, Barve (2012): "Challenges to Waste Management Practices in Indian Health Care Sector", *IPCBEE*, 32, 62-67.

Letha, Sinha (1990): "Role and Rationale of All India Services", *Indian Journal of Public Administration*, XXVI(4), October-December.

Logan, Ikubolajeh Bernard and Kidane, Mengisteab (1993): "IMF-World Bank Adjustment and Structural Transformation in Sub-Saharan Africa", *Economic Geography*, 69(1), January, 1-24.

Malley, L.S.S.O. (1965): *The Indian Civil Service*, Frank Class and Company, London.

McDonald, David A. and Ruiters, Grey (2005): "Rethinking Privatisation, Towards a Critical Theoretical Perspective", *Public Services Year Book*.

Mikhal, Drugor (2009): "Competition in Bureaucracy and Corruption". *Department of Economics, University of Oxford*, January, 1-25.

Nabae, Koji (2003): "The Health Care System in Kerala: Its Past Accomplishments and New Challenges", *Journal, National Institute of Public Health*, Department of Public Health, Toho, 140-145.

Nkrumah, Kwame (1999): "Excerpt from Kwame Nkrumah's Neo-Colonialism: The Last Stage of Imperialism", *The Crisis*, July-August.

Orlando, Plaza and Nelly, Stromquist P. (2006): "Consequences of Structural Adjustment on Economic and Social Domains: Two Decades in the Life of Peru", *Annals of the American Academy of Political and Social Science*, 606, July, 95-115.

Parvati, Iyer and Dinesh, Abrol (2008): "Financing of Health", *India, Science and Technology*, www.nistads.res.in accessed on 08-07-2010.

Pellegrino, E.D. (1999): "The Commodification of Medical and Health Care: The Moral Consequences of a Paradigm Shift from a Professional to a Market Ethic", *Journal of Medicine and Philosophy*, 24(3), 243.

Pohare, P.V. (2011): "Impact of Globalisation on Indian Agriculture", *International Research Journal*, II(26), March.

Raju, Narayana Swami (2011): "Land Acquisition and Development-Induced Displacement: A Case Study from Kerala", *Pragathi*, 5(115), 5-22.

Raman Kutty, V. (2000): "Historical Analysis of the Development of Health Care Facilities in Kerala State, India", *Health Policy and Planning*, Oxford University Press, 15(1), 103-109.

Ramaswamy, P.R. (2002): "The Challenges of Globalisation for Civil Servants", *IJPA* XLVIII(1), January-March, 50-60.

Rao, Mohan., Nayar, K.R., Rama, Baru V. and Ritu, Priya (1995): "Health and Structural Adjustment, Major Shifts at Policy Level", *Economic and Political Weekly*, 30(20), May 20, 1156-60.

Rao, P.H. (2012): "The Private Health Sector in India: A Framework for Improving the Quality of Care", *ASCI Journal of Management*, 41 (2), 14–39.

Rao, T.M. (1980): "The Civil Servants are Not on the Job", *The Statesman*, Calcutta. November.

Reinhart Philip (2012): "The Human Right to Water", *Pragathi*, Quarterly Research Journal, 6(121), July-Sept., 47-59.

—— (2012): "Globalisation: The Higher Stage of Capitalist Expansion", *University College Journal of Politics and Society*, Research Journal, Department of Political Science, University of Kerala, 7(1 and 2), March, 27-40.

—— (2011): "De-regulation, Drug Prices and the Human Right to Health", *Pragati*, 5(117), July-September, 62-63.

—— (2010): "Commodification of Health Care: The Expansion of Market to an Under Marketised Sphere", *Holistic Thought*, IX(2), July-December, 158-67.

—— (2007): "Special Economic Zones, Neo-Liberalism and an Exclusive Development Process in India: A Critique", *Holistic Thought*, VI (1 and 2), 99-108.

Richard, Bocking (2003): "Reclaiming the Commons", *Canadian Unitarian Council*, Toronto, April 27.

Robbins, Peter T. (2003): "Transnational Corporations and the Discourse of Water Privatisation", *Journal of International Development*, 8(15), 1073-82.

Samir, Amin (2001): "Imperialism and Globalisation", *Monthly Review* 53(2), July.

Sathyanarayana, T. (2003): "Liberalisation, Public Administration and the Public", *IJPA* XLIX(1), January-March, 24-32.

Science Daily (2008): "Global Warming Affects World's Largest Freshwater Lake", *National Science Foundation*, 1 May.

Sezhiyan, Era (2007): "Globalisation of Indian Economy, Globe for the Rich-Zero for the Poor", *Mainstream*, XLV(20), May 4-10, 7-11.

Sonia, Andrews and Sailesh, Mohan (2002): "User Charges in Health Care: Some Issues", *Economic and Political Weekly*, 37(37), Sept. 14-20, 3793-3795.

Srini, Sitaraman (2008): "Privatisation, Efficiency, Gender, Development, and Inequality-Transnational Conflicts over Access to Water and Sanitation", *Human Rights and Human Welfare*, 8, 91-113.

Stefan, Timmermans and Rene, Almeling (2009): "Objectification, Standardisation and Commodification in Health Care: A Conceptual Readjustment", *Social Science and Medicine*, 69, 21-7.

Urmi, Goswami (2012): "Investing in Social Sector", *Yojana*, April, 38-42.

Veena, Gokhale (1991): "India's Narmada Valley Hydro Project", *Environment and Policy Magazine*, 1, 1-4.

Victor, A. Thompson (1964): "Administrative Objection for Development Administration", *Administrative Science Quarterly*, Vol. 9, June.

Wiliam, Joe and Mishra, U.S. (2009): *Household Out-of-Pocket Healthcare Expenditure in India: Levels, Patterns and Policy Concerns*, Working Paper 418, Centre for Development Studies, Thiruvananthapuram.

Yojana (2012): "Towards Rapid, Inclusive and Sustainable Growth", *Yojana*, Special Issue, Approach to 12th Five Year Plan, January.

Magazines/Periodicals

Ajoy, Ashirwad Mahaprashata (2011): "Uttar Pradesh", in "Standing Up to the State", *Frontline*, 28(12), June 17, 9-11.

——(2011): "Chhattisgarh", in "Standing Up to the State", *Frontline*, 28(12), June 17, 13-16.

Anupama, Katakam (2012): "Towards Trial", *India Today*, 29(14), July 27, 24-26.

—— (2010): "House of Scandal", *India Today*, 27(24), July 14-27, December 3, 28-32.

—— (2010): "House of Scandal", *India Today*, 27(24), July 14-27, December 3, 28-32.

Anil Kumar, Jain and Parul, Gupta (2008): "Globalisation: The Indian Experience", *Mainstream*, XLVI(8), Feb. 8-14, 15-20.

Business Leads (2003): "Macro-economic Overview of India: Agriculture", *Business Leads*, April 30.

Chandrasekhar, C.P. (2012): "A Big Step Forward", *Frontline*, 29(8), May 4, 10-2.

Dhiraj, Nayyar and Sandheep, Unnithan (2011): "The Great Indian Robbery", *India Today*, XXXVI(5), January 31, 18-24.

Dutt, Ruddar (2007): "India as an Economic Superpower, Myth and Reality", *Mainstream*, XLV(30), July 13-19, 7-11.

Economy (2012): "Economic Survey 2011-12", *Dhankar Publications*, New Delhi.

Joe, Mathew C. (2010): "NPPA Study Finds Huge Gap in Cancer Drug Prices", *Business Standard*, October 13.

Mathew, Aerthayil (2008): "Agrarian Crisis in India is a Creation of the Policy of Globalisation", *Mainstream*, XLVI(13), March 14-20, 8-11.

Mathew, Kurian V. (2007): "Financial Liberalisation and the Third World: A Study with Reference to India", *Mainstream*, XLV(11), March 2-8, 7-10.

Nagaraja, G. (2012): "Welfare Mission", *Frontline*, 29(8), May 4, 120-2.

Purnima, S. Tripathi (2012): "Battle of Bastar", *Frontline*, 29(8), May 03, 32-34.

—— (2010): "Damning Audit", *Frontline*, 27(24), December 03, 49-52.

—— (2010): "Recruitment Now", *Frontline*, 27(14), July 16.

Pushpa, Iyengar (2011): "Under a Dangerous Motto", *Outlook India.com*, August 22, http://www.outlookindia.com/article.aspx?277990, accessed on 24-12-2012.

Ramachandran, R. (2012): "Western Warning", *Frontline*, 29(8), May 4, 18-21.

Reinhart, Philip (2009): "Economic Development and Social Justice", *Competition Success Review*, XLV(11), May, 48-50.

Sushanta, Talukdar (2011): "North-Eastern States", in "Standing Up to the State", *Frontline*, 28(12), June 17, 17-18.

Venkatesan, V. (2012): "Posco in Limbo", *Frontline*, 29(8), May 04, 35-37.

Venkitesh, Ramakrishnan (2011): "The Great Land Grab", *Frontline*, 28(12), June 17, 4-8.

Newspaper Online Articles

Express News (2011): "Big Scams are Big News but Silent, Pervasive Corruption is Real Evil", *The New Sunday Express* (Magazine), Kochi, November 13, 8.

ENVIS (2007): "E-Waste Indian Perspective", *ENVIS*, Urban Municipal Waste Management Newsletter, November.

Global Exchange (2010): *SUEZ-LYONNAISE DES EAUX*, "Some of the *Most Wanted* Corporate Human Rights Violators", http://www.globalexchange.org.

Gurumurthy, S. (2010): "Dishonesty, Fraud, Breach of Trust", *The New Indian Express*, Kochi, 14 June, 9.

IRC (2003): *Sale of River Bhavani, India Resource Centre*, http://www.indiaresource.org /issues/water/2003/bhavaniriver.html, accessed on 10-11-2009.

Josprakash, C.R. (2013): "Panimudakkunnathu Enthinu Vendi", (M) *Kerala Kaumudi*, Kochi, 8 January, 6.

Jyoti, Punwani (2010): "Who didn't help Carbide?" *The New Indian Express*, Kochi, June 17.

Nardeep Singh, Dahiya (2012): "Stainless Steel", *The New Sunday Express* (Magazine), Kochi, 6 May, 1-2.

Priya, Ranjan Das (2008): "Slow Down My Foot, Economy is in the Black", December 18, http://www.mydigitalfc.com/economy/slowdown-my-foot-economy-black-483.

Sainath, P. (2011): "From Questionable Social Subsidies to Unquestioned Corporate Welfare", *Daktre*, 18 September, http://www.daktre.com/2011/09/sainath-talk/, accessed on 30-01-2013.

—— (2010): "Farm Suicides: A 12-Year Saga", *The Hindu*, January 25.

—— (2009): "Neo-liberal Terrorism in India: The Largest Wave of Suicides in History", *Counterpunch*, 12 February.

Santhosh, M.B. (2011): "Maruninum Venam Milma Model", (M) *Kerala Kaumudi*, Kochi, 12 October, 6.

Srivatsa, Krishna (2012): "Is Indian Bureaucracy the Worst?", *The Economic Times*, 16 January.

Upendra Nath, Sharma (2012): "No Lessons Learnt From Bhopal Gas Tragedy", *The New Indian Express*, Kochi, 80 Years Special Edition, 49.

Vandana Siva (2011): "The Great Land Grab: India's War on Farmers", *Al Jazeera*, http://english.aljazeera.net/indepth/opinion/2011/06/20116711756667987.html accessed on 07-06-2011.

Newspapers

Kerala Kaumudi, Kochi Edition, Kerala
Malayala Manorama, Kollam Edition, Kerala
Mathrubhumi, Kollam Edition, Kerala
The Deccan Chronicle, Online Edition
The Economic Times, Online Edition
The Financial Express, Online Edition
The Hindu, Thiruvananthapuram Edition, Kerala
The Hindustan Times, Online Edition
The Indian Express, New Edition, New Delhi
The New Indian Express, Kochi Edition, Kerala
The Pioneer, Online Edition, New Delhi
The Telegraph, Online Edition, Calcutta
Times of India, Online Edition, New Delhi

Websites

Abhilasha (2013): Abhilasha Website, http://210.212.211.3/abhilasha/about.html
Businessweek: www.businessweek.com /magazine
Daily Bhaskar: www.daily.bhaskar.com
Daily News and Analysis: www.dnaindia.com
Earth Policy Institute: www.earth-policy.org
Government of India: www.india.gov.in
India Today: www.indiatoday.intoday.in
Jalanidhi (2010): *Kerala Rural Water Supply and Sanitation Agency*, jalanidhi.ac.in
Outlook: www.outlookindia.com
UN Water: www.unwater.org

Index

A

A.D. Gorwala Committee, 65

Recommendations, 66

Abhilasha Project

launch, 119

works, 119

Ability to pay

in corruption, 132

Accumulation

of wealth, 162

Acharya, B.P. (IAS)

Chargesheet, 149-50

Adarsh Housing Scandal, 148

CBI Chargesheet list, 48

Administration

transparency in, 23

Administrative Reforms, Committee, 65

Administrative Reform Commission

First, 68

Second, 69

Reports, 70

Recommendations, 71

Administrative Reform, 64

Agriculture

impact of liberalisation on, 96-97

crisis - causes, 98

Air Pollution, 200

diseases, 200

..inducing agents, 200

Aitchison Commission

Recommendations, 35

All India Services, 59

numbers, 36

term, 37

need/importance, 62-64

Alma-Ata Declaration 1978, 184

Amaratya Sen

on Development, 93

Anaemia

statistics, 100

Andhra Pradesh Scam
    CBI Chargesheeters, 149
Arrest and detention, 48
Arvind and Tinu Joshi
    attachment of property, 153

B

Basic Facilities Report, 100
Below Poverty Line
(BPL) figures, 98
Bhopal Gas Tragedy, 167
    UCC Settlement, 167
    Compensation, 168
Bio-Medical waste, 197-98
Black money, 154
BPL/APL classification, 163
Bribe payment /Contact influence
    impact, 129
British Administration, 31
British Parliament, 31
Bureaucracy
    term, 15-16, 229
    function, 17
    and citizens relation, 72
    challenges before, 86
    expectations from, 108
    Post independence, 57
    legacy, 58
Bureaucrats-Politicians Nexus, 135

C

CAG Report
    on Coal Allocation, 102
    violations list, 114
    aspects, 115
Cancer Drugs Prices, 190
    Variants, 258
Capitalism, 25
Caste and Religion
    shield in corruption, 138
Central Civil Services Authority, 74
Central Legislative Council, 40
Central Public Servic Commission, 37
Central Service Classification, 59
Central government, 180
Central Vigilence Commission, 127
Charter Act 1833, 39
    1853, 39
Chaturvedi, T.N.,
    on Civil Services, 58-59
Chicago Boys
    philosophy, 79
Civil Servants
    research, 87
    and Public, 22
    term, 32
Civil Service
    Exam, 73
    entry methods, 36
    roles, 58
    changes, 59
Cadre Controlling Authority, 59

CMS India
- corruption study, 130

Charter Act, 33

Coal Block Allocation
- charges against, 114
- scam, 146
- companies profiting, 146

Coalition Politics, 23

Coca-Cola bottling Plant
- violations, 216-17

Collective Imperialism, 78

Collector of Revenue, 32

Colonialism, 27

Commons, 232

Commission of Inquiry
- GOI, 68

Commodification, 212, 233
- of water, 172, 174, 233
- of health, 233

Commercialisation, 97

Commonwealth Games
- Scam, 150
- officials booked, 150-51

Community Development, 58

Comparative Adminstrative Group, 92

Comunicable Disease
- resurgence, 85

Constitution, 43

Constitution of India, 43

Constitutional Amendments, 44

Constitutional Framework, 43

Constitutional Remedies
- - Right to, 51

Cooling-off Period
- post retirement, 112

Cornwallis, Lord, 32

Corporate lobbying, 112

Corporates
- free Play of, 81

Corruption, 24, 236
- Phenomenon, 125-26
- principals/features, 131
- history of, 126
- study, 128-29, 130
- with/without damage, 133
- degrading face, 134
- forms (CVC), 127
- impact, 24

Covenanted Civil Service, 32

Courts of Directors, 33

Cultural and Educational Rights, 50

D

Deforestation, 208

Delhi Airport Modernisation, 114
- charges against, 114

Delicensing, 87

Development and
- globalisation, 94
- .. government role, 94

Development, 91, 230

third world, 19
concept/definition, 20
and HR, 162
induced HR violation, 164
definition (UN), 161
Bureaucrats role in, 161-62
and globalisation, 94
uni-dimensional concept, 91-92
goal, 92
Directive Principles, 51-52
Articles 36 to 51, 51-54
Disinvestment
Plans, 95
Policy, 101
Displacement, 164, 166
in land acquisition, 165
Disproportianate wealth
IAS cases, 152-53
District Collector
post, 32
District Revenue Officer, 117
Draft Water Policy
of India, 175
Drop Outs
reasons, 99
Drug Prices
Deregulation, 188
Differences, 189
Drug Pricing, 234
Drug/Price control
-Kerala, 195-96
Dyarchy
establishing, 40
abolishing, 41

E

East India Company, 31
administration, 31
Economic Reforms (India)
introduction, 95
Economic Security
impact of corruption on, 139
e-governance
initiative, 118
pioneers, 118
Employment
impact of liberalisation on, 98
Endosulfan spraying, 200
harmful effects, 200-201
Endosulfan (Kadsaragod)
victims compensation, 168
Environment protection
in Constitution, 210-11
laws, 211
Environmental Conservation
and Bureaucracy, 215
Ethics in Governance, 72
European Union, 78
e-waste, 198-99, 236
risks, 199
Exploitation of labour, 27

F

Farmer suicides, 97

First Administrative
reforms, 68
Foreign Capital, 26
Foreign Direct Investment, 91
Foreign Investment, 95
Foreign Training
of Bureaucrats, 108
Forest Area Encroachment, 220-222, 235
egs, 221
Fort Williams College, 33
Free Market Economy
impact, 107
Free Market Fundamentalism, 86
Free Market-model, 185
Free Market Programmes, 83
Freedom of Religion, 49
Fresh Air, 213
scarcity, 213
future of, 214
Fundamental
Duties, 54-55
Freedoms, 48
Fundamental Rights, 45-46

G

Gazetted and
non-Gazetted class, 59
Global Financial Crisis, 87
Global Hunger Index, 100
Global Warming, 208
adverse effects, 209
Globalisation, 24-26
the Push factor, 26
criticism, 104
objective, 95
and environment protection, 212
and Health Care, 186
phenomenon, 77
and Uni-polarity, 78
events after, 776
GOI Act
1935, 37, 41
1858, 39
1919, 40
Good Governance Institute, 74
Government expenditure
on IAS Training, 110
Government Health care, 187
Government of India, 98
Green Bureaucracy, 223-25
Green captivism, 212
Green, 232

H

Hastings, Warren, 32
Health care, 184
Bureaucracy role, 197
Use trends, 85
commodification, 185

spending by Government, 186-187

visits-costs, 191

Health Insurance cards

- Kerala, 192

Health

meaning, 183

and Human Development Index, 183

as Fundamental Right, 184

Higher bureaucracy, 18

behaviour in, 108

development role, 18

function, 18

Higher Civil Servants, 38

HR Protection

and Bureaucracy role, 160

Human Rights

and development, 160

idea, situation, 178

Human rights violations, 233

Human development Index, 183

Human Need, 185

Human Trafficking

provisions against, 49

I

IAS, 38, 59

cadre strength, 253

Drain, 110

Expenditure-foreign visits, 255

officers arrested

/under scanner, 149

2010 to 2012, 151-52

officers strength, 111

deployment, 111

retirement/re-employment, 112

Officers with integrity list, 113

ICS First Exam, 36

IFS, 59

Income Disparities

Rise, 84

Income

Inequalities, 163

Indian Civil Service, 32

evolution, 32

Indian Council Act

1861, 40

1892, 40

1909, 40

Indian Independence Act

1947, 41

Infant/Maternal mortality, 100

International Competition, 80

International Peace

and Security, 54

IPS, 59

Islington Commission 1915, 36

J

Jalanidhi Project, 175-76

World Bank Role, 175

Jan Aushadhi Shops, 196

K

Kalmadi, Suresh
- charges, 150

Kerala
- death rate, 194
- drug control, 195-96

Kerala Health Care
- Study, 193
- State Government role, 193, 195
- Achievements, 193-94
- statistics, 194
- challenges, 195

Kerala Medical Services
- Corporation, Ltd.
- low price drug procurement, 190

Kharge Vikas, 118

Khemka, Ashok
- stand on Corruption, 116

Kurien V.J.,
- success story, 116

Kurien, P.H.,
- work on affordable medicine, 197

L

Land acquisition
- protests, 164-65
- rehabilitation and compensation, 166-67

Land Fills, 199

Lee Commission, 37

Liberalisation, 24
- initiatives, 101
- dimensions, 25
- rationale, 103

Liberalisation as
- solution for corruption, 143
- promoter of corruption, 154

Liberalisation Privatisation
- and Globalisation (LPG),
- policies, 107

Liberalisation (India)
- factors inducing, 95
- impact on Agriculture, 95

Licence Permit Raj
- and corruption, 143

Literacy Rates, 99

Local Governance, 72

Lord Warren Hostings, 32

LPG, 107

M

Macaulay Committee
- Recommendations, 33-34

Malnutrition Report
- (HUNGAMA), 100

Mangrove Forests
- Kerala encroachment, 223

Marx, Karl
- on bureaucracy, 17

Michels, Robert
  on bureaucracy, 18
Mid Career training Programme
Mussorie
  details/expenses
  -2010-12, 256
Ministries/ departments, 59
Minority Institution
  Right to, 50
Montague Chelmsford
  Report-1918, 36
MNCs
  entry, 232
  impact on environment, 213
Montagu-Chelmsford
  Reforms, 40
Monthly Per capita Expenditure
  Rural/Urban, 99
MRTP Act, 95
Mutual trust
  in corruption, 132

N

National Development Council
  Meeting (56th), 94
National income, 92
National Family Health Survey, 187
Neethi Medicals, 196
Negative/Positive role
  of Bureaucracy, 220
Neocolonialism, 25
Neo-liberal
  advocacy, 27
  Development Strategy, 234
  School and Development, 91
  success stories, 79
Neo-Liberalisation Theory
  roots, 78
  interpretation, 79
  proponents, 79
  tenets, 81
Neo-liberalism, 231
  reforms, 232
  criticism, 104
New Economic Policy, 101, 107
New Industrial Policy (NIP), 95
  and initiatives of Government, 95
New International
  Economic Order (NIEO), 27
NREGS services bribes in, 129

O

Ocean level
  rise, 209
Organisation
  establishment, 34
Oxygen Zone, 214

P

Panandikar, V.A.,
  study, 18
Pantaprazole
  Price, 257
Parliamentary government, 66
Parallel Economy
  /size study of, 154

Paul H Appleby Report
Recommendations, 67
Per capita daily consumption
figures / BPL figures, 98
Performance Management
System (PMS), 74
Personnel Administration Institute, 73
Pharmaceutical Industry
liberalisation impact, 188-89
Pitts India Act
1784, 39
Plachimada-Coca-Cola
bottling Plant
violations, 216-18
negligence, 218-219
rationale, 219
Police Forces personnel
numbers/ratio, 121
Political interference, 109-10
Political Parties
Riches growth, 146
tax free income, 147
donations to, 147
contributors to, 147
Population vs Governmnet
Servants-Kerala, 257
Post Independence
Civil Services, 38
period developments, 57-58
Poverty line, 98-99
Poverty, 163
Preamble, 44-45
Private good, 185
Private Health care, 187-88
Private Sector
absorption of IAS Officers, 111, 113
Privatisation, 81,102, 234
Protection of Life
and personal liberty, 48
Protection of Monuments, 53
Provincial Autonomy, 38
Public Administration
Reforms, 67
Public Distribution System, 163
and TDS, 163
Public Expenditure
Cuts, 85
Public Health Care, 201
Public Servants
ratio of population, 120-21
Public Money
wastage, 164

Q

Quality of Life
scenario, 99
Queen Victoria's
Proclamation, 34

R

Rai,Vinod
-CAG praise, 14-15

Rajiv Gandhi, 95
Raja, A.,
    Telecom scam, 145
Recruitment and Service Conditions
    All India/Central Services, 60
    Constitutional provisions, 60
Reddy Jaipal
    reshuffle, 103
Regan/Thatcher
    government policies, 80
Regulating Act
    1773, 31, 38
Repeat visits
    for services, 169
Right
    Against Exploitation, 49
    to Education, 48
    to Equality, 46-47
    to Freedom, 47
    to Information, 71, 75
Rise in Debt
    impact, 97
River Pollution
    controlling, 173
    Performance Audits, 173
Royal Commision
    on Superior Civil Services, 37
Rural Employment
    Guarantee Act, 75

S

Sagayan, U
    stand on Corruption, 117
Sahni, Rajneesh
    role as Collector, 118
Sala Bureaucracy, 88, 232
Scams/scandals
    list-India, 125
Scheduled Castes, 100
Scheduled Tribes, 100
Secular, 44
SEZ, 164
    rise in, 102
and displacement, 164
    violence due to, 164
Sidhanta Singh
    Odisha Pollution work, 117
    Mangalore drive, 117
Silent Valley
    Positive role of Bureaucracy, 220
Singur and Nandigram
    violence, 164
Slum Population, 99
Social Change, 27, 93
Social Economic Zone, 102
Social Justice, 92
Social Sector
    post globalisation, 84
Sorafenib Drug
    (Cancer generic version), 197

Soviet Disintegration, 78
Spectrum Allocation
  2 G scam, 114, 145
  companies profiting, 145
Srilakshmi Y., (IAS)
  Charges against, 149
Structural Adjustment Programmes, 82
Structural Adjustment Policies
  (SAP), 81-82
  Phases, 83
  Conditionalities
    -Logan and Kindane, 83
  impact in third world, 84
Sustainable development, 21, 211
Swiss banks
  money transfers, 154

T

Tata's Greenfield Project
  -Lohandigude, 221
Tax havens, 154
Third World Bureaucracy, 232
Tottenham Commission, 38
Transparency International
  study on corruption, 125, 128-29
Trickle-Down theory, 80, 92

U

UN Declaration
  on Right to Development, 160
Unemployment
  /Underemployment
  rise, 82
Uni-dimensional
  concept, 91
Uniform Civil Code, 53
Uni-Polarity in
  International Relations, 78
Universal Declaration
  of Human Rights, 159
Upright Officers
  removal, 136-37
  life risk, 136
UPSC, 37, 59

V

Vakati Karuna
  work as Joint Collector
  Warrangal, 118
Vani Mohan Dr G.,
  welfare programme
  as Collector, 119-20
Voluntary Retirement
  IAS, 108, 111
  Quitters list, 109
    ..reasons, 109-10

W

Warming of Climate
  system, 210
Waste generated
  CAG Report, 199

Waste Management, 198, 202, 236
Water, 232
Water consumption
    in Agriculture, 176
    role of bureaucracy, 173, 177-78
Water Pollution, 201
    diseases, 201
Water, 170
    as HR, 170, 172
    Right to, 171
    ..security aspect, 177
    commodification, 172, 174
Weber, Max
    on bureaucracy, 16-17
Weberian Bureaucracy, 230-31
Wellesley, Lord, 33
Wet Land ecosystem
    encroachment, 222-23
Women impact of globalisation, 85
World Bank
    Water Project, 175-76

Y

Yamuna expressway
    displacement, 165
        .. Mayawati role, 166